Practical Global
Tort Litigation

Contextual Approach Series
in Comparative Law

* * *

Series Editor, Andrew J. McClurg

Practical Global Tort Litigation

United States, Germany and Argentina

Andrew J. McClurg

Adem Koyuncu

Luis Eduardo Sprovieri

Carolina Academic Press

Durham, North Carolina

Library of Congress Cataloging-in-Publication Data
McClurg, Andrew J., 1954-
Practical global tort litigation : United States, Germany, and Argentina / by
Andrew J. McClurg, Adem Koyuncu, Luis Eduardo Sprovieri.
    p. cm. -- (Contextual Approach Series in Comparative Law)
Includes bibliographical references and index.
ISBN-13: 978-1-59460-192-7 (alk. paper)
ISBN-10: 1-59460-192-5 (alk. paper)
  1. Torts--United States 2. Actions and defenses--United States. 3. Torts--
Germany. 4. Actions and defenses--Germany. 5. Torts--Argentina. 6. Ac-
tions and defenses--Argentina. I. Koyuncu, Adem. II. Sprovieri, Luis Ed-
uardo. III. Title. IV. Series.

K923.M38 2007
346.7303--dc22

                                                2007008948

CAROLINA ACADEMIC PRESS
700 Kent Street
Durham, North Carolina 27701
Telephone (919) 489-7486
Fax (919) 493-5668
www.cap-press.com

To Douglas P. McClurg, my mentor and hero.
We still miss you every day.
AJM

To my family.
AK

To my daughter Lucia and my son Juan,
hoping that they will live in a borderless world
that will still foster social awareness and transcendent values.
LES

Contents

PREFACE

This book and the Contextual Approach Series (CAS) had their genesis at the Florida International University College of Law, South Florida's public law school, where I taught as a member of the founding faculty from 2002–06. The FIU College of law is one of the most international of all U.S. law schools, drawing its students from many diverse cultures and nations. Adopting a pervasive approach to teaching comparative and international law, the FIU College of Law curriculum uniquely requires that all courses, including domestic law courses, contain a comparative and/or international law component. Comparative law is the study of similarities and differences in the law and legal traditions of different nations. International law is the "law of nations." It covers the entire field of both public and private transnational relationships.

To satisfy the comparative/international law requirement in my Torts and Products Liability courses, I searched long and hard for manageable, self-contained materials comparing the U.S. common law tort litigation system with tort systems in countries following the civil law tradition, which make up much of the world. While the search turned up a large body of outstanding comparative law scholarship, only a small amount addressed tort law and litigation, in part because extensively developed tort law is a relatively recent and still ongoing phenomenon in most countries. Another discovery was that most comparative law literature is historical, theoretical or thematic in nature. Not many materials attempt to explain how law "really works" in other nations as compared to the U.S. common law system.

One obvious explanation for this gap is the sheer enormity of the task. To say that comparing legal systems is difficult is euphemistic. Think how impossible it would be, for example, to "compare the law" of New York and Wyoming, then consider the proportions of comparing different legal systems of different countries. As a byproduct of this obstacle, comparative law coverage tends to be either very broad or very narrow. Survey-type comparative materials offer wide geographic and subject matter coverage, but do not convey a sense of how law functions in practice. Comparative analyses of specific topics provide much greater analytical depth, but the subject matter often has only narrow application.

Like many faculty members at the FIU College of Law, I tried both the macro and micro approaches to integrating comparative/international law in Torts and Products Liability, with underwhelming success. In Torts, I distributed a nifty chart attempting to compare common law and civil law systems in six pages, assigned a lengthy law review article about the Alien Tort Claims Act, and invited guest speakers such as the Chief Justice of the Costa Rica Supreme Court, a wonderful gentleman, and a distinguished lawyer from Argentina. I made my Products Liability students do presentations about Latin American products liability law. All of these endeavors were interesting, but my students weren't learning much about comparative or international law. There had to be a balance between "Today we're going to compare the law of the entire world," and "Today we're going to explore interpretations of article 1(c)(ii) of the Convention on International Liability for Damage Caused by Space Objects." Feedback from students at FIU affirmed that my difficulties in trying to integrate comparative and international law were not unique. Other professors were facing the same challenges.

It occurred to me that one way to strike a breadth-depth equilibrium and also help bring comparative law to life would be to *contextualize* it by applying the law of different nations to a set of case facts raising legal issues common and important to people in all nations. A case-based approach offers unique advantages. Foremost, it gives writers a foundation for *analyzing* (in addition to expositing) law and students a contextual anchor to which they can attach what they're learning. Legal principles mean little in isolation from facts, which is a principal reason why U.S. law students learn most subject matter by the "case method." Applying law to facts promotes analysis that is not only more focused, precise, and accurate, but accessible and retainable. It is one thing to recite a general rule about the burden of proof in a given legal system, and quite another, as readers will see, to unweave the intricacies of how proof burdens apply to a concrete set of facts. Seeing how different legal systems respond to the same facts highlights similarities and differences directly and in some instances dramatically. A case approach would not intuitively occur to lawyers in non-common law systems, who are trained to think in terms of codes rather than cases, but a "problem approach"—which is essentially the same thing—probably would. Regardless of their legal tradition, lawyers around the world are engaged in the same task: solving legal problems, many of them universal in nature.

I drafted a set of facts about a fictional tort plaintiff named Silvia Winter injured by a shattering glass food container, a prototypical products liability case, then set out to find co-authors in Europe and Latin America, major world regions where the civil law tradition predominates. I was most fortunate to meet up with co-authors Adem Koyuncu, in Cologne, Germany, and Luis Eduardo Sprovieri, in Buenos Aires, Argentina, whose outstanding credentials (see "About the Authors") speak for themselves. As discussed in chapter two, Germany and Argentina are good candidates for this comparative study. Both countries have well-developed products liability systems that function similarly to other nations in Europe and Latin America.

The three of us set out on a comparative law journey spanning three continents, using Silvia Winter's hypothetical case as our instrument for exploration. None of us is an expert in comparative law, but that may have been an advantage for a project of this nature. "As every comparatist knows," writes Mathias Reimann, "it is difficult, and sometimes outright impossible, for an outsider fully to understand the law of a foreign country." Mathias Reimann, *Liability for Defective Products at the Beginning of the Twenty-First Century: Emergence of a Worldwide Standard*, 51 AM. J. COMP. L. 751, 755 (2003). We are each "insiders" with substantial backgrounds in the tort and products liability systems of our respective countries. We approached the project without preconceived notions, sharing the same kinds of questions about how tort litigation functions in other nations.

I tested, unscientifically, the contextual comparative law approach on my Spring 2006 Products Liability students at the FIU College of Law, asking them to read and comment anonymously on sample chapters of this book. As the only U.S. law students exposed to comparative/international law in every course, they were well-qualified survey participants. Their thoughtful comments helped shape the final manuscript while also confirming the value of a problem-based methodology. The following student comment was typical:

> After several semesters of having professors try their hands at fulfilling the comparative component of a class, I think a hypothetical case study might be the most effective way to integrate a comparative component into class material. One of the difficulties that always arises seems to be integrating the comparative part into the whole of the class. Sometimes, a professor picks a very defined topic and hands out a law review article comparing the U.S. on that topic to the rest of the world. In other classes, the professor picks a country and we spend one class day looking at how that particular country deals with the body of law. Some nuggets are retained, but it doesn't seem to be the spirit that the comparative law component was meant to capture.... Taking the same set of facts, and keeping the structure of the

analysis parallel while applying the law of a limited, defined set of countries, seems to me to be a very effective method for comparative study. First, it gives the student context when reading about foreign law. Instead of an expository discussion of what the law is somewhere else, this approach applies the law. I think the application portion is the most valuable component of this method. For example, instead of just reading about how Germany's Product Liability Act limits claims against retailers and distributors, we actually see how this impacts Silvia. ...

Carolina Academic Press also saw the benefits of a problem-based approach to comparative law and started the CAS based on it. Each entry in the series, this being the first, will follow a consistent format of enlisting experts in three countries, the U.S. always being one of the countries, to analyze from a real world comparative perspective a set of problem facts raising universal legal issues in a particular subject area. The series will explore a rich array of legal topics in countries from all corners of the planet.

Accessibility is a guiding principle of the CAS. The goal is to craft texts accessible to people without prior expertise in either comparative law or any of the three legal systems under study. *Practical Global Tort Litigation* is designed for any reader, in or outside the U.S., interested in learning how one common variety of products liability case would be handled, procedurally and substantively, in the U.S. common law system as compared to representative civil law systems in Europe and Latin America. As a law school text, the book is intended as a supplemental text in basic torts and products liability courses for professors who want to expose their students to a comparative legal perspective, or as a primary or supplemental text in comparative law courses or advanced courses in torts, products liability, civil procedure or litigation.

We hope you enjoy reading it as much as we enjoyed writing and learning from it.

Andrew J. McClurg
Herbert Herff Chair of Excellence,
The University of Memphis
Cecil C. Humphreys School of Law

ACKNOWLEDGMENTS

Many people generously helped us in this project, and we're grateful to all of them.

In the U.S., Jennifer Shannon and Jury Verdict Research donated their case valuation services. Dr. Robert W. Bailey and Dr. David M. Baroff provided medical advice in structuring our hypothetical case, and Bailey estimated Silvia Winter's U.S. medical expenses. Several distinguished lawyers and scholars shared their knowledge and experience, including the Honorable Timothy J. Corrigan; Professors Thomas E. Baker, William G. Childs, Elizabeth Price Foley, José Gabilondo, Jerry W. Markham, Jonathan Miller, M.C. Mirow, David G. Owen, Ellen S. Pryor, and Howard Wasserman; and practitioners Thomas Baur, Jane Lester, C. Rufus Pennington, III, and Mark Schleben. Professsor Mary Pat Treuthart edited the manuscript with her usual skill and flair. The students in McClurg's Spring 2006 Products Liability class at the Florida International University College of Law offered insightful comments on sample chapters, many of which influenced the final product. McClurg is especially indebted to his multitalented, multilingual former research assistants at the FIU College of Law: Tanya Baur, Lorella Dal Pezzo, Gaspar Forteza, and Guillermo Mancebo. Forteza, in particular, saved the day on numerous occasions and deserves special credit. FIU College of Law librarians Marisol Floren-Romero, Jan Stone, and Sailaja Tumrukota went above and beyond the call of duty in tracking down hard-to-find Argentine and German legal sources. Dean Leonard P. Strickman, Associate Dean Ediberto Román, and the FIU College of Law provided substantial research support, as did The University of Memphis Cecil C. Humphreys School of Law. Karol Landers at The University of Memphis found errors in the manuscript that everyone else missed, and, with the help of research assistant Maggie Cooper, logged many tedious hours compiling the index. Finally, we couldn't have done any of this without the help, support, and vision of all the great folks at Carolina Academic Press.

In Germany, we received valuable counsel from a number of distinguished scholars, including Markus Geisler, partner at Mayer, Brown, Rowe & Maw

LLP in Cologne, who offered his insights regarding both German and U.S. litigation procedures, and Joachim Hindemith, who lent his in-depth experience as a plaintiffs' personal injury lawyer. Dr. Ulrich Gupta and Dr. Christof Burger estimated Silvia's medical expenses in Germany. Legal trainee Philipp N. Basch provided helpful research assistance. Koyuncu is especially thankful to all members of the Mayer, Brown, Rowe & Maw LLP team in Cologne for supporting this project.

In Argentina, librarian Sandra Romagnoli provided research assistance, law student and paralegal Gloria Sivero visited courts for unpublished opinions, and Soledad Saavedra contributed her clerical assistance and tireless support. Dr. Roberto Bitton estimated the cost of medical treatment for Silvia's injuries in Argentina. Last but not least, Sprovieri is grateful to the many staff members at Baker & McKenzie's Buenos Aires office who struggled with his handwriting and succeeded.

Practical Global Tort Litigation

United States, Germany and Argentina

CHAPTER 1

ROADMAP TO A CONTEXTUAL COMPARATIVE LAW JOURNEY

This is a story about an ordinary products liability case with an extraordinary plaintiff: Silvia Winter. Silvia was a thirty-year-old university student studying to be a physical therapist when a glass jar of peanuts shattered as she attempted to place the lid on it, injuring her hand and wrist. What makes Silvia so special? She exists in three incarnations in three countries on three continents. "U.S. Silvia" is a citizen and resident of Miami, Florida, United States. "German Silvia" is a citizen and resident of Cologne, Germany. "Argentine Silvia" is a citizen and resident of Buenos Aires, Argentina. This book tracks Silvia's hypothetical products liability lawsuit seeking to recover damages for her injuries as it progresses through the legal system of each country. Like all stories, Silva's requires "back story"—in our case, to provide a contextual anchor for her perilous multinational legal journey. Before meeting Silvia, we'll give you some background about the legal systems of the U.S., Germany, and Argentina and the sources of law in common law and civil law systems, both generally and as they pertain to products liability law.

This book needs a product warning of its own. It is intended as a basic primer on comparative tort law and litigation in the U.S. common law system and a major civil law system from Europe (Germany) and Latin America (Argentina), using one common kind of products liability case as the vehicle for exploration. The emphasis is on clear, concise explanation and analysis of these topics:

• An overview of the legal systems of the U.S., Germany, and Argentina (chapter two);

• Sources of law in civil and common law countries, concentrating on sources of products liability law in the three countries under study (chapter three);

• Fact gathering and presentation procedures (chapter five);

• Expert witnesses (chapter six);

• Burdens of proof and causation (chapter seven);

3

• Theories of recovery in a products liability case involving a manufacturing defect (chapter eight);
  • Defenses in such a case (chapter nine); and
  • Damages and attorneys' fees (chapter ten).

Even though the focus is on a single set of facts, considerable generalizing is required in a book that attempts to concisely cover an entire litigated case in three countries. Volumes could be, and in many cases have been, written about the myriad topics and doctrines discussed. Moreover, within each country, different legal systems function simultaneously, with many variations among them. The U.S., for example, is comprised of not one, but fifty-one legal systems: the federal system and a separate system for each of the fifty states. Multiple judicial systems also function in Germany and Argentina.

The book attempts to deliver a big picture overview of a litigated tort case while at the same time not skimping on important details. We do not delve deeply into historical, cultural or other explanations for why legal rules developed the way they did. Any such effort in a book intended as a basic primer would have come up far short or, alternatively, would have converted the project into a much different book or set of books. Similarly, although chapter ten discusses some of the social infrastructures that shape tort litigation in the U.S. versus civil law countries, those infrastructures are not extensively analyzed. Several excellent existing works explore the historical and social evolution of common and civil law traditions, while others provide in-depth analysis of tort and products liability law in specific countries or regions. Readers interested in learning more detail should consult those works, some of which are listed in the bibliography.

One consequence of these omissions is that readers should be cautious in assessing the many convergences in doctrinal rules among the three countries highlighted herein, realizing that they may obscure underlying non-apparent differences. Similarly, with regard to divergences, Basil Markesinis cautions that simply because a particular legal feature appears to be missing in one system does not mean it is not accounted for in other ways. *See* Basil Markesinis et al., Compensation for Personal Injury in English, German and Italian Law 198 (2005).

Structural limitations include the fact that Silvia's products liability case involves only one of the three major categories of product defect: manufacturing defects. Discussion of design and informational defects is omitted. Because the book is intended to survey an entire litigated case, dispute resolution mechanisms such as mediation and settlement, by which most cases are resolved in all nations, are discussed only tangentially.

To facilitate coherent side-by-side comparisons, we opted in most places for a compartmentalized format in which the law of our respective nations is set forth under separate subheadings, beginning with the U.S., followed by Germany, and then Argentina. We considered and rejected as too unwieldy and confusing the alternative approach of trying to weave together the intricacies of the law in all three nations line by line.

We strived to construct a neutral comparative account. The purpose is to inform, not persuade. Except for brief editorial comments in the final chapter, we leave it to others, including readers, to pass judgment on the relative merits of any particular aspect of the legal systems studied.

Here is some other useful advance information:

Abbreviations. The sources below, mentioned often, are abbreviated as indicated. However, full titles are used from time to time as appropriate to refresh readers' memories.

> Argentine Civil Code—ACC
> Argentine National Code of Civil Procedure—NCCP
> Argentine Consumer Protection Law—CPL
> German Civil Code—GCC
> German Code of Civil Procedure—GCCP
> German Product Liability Act—PLA
> U.S. Restatement (Third) of Torts: Products Liability
> (1998)—*Products Liability Restatement*

Monetary and Statistical Comparisons. We gave in to the temptation to make a direct monetary comparison of Silvia's estimated damages award in each country should she prevail on the merits. Comparatists avoid making direct damages comparisons among nations, for good reason. Money figures become outdated because of inflation, deflation, and other reasons. Moreover, without accounting for all the social and other factors that influence damages awards in different countries, which is probably impossible, comparisons can take on an "apples and oranges" appearance. Our situation is even more problematic because Silvia's damages are being projected in advance. We recognize the limited value of attempting to estimate and compare damages in a hypothetical products liability case for three countries, but thought readers would want to know "the ending" to Silvia's story. More important, the projections provide a contextual basis for exploring some of the key explanations for disparities in tort damages awards between the U.S. and other nations. Don't focus on the specific numbers. They're offered only as rough comparative benchmarks. While the specific monetary amounts may be or become inaccurate, the *general relative comparisons* among the three countries are more likely to remain stable.

In discussing money, euros (Germany) and pesos (Argentina) are exchanged for U.S. dollars using the following 2006 approximate average currency exchange rates: $1.2 = 1 euro; $1 = 3 Argentine pesos. Currency exchange rates fluctuate, of course, and some currencies are more stable than others. Again, the figures are used only to provide a general comparative perspective.

Some statistics are cited, usually to support generally accepted propositions. Statistical evidence in a concise work such as this one is necessarily incomplete, omitting conflicting data and explanation as to how the figures were arrived at. As with the monetary references, readers should not put too fine a point on precise statistical figures. Many of the figures, both currency amounts and statistical percentages, were rounded to the nearest whole numbers for easier consumption.

Translations. Quotations of German and Argentine legal sources in this book were translated to English from German and Spanish by co-authors Koyuncu and Sprovieri and McClurg's research assistants. To enhance accuracy, these translations were compared to other translations, where available. One truth confirmed many times during the composition of this book is that there is no such thing as a single accurate translation of a legal principle or legalese from one language to another. When one consults five different translations to English of a particular German or Argentine legal principle, one encounters—literally—five different translations. All convey the same substance, but, invariably, differences appear in the precise words and sentence structure.

Summary Charts. Beginning with the comparison of specific areas of procedural and substantive law in chapter five, charts are inserted at the end of each chapter highlighting key similarities and differences discussed in the chapter. Intended only as handy reference guides, the charts do not contain detailed explanation or qualifications to make them precisely accurate.

With all of the above disclaimers and limitations, this book is unique in its problem approach to comparative law. By contextualizing comparative law—that is, by applying the substantive and procedural law of different countries to a consistent set of facts—the intention is to showcase similarities and differences among the U.S. common law tort system and the civil law tort systems of Germany and Argentina in a way that is understandable, interesting, and digestible. We seek to *show* in addition to tell. So what are we waiting for? To continue our journey metaphor, it's time to crank the ignition and begin the trip.

CHAPTER 2

THREE LEGAL SYSTEMS ON THREE CONTINENTS—UNITED STATES, GERMANY, AND ARGENTINA

Most comparative law study, including this book, focuses on the two most influential worldwide legal traditions: common law and civil law. The common law—a system in which judge-made precedent traditionally formed the primary source of law—developed in England beginning at the time of the Norman Conquest in 1066 A.D. and was carried to other nations, including the U.S., through British territorial expansion. Other notable common law countries include Australia, Canada, Ireland, and New Zealand. Civil law—a system in which codes and other statutes are the primary source of law—is rooted in Roman law dating back to 450 B.C. The underpinnings of modern civil law are found in the French Civil Code of 1804, often called the Napoleonic Code, and the German Civil Code of 1896. The civil law traditions of these two countries have played a dominant role both in the distribution and shaping of civil law throughout the world.

Civil law is both much older and more widely distributed than the common law tradition. All of Western Europe and Latin America operate under civil law systems, as do parts of Africa and Asia. The legal systems of Eastern Europe also were built on a foundation of civil law. Following World War II, socialist law was overlaid on those systems by the former Soviet Union. With the fall of Soviet socialism, the civil law foundation of Eastern European countries is re-emerging. *See generally* JOHN HENRY MERRYMAN, THE CIVIL LAW TRADITION: AN INTRODUCTION TO THE LEGAL SYSTEMS OF WESTERN EUROPE AND LATIN AMERICA 1–5 (2d ed. 1985) (discussing worldwide distribution of common law and civil law systems).

It's not possible to differentiate common law and civil law systems in anything approaching black and white terms. The variations among the legal systems of different nations, even nations that fall under the same classification as "common law nations" or "civil law nations," are enormous. They include

differences in both procedural and substantive rules of law, as well as fundamental structural differences such as the extent to which a system adheres to
the principle of judicial review. Even in countries following similar legal traditions, social and economic differences dramatically impact how those rules
are applied in practice and the results that flow from their application. It has
been observed, for example, that the modern version of England's common
law system has more in common with civil law systems on the European con-
tinent than with the U.S.

Complicating categorization further, many legal systems are mixed systems
combining elements of both Anglo-American common law and European civil
law, and in some cases, Islamic law. South Africa's legal system is a combination of Roman-Dutch civil law and English common law. Pakistan's legal system is grounded in English common law mixed with elements of Islamic law,
while India's is a combination of common law and Hindu law. The U.S. state
of Louisiana is a mixed civil law-common law jurisdiction. In some civil law
countries, U.S. law has been particularly influential. This is true in many Latin
American countries, including Argentina.

With 192 nations on the planet, and so many variations among their legal
traditions, selecting any three countries for comparative study is susceptible
to criticism as being arbitrary. Nevertheless, the U.S., Germany, and Argentina
are fitting subjects for a tri-continent "common law vs. civil law" comparative
products liability study. The U.S. is the largest common law system in the
world and the U.S. litigation system is the most intricately developed and oft-
used, while Germany and Argentina are major civil law systems on their respective continents.

Germany boasts Europe's largest population and economy and the Ger-
manic civil law tradition is rivaled only by France in terms of its world influence. Because Germany is a world leader in producing consumer and industrial products, the country has a highly-developed products liability legal
system. In light of the ongoing European legal harmonization process, German litigation procedures can be regarded as representative of many European
communities. Substantively, all members of the European Union have now
implemented the European Union Product Liability Directive of 1985, a statement of uniform products liability principles.

In Latin America, where litigation practice in general and personal injury
law in particular are less well-developed than in the U.S. or Western Europe,
Argentina is viewed as a progressive legal leader. This is particularly true in
products liability law, a fast-growing field of Argentine law and a good proxy
to understand how law works in practice in Argentina. In addition to relevant
code and other statutory provisions, a well-developed set of judicial precedent

is available addressing the main issues in products liability, as well as a wealth of scholarly commentary. A study of products liability in seven Latin American countries concluded that Argentine law has had the most impact on the other nations in the study and was the most innovative and likely to adopt new theories. Alejandro Hernandez Maestroni, *Overview of the Study Undertaken by the National Center for Inter-American Free Trade, in Symposium— Products Liability in Latin America*, 20 ARIZ. J. INT'L & COMP. LAW 1, 6 (2003).

Argentina's courts and legal profession function quite similarly to their Latin American counterparts. The country is part of a far-reaching trade and legal harmonization pact in South America known as Mercosur, a shortening of *Mercado Común del Sur* or Southern Common Market. Signed in 1994 by Argentina, Brazil, Paraguay, and Uruguay, Mercosur is intended to harmonize trade policies in all sectors to facilitate free trade among its members. Chile and Bolivia also have entered into agreements with Mercosur. The member countries have a combined population exceeding two hundred million people, more than two-thirds of the population of South America. Mercosur may ultimately lead to legal harmonization similar to what has occurred in the European Union. Already, Mercosur has proposed rules addressing consumer protection, although they have not been adopted.

Including a civil law nation from Europe and one from Latin America adds an extra comparative dimension. While both Germany and Argentina are civil law countries, large cultural and economic differences exist between them and between their continents that influence their legal traditions. Most comparative law analysis pertaining to products liability has focused on Europe and Great Britain. Even the U.S. hasn't received much attention, but Latin America has been largely ignored, which is not surprising given the link between products liability issues and economic development. That should change as Latin American markets continue to emerge. Although Latin American economies remain somewhat volatile, in 2004–05 Latin America posted its strongest economic growth in a quarter century. In today's global marketplace, the citizens of virtually all nations are actively involved in buying and selling mass-produced products, both from within and without their borders.

Comparing Geographic and Demographic Data

Not sure exactly where Argentina is located? Wondering if Cologne, Germany has anything to do with fragrances of the same name? Can't remember where the U.S. ranks in worldwide population? No problem. To give readers at least a barebones frame of reference, some demographic and geographic statistical information is offered about the respective countries and cities where our hypothetical lawsuit will be filed. Most of the information below comes from *The World Fact Book* compiled by the U.S. Central Intelligence Agency (available at http://www.cia.gov/cia/publications/factbook/). Although some might be reticent about relying on information provided by the notorious American spy agency, *The World Fact Book* is regarded as a reliable, up-to-date source, collecting information from U.S. agencies and organizations such as the Bureau of the Census, Department of Defense, Department of Labor, and the National Science Foundation. Readers must consult history, sociology, and anthropology texts for deeper cultural understanding and travel guides for more colorful descriptions. Borrowing from Sgt. Joe Friday in the 1960s U.S. television series, *Dragnet*, these are "just the facts," and very basic ones at that.

United States

Located in North America between Canada and Mexico, the United States has a population of approximately 298 million people, including a labor force of 149 million, and a land area of 9,161,923 square kilometers. It is the world's third largest country both in size (after Russia and Canada) and population (after China and India). The U.S. is comprised of fifty states, including Alaska and Hawaii, and the District of Columbia, where the capital is located.

The U.S. has the largest economy in the world. The Gross Domestic Product (GDP) in 2005 was $12.47 trillion, or $42,000 per capita. Twelve percent of the population lives below the poverty line. While highly diversified, the economy is primarily service-based, with 79% of the GDP coming from services, 21% from industrial processes, and 1% from agriculture.

The U.S., of course, imports and exports massive quantities of consumer products and other goods and materials. Exports break down on a percentage basis by type of product as follows: 9% agricultural products, 27% industrial supplies, 49% capital goods (e.g., aircraft, computers, telecommunications equipment), and 15% consumer goods. Imports are divided as follows: 5% agricultural products, 33% industrial supplies (including oil), 30% capital goods, and 32% consumer goods.

Ethnically, the U.S. population is roughly 69% non-Hispanic white, 13% Hispanic, 13% black, 4% Asian, and 1% Native American and Alaska native. Religiously, the population is divided as follows: 52% Protestant, 24% Roman Catholic, 2% Mormon, 1% Jewish, 1% Muslim, 10% other, and 10% either nonreligious or no religious preference. English is the dominant language (82%), with Spanish being the second most prevalent language (11%).

Ninety-seven percent of the U.S. population over the age of fifteen can read and write.

Miami-Dade County, Florida, where our hypothetical case will be filed, is a cultural and ethnic melting pot of 2.3 million people. Located on the southern Atlantic coast of Florida, Miami-Dade is the eighth largest county in the U.S. The city is known for its beautiful beaches, Latin-Caribbean culture, South Beach nightclubs, and professional sports franchises such as the Miami Dolphins and Miami Heat. Nearly 60% of the population is Hispanic. Fifty percent of the residents were born in another country.

Germany

Located in the middle of Europe, Germany has a population of 82.5 million people, including a labor force of 43 million, and a land area of 349,223 square kilometers, slightly smaller than the U.S. state of Montana. Germany is Europe's most populous country, bordered on the north by Denmark and the North and Baltic Seas, on the south by Switzerland and Austria, on the east by Poland and the Czech Republic, and on the west by France, Belgium, the Netherlands, and Luxembourg. Germany is a constitutional federal republic divided into sixteen states.

Germany's affluent and technologically powerful economy is the largest economy in Europe and the fifth largest economy in the world. The Gross Domestic Product (GDP) in 2005 was $2.76 trillion, or $29,800 per capita. Similar to the U.S., Germany's diverse economy is primarily service-based, with the GDP comprised of 70% services, 29% industrial processes, and 1% agriculture.

Germany is among the world's largest and most technologically advanced producers of iron, steel, coal, cement, chemicals, machinery, vehicles, machine tools, electronics, food and beverages, ships, and textiles. In 2005, Germany exported $1 trillion in such materials and goods, while importing machinery, vehicles, chemicals, foodstuffs, textiles, and metals to the tune of $800 billion.

Ethnically, Germany's population breaks down as follows: 92% German, 2% Turkish, 6% other (largely Greek, Italian, Polish, Russian, Serbo-Croatian, and Spanish). Religiously, the country is divided as follows: 34% Protestant, 34% Roman Catholic, 4% Muslim, and 28% other. German is the dominant language, although English is widely spoken. Ninety-nine percent of the German population over the age of fifteen can read and write.

Cologne (Köln in German), the city where our hypothetical lawsuit will be filed, is the oldest large city in Germany. Founded by the Romans, Cologne is located in the German state of North Rhine-Westphalia, along the Rhine River between Düsseldorf and Bonn. With a population exceeding one million, Cologne is the fourth largest city in Germany and the sixteenth largest city in the European Union. Cologne is the capital of carnival in Germany, and the city's Roman Dome is the nation's most visited tourist attraction. Among the city's noteworthy contributions to popular products, Cologne is known for its Kölsch beer, which like champagne, is a protected regional appellation. Cologne was home to the original Eau de Cologne, a light perfume first produced in 1709 by Italian Giovanni Maria Farina. The city's largest employer is also a product producer: the U.S. Ford Motor Company.

Argentina

Located at the southern tip of South America, Argentina has a population of approximately 40 million people, including a labor force of approximately 15 million, and a land area of 2,736,690 square kilometers, roughly one-third the size of the U.S. It is South America's second largest country, after Brazil. The country's long western border abuts Chile, while the eastern border offers 4,700 kilometers of undulating coastline on the Atlantic Ocean. Argentina is bordered on the north by Bolivia, Paraguay, Brazil, and Uruguay. The country is a federal democratic republic divided into twenty-three provinces.

Argentina is a country rich in natural resources and maintains a diverse industrial base and export-oriented agricultural sector. Plagued by economic problems for decades, including rampant inflation, capital flight, and large foreign debt, the country plunged into economic crisis in the late 1990s. The past few years, however, have seen a dramatic turnaround in the economy. In 2005, Argentina's GDP grew 9.1%, expanding to $182 billion, or $13,700 per capita. Nevertheless, inflation remains a problem and approximately 39% of Argentina's population continues to live below the poverty line. The country's GDP is derived 54% from services, 35% from industry, and 11% from agriculture.

Among Argentina's major exports are edible oils, fuels and energy, cereals, feed, leather, beef and poultry, and motor vehicles. Chief imports include machinery and equipment, motor vehicles, chemicals, metals and manufactures, and plastics. Argentina is the fourth largest exporter in Latin America, behind Mexico, Brazil, and Venezuela.

Ethnically, Argentina's population is 97% white (of mostly Spanish and Italian descent), and 3% mestizo (mixed white and Amerindian ancestry), Amerindian, or other non-white groups. Religiously, the population is divided as follows: 92% Roman Catholic (but with less than 20% practicing), 2%

Protestant, 2% Jewish, and 4% other. Spanish is the official and dominant language; however, English, Italian, German, and French are widely spoken. Identical to the U.S., 97% of the population over the age of fifteen can read and write.

Buenos Aires, where our hypothetical case will be filed, is the capital of Argentina, as well as its largest city, with a sprawling metropolitan area population exceeding thirteen million people, making it one of the largest urban centers in the world. Located on the southern shore of the River Plate, Buenos Aires occupies more than 8% of the total land mass of the country. Buenos Aires is a vibrant cosmopolitan city nicknamed the "Paris of South America." The city's residents, who call themselves *porteños*, have a passion for, among other things, great steaks, tango, and soccer.

Comparing Court Systems, Judges, and Legal Professions

Before one could begin to understand how an automobile transmission works, he or she would have to know what an automobile looks like. Similarly, before attempting to understand how a tort case is handled in a particular legal system, one needs at least a snapshot of the overall system. Here's an overview of the court structures, judiciaries, and legal professions in the U.S., Germany, and Argentina.

United States

Courts. The U.S. is a federalist system in which a federal, or national, court system operates both independently from and interdependently with separate court systems in each of the fifty states. Each system (that is, the federal judicial system and the judicial system of each state) has a set of trial courts, one or more intermediate appellate courts, and a single high court, called the Supreme Court in the federal system and in most states. The classic representational diagram is a triangle or pyramid with the trial courts lining the bottom, a much smaller number of intermediate appellate courts filling a layer in the middle, and a single high court at the top. Most courts in the U.S., both state and federal, are courts of general jurisdiction, although some specialized courts also exist. In the federal system, these include bankruptcy and military courts, as well as a tax court and court of claims. States often have specialized courts in areas such as family law and probate law.

The federal court system is made up of ninety-four trial courts known as U.S. District Courts spread across the country, thirteen intermediate appellate courts known as U.S. Courts of Appeal (eleven regional courts of appeal, plus courts of appeal for the Federal Circuit and the District of Columbia Circuit), and the U.S. Supreme Court. Federal district courts and judgeships are allocated roughly according to population and corresponding caseload. Thus, largely rural Idaho and North Dakota have only one federal district court with two judges each, whereas populous Florida (home to "U.S. Silvia") has three district courts and thirty-one district court judges.

Civil subject matter jurisdiction in the federal court system is primarily limited to cases involving federal questions (e.g., a dispute involving a federal statute or a provision of the U.S. Constitution) or those where the opposing parties are citizens of different states and the amount in controversy exceeds $75,000. *See* 28 U.S.C. §1331 (federal question jurisdiction); 28 U.S.C. §1332 (diversity of citizenship jurisdiction). Tort law, including products liability law, has traditionally been a matter of state law and most tort cases are filed in state courts. Diversity of citizenship jurisdiction, however, allows some tort cases to be brought in federal court. When federal subject matter jurisdiction is based on diversity of citizenship, federal courts are required to apply the substantive legal rules of the state in which the case arose under the *Erie* doctrine, from *Erie R.R. v. Tompkins*, 304 U.S. 64 (1938). Thus, a federal court hearing a tort case filed in Florida would be required to apply the substantive common law and statutory rules of the state of Florida to the case.

In addition to the federal judicial system, each state has its own unified judicial system, also made up of trial courts, intermediate appellate courts, and a state high court. Most civil disputes of all kinds, including, as noted, most tort suits, are filed in state court. Even in situations where federal diversity of citizenship jurisdiction exists, most U.S. tort plaintiffs prefer litigating in state courts, where civil justice is generally faster, less formal, and less expensive. It is not uncommon, however, for defendants in diversity cases to remove cases to federal courts, which are thought to be less subject to the caprice of state judges, many of whom are elected.

Contrary to the view of the American justice system generated by movies and television, very few civil cases that are filed actually go to trial in the U.S. Most cases settle or are dismissed. With regard to tort cases, U.S. Department of Justice statistics show that only 2% of the 98,786 tort cases that were terminated in the U.S. district courts in fiscal 2002–03 were decided by a trial. Another popular misconception about the U.S. tort system, at least among laypersons, is that plaintiffs always, or at least usually, win. In actuality, plaintiffs lose about as often as they win. Plaintiffs won 52% of state court tort trials in the nation's seventy-five largest counties in 2001, a figure that has remained relatively steady since 1992. They fared somewhat worse in products liability cases than in other kinds of tort suits, prevailing 44% of the time.

Trials are presided over by a single judge in both the federal and state systems. The right to trial by jury, a fundamental distinguishing feature from civil law systems, is guaranteed by both the federal and forty-seven state constitutions. Again running contrary to public perception, a majority of civil cases that go to trial in the U.S. are "bench" trials; that is, trials before judges rather than juries. Although the right to jury trial is constitutionally guaranteed, one of the parties must demand a jury or the right will be deemed waived. In the majority of cases involving business disputes, the parties are content with a trial before a judge only. In personal injury cases, however, plaintiffs almost always demand a jury trial. In 2001, in the seventy-five largest U.S. counties, roughly 12,000 tort, contract, and real property disputes were resolved by a full trial. Ninety-one percent of the tort trials were jury trials, compared to 43% of the real property trials, and only 27% of the contract trials.

Assuming a party can point to an alleged error in the trial court, an appeal as of right exists to an intermediate appellate court in the federal and most state systems. In reality, only a small percentage of cases are appealed. For example, in 2001, only 13% of the tort cases terminated in the state courts were appealed.

Judges. Federal judges are nominated by the President and must be confirmed by the U.S. Senate. They are appointed for life. A majority of states still rely on popular elections to select some or all of their judges for a term of years, although the trend, particularly for appellate judges, is toward eliminating judicial elections in favor of judicial appointments by governors or legislatures, usually with the help of judicial nominating commissions. Even appointed state judges often are subject to regular retention votes, an arrangement in which citizens are asked to vote "yes" or "no" every few years as to whether the judge should be retained on the bench. Unless the judge has become controversial for some reason, these merit retention votes usually operate as perfunctory stamps of approval.

Judges in the U.S. rarely begin their legal careers as members of the bench. Becoming a judge is an honor usually reserved for a select group of lawyers who have established themselves and their reputations over many years as practitioners.

Given the starring role of judges in a common law system, including the general recognition (if not complete popular acceptance) of the principle of judicial supremacy, U.S. judges stand out much more than their counterparts in civil law countries. Most U.S. law students can rattle off the names of legendary judges such as Benjamin Cardozo, Learned Hand, Oliver Wendell Holmes, and John Marshall, as well as current U.S. Supreme Court justices. Some judges of lesser status become household names among laypersons due to their handling of cases attracting substantial media attention. This is not the case in civil law countries, where most judges labor in obscurity.

Legal profession. Statistics compiled by the American Bar Association show that in 2005 the U.S. had 1,104,766 lawyers, approximately one lawyer for every 270 citizens. Approximately 28% of U.S. lawyers are women. Not surprisingly, the majority of lawyers are concentrated in heavily populated areas. New York has the most lawyers (142,538), while North Dakota has the fewest (1,393).

In 2005, the U.S. had 191 law schools accredited by the American Bar Association, as well as some unaccredited law schools. Enrollment at accredited law schools stands at about 148,000 students, divided almost evenly between men and women. Law school is a three-year graduate program leading to a Juris Doctor degree. (Warning: If you are a U.S. law student and this comes as news to you, step back and reassess your career plans.) A four-year undergraduate degree is a prerequisite to law school admission. To qualify to practice, a law school graduate must take and pass an intensive state-administered examination known with fear and trepidation among law students as "the bar exam."

Germany

Courts. Germany operates under a system of general jurisdiction courts, as well as separate systems of administrative, labor, social welfare, and tax courts. There is also a Federal Constitutional Court, which holds the power of judicial review over the constitutionality of all German judicial, legislative, and administrative acts. This court is perhaps the ultimate concession to the fact that, even in a civil law system where legislatures theoretically reign supreme over courts, all law has to be interpreted. The courts of general jurisdiction handle most criminal and civil cases, including tort cases.

Germany is composed of sixteen states, each of which maintains its own court system. The analogy to a triangle in the U.S. court system accurately describes the hierarchy of German court systems as well. The courts of general jurisdiction operate on four levels: the Local Courts (*Amtsgericht*) (handling family law matters, as well as small civil disputes), the State District Courts (*Landgericht*) (handling the bulk of serious civil litigation, including tort cases), the State Appeals Courts (*Oberlandesgericht*) (handling appeals from the State District Courts), and the Federal Court of Justice (*Bundesgerichts-*

hof). The Federal Court of Justice, located in the city of Karlsruhe, is the supreme court of last resort in both civil and criminal matters. For clarity, it is referred to in this book as the Federal Supreme Court.

A typical tort case involving serious injuries would be filed in the State District Court for the state in which the injury occurred. The State District Courts have jurisdiction in civil cases where the amount in controversy exceeds 5,000 euros (roughly $6,000). If the amount in controversy is less than 5,000 euros, jurisdiction lies in the Local Courts. Currently, there are 116 State District Courts spread throughout the country. Civil law countries do not use juries. Traditionally, the case would be heard by a panel of three professional judges. Reforms adopted in 2002, however, require that some cases, including most cases like Silvia's, be assigned to a single judge.

In civil cases where the amount in controversy involves more than 600 euros, appeal may be taken as of right to the State Appeals Court. Currently, twenty-four such appellate courts exist. Appellate cases, including tort cases, are assigned by subject matter to be heard by specialized panels, ensuring that the judges will possess expertise in the particular area. This is different from the U.S., where judges on courts of general jurisdiction do not specialize in particular subject areas.

For most cases, the State Appeals Courts function as the court of last resort. The only place to go from there is the Federal Supreme Court. There are no state supreme courts. Appeals to the Federal Supreme Court, where cases also are assigned to specialized panels, used to be more or less a matter of right if the amount in controversy exceeded a certain amount, but the reforms of 2002 enlarged the discretionary authority of the court to accept or deny review in most cases, much like the U.S. Supreme Court exercises the bulk of its jurisdiction through discretionary review. Today, civil lawsuits reach the Federal Supreme Court only if they raise new questions of law or if there is a divergence of authority in the State Appeals Courts.

Judges. Contrary to the U.S., in Germany, as in other civil law countries, judges function as relatively low-profile civil servants. Becoming a judge in Germany is just one of the many options available to persons who graduate from a university law program. It's a "career choice," although, realistically, only the top students have a chance of landing judicial positions. Candidates who pass exams and receive special training in a post-graduate internship program can begin serving on the bench in a short time. After a probationary period of a few years, the judge receives lifetime tenure. The training, exam, and probationary requirements promote a uniformly well-qualified (as well as uniform in terms of judicial attitudes toward case handling) bench. Yet, while this description is accurate as a sterile summary, it obscures the tremendous importance that government posts and government institutions hold in modern civil law societies. While judges in civil law systems may not achieve the fame or notoriety of some of their U.S. counterparts, holding a judgeship in the large and prestigious public sector of a civil law culture is a significant honor.

Judges usually begin their careers in the lower courts, and, like other civil servants, may apply for promotion to higher courts based on their records and seniority. Due to the deeply rooted ideology of strict separation of powers in civil law systems, as well as the standardized training and the civil servant system in which judges operate, one does not find "activist" judges in Germany. Unlike some U.S. judges, German judges rarely forge new, creative paths in the law. That is not their role. Even if a judge did strike a new path in a particular case, he could change his mind and go the opposite way in the next case, forever obliterating the former position without a wrinkle. Such is the nature of civil law systems.

Legal profession. As of 2004, there were approximately 121,000 attorneys licensed to practice in Germany, with a gender split of roughly 73% men and 27% women. Germany has approximately one lawyer for every 682 inhabitants, a much lower per capita ratio than in either the U.S. or Argentina.

Germany has forty law schools, with more than 93,000 students, including both German and foreign students. Slightly more than one-half of German law students are women. Legal education in Germany is structured much differently than in the U.S. Whereas U.S. legal education is a three-year (four years for part-time students) post-graduate professional degree program, academic legal education in Germany is more like a "major" studied in undergraduate university programs. This is the case in most civil law nations. The normal program leading to a degree in law is five years. However, that is only the first part of a German lawyer's education. Toward the end of a university program in law, students must take and pass their first state exam, known, appropriately enough, as the "First Exam." At that point, lawyers-to-be enter phase two of their training. This second block is called the *Referendariat*, which is essentially a two-year legal clerkship during which students receive practical training working at a law firm, court, prosecutor's office or other government agency. After the *Referendariat*, students must pass the "Second Exam," which is akin to the bar exam in the U.S. Passing the Second Exam earns one the title of *Volljurist*, or "full jurist," and entitlement to practice law. Because of this lengthier two-part system, German lawyers generally enter their work life a couple of years later than their American counterparts.

Argentina

Courts. Given that Argentina's constitution, adopted in 1853, was modeled after the U.S. constitution, it is not surprising that the structure of the country's judicial system resembles that in the U.S., with both a federal judiciary and separate judicial systems for each of the nation's twenty-three provinces, which can be analogized to U.S. states.

Moreover, in 1994, an amendment to the Federal Constitution vested the federal capital city of Buenos Aires, where our hypothetical suit will be filed, with autonomy similar to that of a province. Despite this grant of autonomy, the nation has been reluctant to surrender its local prerogatives in the capital city, one of them being the administration of justice. The result is that the city of Buenos Aires maintains a somewhat confusing, to outsiders at least, court structure in which two parallel "federal" court systems coexist: the true "federal" courts (described below) and what are referred to as the "national" courts.

The national courts are courts of general jurisdiction that deal only with local matters in the federal capital city. In other words, although they are technically part of the federal judicial system, they are "national" in name only. The city of Buenos Aires also created its own system of local courts after being granted autonomy in 1994, but those courts have only limited jurisdiction because of the federal government's reluctance to surrender judicial power in the capital. While discussions continue about transferring the national courts from the federal system to the city, some national court judges have protested that they are federal judges and will fight against relinquishing that status. The bottom line is that for the foreseeable future the national courts in the city of Buenos Aires fill the role of general jurisdiction trial courts in nearly all criminal and civil cases.

As is true of both the U.S. and Germany, Argentina's federal and provincial court systems, as well as the national court system in the city of Buenos Aires, are structured in a hierarchical form, with trial courts (called "first instance courts") at the bottom, intermediate appellate courts ("second instance courts") in the middle, and a high court at the top.

The federal courts consist of several local and territorial-level courts, seventeen appellate courts, and the Supreme Court (*Corte Suprema de Justicia de la Nación*). Much like in the U.S., the federal courts are endowed with original jurisdiction to hear matters of diversity (i.e., where the conflict is between persons from different provinces) and those in which the subject matter is federal in nature (i.e., trademark and patent infringement, admiralty, and disputes between any person and the federal government). The Supreme Court also has original jurisdiction in certain cases, such as those involving claims against a province, claims by one province against another, and cases involving foreign states or their ambassadors.

Mirroring the federal system, the provincial judicial systems consist of three levels of courts: the trial courts, intermediate appellate courts, and the Provincial Supreme Courts (*Tribunales Superiores de Justicia*). The Provincial Supreme Courts are made up of three or nine-judge panels, depending on the province. Like Germany and most civil law countries, in addition to courts of general civil and criminal jurisdiction, some Argentine provinces have a series of specialized courts in the areas of administrative, commercial, and labor matters.

The national courts in the city of Buenos Aires are structured similarly to the provincial courts, with a system of specialized trial courts and an intermediate appellate court for each specialty area (e.g., civil, commercial, etc.). Unlike the provincial court systems, however, each of which has its own supreme court, the court of last resort for the national courts in the city of Buenos Aires is the Federal Supreme Court of Argentina.

As in the U.S., every court is vested with the power to judge the constitutionality of a law. This is known as the "diffuse" constitutionality test. It contrasts with the centralized control in place in some European civil law countries, such as Germany, in which only one national "constitutional" court has the authority to rule on matters of constitutional compliance. In part because of the diffuse constitutionality test and the fact that Argentine court judgments lack official precedential value, forum shopping is prevalent. Many litigants favor judges sitting in Buenos Aires and a few other large cities. The judiciary of small or unpopulated provinces is rather unreliable, usually favoring local residents.

Ordinary civil cases, including tort cases, are filed in the ordinary "local" court of the province in which they arose, or in our hypothetical case, in an ordinary "national" court in Buenos Aires. Civil cases are heard by a single judge. Interestingly, the Argentine constitution guarantees a right to trial by jury, but the right has not been implemented. The right to trial by jury is, however, being seriously studied by the federal government and is being experimented with in parts of the country in certain cases. In the province of Córdoba, for example, legislation has been passed adopting juries for some serious criminal cases. Some Argentine political scientists predict that jury trials ultimately will be extended nationwide for all types of cases, which would make Argentina quite unique among civil law countries.

Either party may appeal the trial court's judgment as a matter of right to an intermediate appellate court known as a *Cámara*, made up of three-judge panels similar to the panels of most intermediate appellate courts in the U.S. Contrary to the U.S., where only a small percentage of cases are appealed, nearly all first-instance court decisions are challenged on appeal. In fact, certain rules regulating the legal profession make it an ethical violation not to challenge on appeal a decision against a client. The decision of the *Cámara* will, in most ordinary civil cases, be dispositive. Appeals to the Supreme Court are limited to special circumstances not present in garden variety tort cases.

Judges. As of 2003, Argentina had 4,400 judges, including 820 federal judges. The selection of judges is accomplished through various mechanisms, depending on where the particular position to be filled stands in the judicial hierarchy. As in the U.S., justices of the federal Supreme Court, known as "ministers," are appointed by the president, subject to Senate confirmation. The appointment of lower court judges, however, is accomplished differently. By constitutional mandate, a special council called the *Consejo de la Magistratura*, composed of members of Congress, practicing lawyers, jurists, and legal scholars, nominate candidates through a rather strict and complex examination and scrutiny process. The President then nominates candidates from this pool subject to Senate confirmation.

Judges serve lifetime appointments, subject to good behavior and voluntary resignation. No power can remove them, save Senate impeachment for Federal Supreme Court ministers or impeachment by specially convened juries in the case of lower court judges. It is as difficult to remove an Argentine judge from office as it is to remove a judge in the U.S.

Judges, of course, are supposed to be impartial, and lifetime appointments would seem to facilitate impartiality. In reality, however, there has been much anecdotal evidence of judicial impartiality and corruption over the years. As one example, during the most recent economic crisis, in which the government froze bank accounts, citizens could apply to a local court for an order to unfreeze their funds. By some accounts, certain judges sitting in small provincial cities were all too willing to grant such orders—in return for a percentage of the assets. In contrast, some federal judges sitting in Buenos Aires and other large cities made it a personal crusade to unfreeze as many deposits as possible in an effort to honor the people's constitutional rights. The latter faced and withstood fierce attack from the executive branch.

Although judicial reform has been an ongoing process, some commentators argue that the problems that pervade the Argentine judiciary will be difficult to eradicate. According to a report prepared by the World Bank, factors seen as facilitating corrupt practices in the Argentine judicial system include backlogs and delay, the lack of clear administrative procedures and accurate case monitoring, and widespread acceptance of ex parte communications with judges. Of course, some degree of judicial corruption exists in all systems, but, at least according to public perception, it may be more institutionalized in Argentina. Polls show that Argentine citizens consider corruption to be a serious problem in the nation's judicial systems.

Legal profession. Reliable statistics regarding the legal profession do not exist for Argentina. Various sources cite different figures for the same statistic. With that caveat in mind, we selected what appear to be the most reliable figures. Approximately 130,000 lawyers practice in Argentina, which translates to one lawyer for every 308 inhabitants, a ratio not dissimilar to that in the U.S.

Argentina has thirty-four public and private law schools, in which approximately 130,000 law students are enrolled. The largest legal education program in the country, by far, is at the University of Buenos Aires. As in Germany, basic law degrees are obtained through undergraduate university studies that generally consume five years. Unlike the U.S. and Germany, no proficiency exam is required to practice law in Argentina. We can almost hear the startled reactions of U.S. and German law students: "What? No licensing exams?" That's right. There is no bar exam as in the U.S. or first and second exams as in Germany. All one needs to practice law is a degree.

Before you consider moving to Argentina and enrolling in law school, it should be noted that this practice has become controversial in recent years, with reputed scholars and practitioners advocating reform. The argument to institute proficiency exams flows from the fact that the current practice was established when there were fewer law schools and stricter education standards. In other words, law schools were expected to perform the screening function served by bar exams. After the Federal Ministry of Education relaxed the requirements for authorizing a university to grant law degrees, many new law schools were established. It may well be that in the future proficiency exams will be implemented in Argentina as a prerequisite to practice law.

Argentina has seventy-six bar associations. The largest, again by a wide margin, is the Public Bar of Lawyers of the Federal Capital (*Colegio Público de Abogados de la Capital Federal*) in Buenos Aires, with more than 64,000 members. Approximately 40% of the lawyers licensed to practice in the federal capital are women. Given Argentina's volatile economy over the years, being a lawyer in Argentina has not offered the same economic opportunities for most lawyers that are available to U.S. lawyers.

CHAPTER 3

Sources of Law

The last preliminary stage before setting forth and analyzing Silvia Winter's hypothetical case is to gain insight into the sources of law in common law versus civil law countries, as well as the specific sources of products liability law in the U.S., Germany, and Argentina. "Where does law come from?" is a question that goes to the heart of the core differences between common law and civil law traditions. As will be seen throughout this book, the answers in real life are quite different from popular perception.

Where Does Law Come From? — An Overview

Common Law: As the Case May Be

It is regularly said that the central distinguishing feature of a common law tradition is that the primary source of law is a body of case law developed by judges known as "precedent." The inventory of judicial precedent in the U.S. is large. West's National Reporter System, which publishes judicial opinions of both state and federal courts, contains more than eleven thousand volumes of precedent from more than six hundred U.S. courts. The system adds more than 130,000 decisions each year. Theoretically, under the doctrine of *stare decisis*, if a case is "binding precedent," the rule of the case must be followed by a court confronted with similar facts in a subsequent case.

Simplistically, binding precedent in state systems consists of cases decided by a higher court of the same jurisdiction that cannot be distinguished from the case at bar. Thus, the decision of a state supreme court is binding precedent on all other courts in that state, including trial courts and intermediate appellate courts. Contrarily, a decision of the high court of a different state would not be binding, although it might be considered persuasive. Similarly, a federal court decision interpreting state law might be considered persuasive, but would not be binding on a state court. In the federal system, decisions by the U.S. Courts of Appeal are binding on the federal district courts in the same federal circuit. Decisions of the U.S. Supreme Court interpreting federal law are "the law of the land," binding in all state and federal courts.

Reality diverges from theory with regard to the binding nature of judicial precedent in the U.S. common law system. Although a system in which precedent controls the outcome of cases would seem to assure a degree of certainty and predictability in adjudicating cases, in practice, common law decision-making allows for great flexibility in reaching decisions.

The conventional view of judging in a common law system is a simplistic one: decisions are arrived at by applying existing rules of law from similar cases to known facts. In the early twentieth century, a school of critical analysis known as legal realism emerged in the U.S. that challenged this conventional view, a view Roscoe Pound labeled "mechanical jurisprudence." Legal realism served as an ancestor to the critical legal studies movement of the late twentieth century. Without embracing everything the realists had to say, their critique of formulaic judging is useful for our overview of common law decision-making.

Realists rejected the notion that judges act as "living oracles" who merely find and apply rather than make law. They believed that neither the body of legal rules nor the process of judicial fact determination is certain enough to provide a sound basis for predicting the outcome of litigation, controlling judicial discretion or evaluating judges and the bases for their decisions. In other words, they essentially argued that there is little precedent that is truly binding. Though the realists did not always make the distinction clear, a rough dichotomy of philosophy existed between "fact skeptics" and "rule skeptics." Jurist and expositor of realist thought Jerome Frank elaborated on the difference in his book, *Law and the Modern Mind* (1963). The fact skeptics were concerned primarily with trial court decisions and the elusive nature of fact determination. Because the judge or jury chooses which facts to believe, and because such selection is frequently based on either conscious or unconscious prejudices, the fact skeptics believed there is little to constrain a trial court from reaching whatever decision it chooses. Because appellate courts have limited power in common law systems to disturb fact-findings made by trial courts, the realists asserted that many trial court mistakes go uncorrected at the appellate level. Precedent, they argued, thus becomes of small value because the determination of the facts by the trial court, either the judge or jury, already has determined which precedent will control.

Rule skeptics focused on appellate court decisions. They were skeptical of the notion that the rules articulated by judges in a written decision provide reliable guidance in predicting the results of future cases, or even that the written decisions represent the true reasons for why the court reached the result it did. Their view was that judges do not decide cases by applying precedential rules to facts to reach a decision, but rather, operate in reverse by first arriving at a decision and then working backwards, searching for rules to support their conclusions. The rule skeptics believed that the rules expressed in judicial opinions mask the true reasons for the decision, including the mores, customs, social, economic, and political backgrounds of the judge.

The realists' basic points must be appreciated. The notion that all, or even most, decisions in common law systems are controlled by the mechanical application of "binding precedent" is not accurate. Even setting aside the cynical views held by some realists regarding the motivations of judges, few cases are identical to one another. A change in a single fact may command a different result from a prior, otherwise similar case. Thus, it should come as no surprise that judges in common law systems are required to make new law on a regular basis despite an ample body of precedent.

Moreover, one must remember that case law constitutes only one slice of the total law-pie in common law jurisdictions. Constitutions, statutes, and administrative regulations fill in the rest of the pie and they are each large slices indeed. The United States Code, the body of federal legislation binding in all fifty states, fills more than 34,000 pages, excluding tables and indices. Merryman has observed that individual U.S. states have as much legislation in force as most civil law countries. Of course, constitutions, statutes, and regulations invariably require interpretation by courts in common law and, as seen below, civil law systems, adding another vast layer of judicial precedent.

Civil Law: An Ode to Codes

Whereas conventional wisdom holds that the primary source of law in common law systems is a body of binding judicial case precedent, the same wisdom holds that the *only* sources of law in civil law systems are codes and other legislation. This orthodoxy took root following the French Revolution in the late eighteenth century, which triggered the emergence of nation-states in Continental Europe and a belief in state sovereignty, both externally and inwardly, as a fundamental concept. Inwardly, this included the view that only the state, not individuals, could make law, a view that was reflected in a belief in the strict separation of power between legislatures and courts. Only the former had the power to make law for the state. *See generally* MERRYMAN, at 19–25.

Legislative power found its primary expression in codes. Codes form the basic blueprint of law in civil law countries. Codes are essentially books of statutes that set forth, in an organized fashion, the law in different subject areas. However, this description, while technically accurate, does not do justice to the importance of codes in civil law nations. In the way they are venerated, codes may be better analogized for common law students to constitutions rather than statutes. While U.S. statutes tend to be unsystematic, topical, specific, and prolix, codes purport to be organized and complete, yet succinct and rich in meaning. Organization is the key. That is what a code is supposed to do: place legal categories in order so that solutions to practical problems can be identified by the lawyers, sanctioned by the judges, and adhered to by everyone else. This helps explain why codes tend to be maintained even when they fall out of pace with the needs of modern societies.

Most civil law countries have separate codes addressing civil law, commercial law, criminal law, and civil and criminal procedure. Rights and obligations of ordinary citizens are addressed in the civil code. Civil codes generally are arranged under headings such as the law of persons, family law, property law, succession law, and the law of obligations.

Tort law falls under the law of obligations, a broad field that covers most acts and transactions that can give rise to legal claims between private parties. The civil law's conception of tort liability is a unified one. Whereas the common law divides tort law into discrete wrongs with discrete elements (e.g., assault, battery, false imprisonment, trespass, conversion, trespass to chattels, intentional infliction of emotional distress, and negligence), civil law does not attempt to pigeon-hole different types of tort-like wrongs. As Mary Ann Glendon and colleagues put it, "it is a law of *tort* rather than torts." MARY ANN GLENDON ET AL., COMPARATIVE LEGAL TRADITIONS 117 (2d ed. 1999). Tort liability in civil law systems is usually derived from a handful of key code sections imposing, in broad terms, civil liability for wrongs that cause damage to persons or property.

The idea of a civil code, one that defines the rights and obligations of persons under various circumstances, is one most U.S. law students would find appealing. Frustrated by the indefiniteness of the common law, students frequently offer classroom comments such as, "Why don't they just write all the rules down in one place? That way, we'd know what the law is!" Without realizing it, they're advocating the ideology of a civil law system.

But can any body of statutory law really provide all the answers to the infinite variety of cases that arise day to day? Civil codes vary in their detail. The widely imitated French Napoleonic Code of 1804 was purposely written concisely so that it could be read and understood by ordinary citizens. Most of its provisions represent broad statements of general principle rather than specific rules of law. A utopian product of the French Revolution, one motivation for the code was to eliminate the need for lawyers by setting forth the law in a simple and straightforward way that could be read and understood by the masses.

At the other end of the spectrum is the Prussian Territorial Law of 1794. It stands as an attempt to implement what so many U.S. law students desperately wish for: a detailed compendium of rules intended to foresee and govern the entire range of human conduct. Enacted under Frederick the Great, the Prussian Code contained more than seventeen thousand provisions setting forth specific rules intended to govern specific fact situations. In theory, judges were prohibited from interpreting the code. Any questions of interpretation were to be referred to a special commission. It didn't work that way in practice. Even seventeen thousand provisions proved to be insufficient to cover all varieties of human conduct. Seventeen million provisions might not be enough. The Prussian Code broke down under its own weight. It was a failure. As an aside, Prussia eventually became part of Germany and the Prussian Territorial Law can be regarded as a predecessor to the national codification of German law that occurred after the unification of the formerly independent German states in 1871.

The highly influential German Civil Code (GCC) of 1896, discussed more extensively below, stands somewhere in between the user-friendly French Code and the unwieldy Prussian Code. The product of twenty years study and crafting in the late nineteenth century, the GCC is a "scientifically" constructed code that, while it does not attempt to regulate the specific details of human conduct, is more precise and cohesively organized than the French Code. For example, the GCC contains thirty sections addressing tort law, while the French Code contains only five sections devoted to tort law. Whereas the goal of the French and other codes was to wipe out and replace preexisting law, the German code was based on a thorough study of the history of German law with the goal of implementing the lessons and essential principles of that history in a way that fit together systematically. *See generally* MERRYMAN, at 26–33 (discussing the French, Prussian, and German civil codes).

In addition to the codes, civil law countries regularly adopt other statutes or acts that are not part of the codes. Acts tend to address more specific subject matters and contain narrower provisions than codes. Acts in civil law countries are no different than legislative acts passed by Congress or state legislatures in the U.S. Nor is there any difference in legal effect between an act and a code provision, as they occupy the same level in the hierarchy of sources of law. If an act specifically addresses a matter, the act applies. In cases where an act leaves room for interpretation or does not answer a specific private law question, the more general provisions of the codes can be consulted. Of course, both code and act provisions often apply in the same case.

Under the strict view of separation of powers that is part of the foundation of the civil law tradition, judges are neither trusted to nor supposed to make law. Only legislators make law. The role of a judge is simply to *apply* the law—code or other statutory provisions—promulgated by the legislators. There is no doctrine of *stare decisis* or notion of binding precedent in civil law systems. In theory, the lowliest trial court judge in a civil law system can ignore decisions of the high court of last resort. To implement this philosophy, the goal is to create a body of statutory law so clear and comprehensive that there is no room for judicial interpretation. Whereas certainty is only one of many competing values in a common law system, it is a primary value of a civil law system.

But just as there is a divergence between theory and reality regarding the nature of precedent in common law systems, the above paragraph, while sound in theory, does not accurately describe the way civil law systems work. Civil law judges make law every day, just like common law judges.

Code provisions in particular usually are written in broad language. The provisions simply do not answer most of the questions that arise from case to case. In some cases, there might not be any directly applicable code provision, or just as problematic, more than one conflicting provision might apply. In these instances, there is no escaping that judges have to make law to resolve the case. While all case decisions must be rooted in a code or other statutory provision, it is common to find judicial decisions in civil law nations in which the court reaches a conclusion by stringing together deductions from a series of broadly worded code provisions, none of which says precisely what the court ends up deducing from them.

The simplistic view that civil law judges mechanically apply clear code or other statutory provisions to reach decisions is myth along the same lines as the myth that common law judges mechanically apply binding precedent to reach decisions. While it is true that, unlike in common law systems, judicial opinions in civil law countries are not binding in other cases, even in the same court, they are very influential. Despite the absence of any principle of *stare decisis*, civil law judges frequently rely on and cite to prior judicial decisions in resolving cases. Merryman writes that the civil law "judge may refer to a precedent because he is impressed by the authority of the prior court, because he is persuaded by its reasoning, because he is too lazy to think the problem through himself, because he does not want to risk reversal on appeal, or for a variety of other reasons." MERRYMAN, at 47. As will be seen herein, most of the law of products liability in Germany and Argentina has been imposed by courts.

Having noted that case law is highly influential in both common and civil law systems, this is an instance where merely observing the "sameness" glosses over deeper differences. Civil law judges do make law every day and some of their decisions, particularly those of high courts, may be influential, but there will likely always be a vast difference in the way common law judges make law and civil law judges make law. Civil law judges are concerned only with making the "law of the case." Their purpose is to solve the case before them, not shape the law generally, a function that is left to the legislators, and in the legal profession, to the scholars. As discussed in the appendix, unlike in the U.S., court decisions in civil law countries often are not published in full format in easily accessible reporting systems. Scores of decisions give little explanation of their reasoning, and receive very little or no attention. Judicial decisions often do not trace a cohesive development of the law. Rather, they constitute a sea of specific-to-the-case applications of legal principles. In one sense, interesting because it cuts against the grain of civil law ideology, civil law judges have more freedom than common law judges to apply whatever law best resolves the case, in part because their decisions need not be constrained by their possible effect on future cases.

Sources of Products Liability Law

The hypothetical case we crafted to use as the vehicle for exploring tort litigation in the U.S., Germany, and Argentina is a products liability case. One reason for pursuing a case-based approach is to narrow the level of abstraction at which comparative law is often discussed. Thus, having addressed generally the sources of law in common law and civil law systems, we turn more specifically to the sources and development of products liability law in our three nations of study. Expanding on the points above, what follows turns upside down some of the traditional notions of the sources of law in common law and civil law nations. Far from being exclusively a case-based system, the U.S. tort system is becoming increasingly dominated by legislative and regulatory controls, whereas most of the specific products liability rules in Germany and Argentina have been implemented not by legislators, but by judges. The sections below do not explain in detail the substantive theories of products liability law and how they function. That is left for chapter eight. Rather, they focus on the origins of those theories and their roots in the law.

United States

The U.S. products liability system evolved in fits and starts throughout the twentieth century as a creation of state common law. Its modern underpinnings can be traced to a handful of judicial opinions penned by legendary state court judges who not only "made law," but did so in big, important ways with far-ranging consequences. Justice Benjamin Cardozo's famous opinion in *MacPherson v. Buick Motor Co.*, 111 N.E. 1050 (1916), opened what had been locked courthouse doors to consumers bringing negligence claims directly against manufacturers of defective products. The decision spurred a nation-wide judicial movement to abrogate the privity requirement in negligence cases, which barred claims unless the consumer had a direct contractual rela-tionship with the manufacturer. Justice John Francis's opinion in *Henningsen v. Bloomfield Motors, Inc.*, 161 A.2d 69 (1960), paved the road toward strict li-ability by eliminating the privity requirement in contractual breach of war-ranty cases and refusing to allow manufacturers to disclaim the implied war-ranty that their products will be free from defects. Justice Roger Traynor completed the transformation to strict liability in his opinion in *Greenman v. Yuba Power Products, Inc.*, 377 P.2d 897 (Cal. 1963), the first decision to openly embrace strict liability in tort for defective products. While none of these de-cisions had binding precedential effect outside of their respective jurisdictions, they influenced the development of products liability law on a national scale.

Two years after *Greenman* was decided, the American Law Institute (ALI) released *Restatement (Second) of Torts* § 402A, imposing strict liability for products in a "defective condition unreasonably dangerous." The ALI is an arm of the American Bar Association. Its members are distinguished lawyers, ju-rists, and legal scholars. The ALI's Restatement projects consolidate current and emerging common law principles in various subject areas and cast them into terse "black letter" statements of the law, followed by commentary and illustrations. The Restatements are a form of secondary authority. They are not binding on any court. Nevertheless, some of the Restatements, particu-larly in the area of tort law, have been extremely influential. Section 402A is the premier example. Discussed in more than 4,700 judicial opinions, it is the most widely cited Restatement provision in any area of law. Voluntarily adopted by most state high courts (and, in some states, legislatively), section 402A became the blueprint for U.S. products liability law nationwide.

Today, state courts remain the major player in the development of U.S. products liability law. Major changes are underway, however, that are work-ing to make U.S. products liability law much more structured and system-atized. The major shift involves the transfer of power to make tort law from judges to legislatures as part of the so-called "tort reform" movement. Virtu-ally all states have passed statutes regulating aspects of tort law that tradition-ally were within the exclusive province of state court judges. Many of these statutes are directed specifically at products liability, but most apply to tort litigation generally. The growing impact of this legislation on the American tort system cannot be overstated.

Some states have enacted comprehensive legislative packages regulating products liability. *See, e.g.,* ARK. CODE ANN. §§ 16-116-101 to -107 (2005); TEX. CIV. PRAC. & REM. CODE ANN. §§ 82.001–.008 (2005); OHIO REV. CODE ANN. §§ 2307.71–.81 (2005). Nearly all states have passed at least some laws addressing specific products liability issues. Florida, for example, where the U.S. version of our hypothetical case will be filed, has passed a variety of statutes regulating products liability issues, including legislation recognizing a state of the art defense (FLA. STAT. § 768.1257), creating a rebuttable presumption that a product is not defective if it complies with government safety standards (FLA. STAT. § 768.1256), and imposing a twelve-year statute of repose for products liability claims (FLA. STAT. § 95.031).

General tort reform legislation also significantly impacts products liability actions, such as laws abrogating or modifying joint and several liability for multiple defendants (passed by more than thirty states), restricting punitive damages (more than thirty states), establishing maximum caps on noneconomic damages (approximately twenty-five states, although roughly one-half of the caps apply only to medical actions), and abolishing or restricting the collateral source rule (more than twenty states).

Each year, bills are introduced in Congress to regulate products liability on a nationwide basis. Sweeping efforts have thus far been unsuccessful, although in 1996 Congress passed a broad products liability bill that was vetoed by President Bill Clinton. A few narrower proposals have met with success. In 2005, for example, Congress passed a law granting broad immunity from tort liability to the firearms industry for injuries inflicted by the misuse of guns. Protection of Lawful Commerce in Arms Act, 15 U.S.C. §§ 7901–7903 (2005).

Preemption of state products liability common law by federal legislation and administrative product safety regulations also is expanding. Preemption is the constitutional doctrine, arising under the Supremacy Clause (U.S. CONST. art. IX, cl. 2), holding that federal law is the "law of the land," trump ing conflicting state law. The effect of preemption can be to impose federal statutory or regulatory standards as binding rules in state products liability lawsuits. For example, in *Geier v. American Honda Motor Company, Inc.,* 529 U.S. 861 (2000), the Supreme Court held that federal agency regulations governing passive restraint devices in automobiles preempted state common law tort claims that automobiles without airbags are defectively designed. Some legal scholars argued that *Geier* abandoned the longstanding presumption against preemption and opened the door to substantial enlargement of the preemption doctrine.

Leading products liability scholar David Owen says that "no issue in modern products liability law is more important" than preemption. DAVID G. OWEN, PRODUCTS LIABILITY LAW § 14.4, 895 (2005). A host of recent activity suggests he is correct. In 2006, federal agencies adopted or considered a variety of rules and preambles to rules that could have the effect of precluding state common law tort actions, a process some have labeled "silent tort reform." The Food and Drug Administration (FDA) promulgated a labeling rule with a preamble taking the position that FDA label approval preempts claims based on inadequate warnings arising under conflicting state law. The Consumer Product Safety Commission, for the first time in the agency's history, adopted a rule limiting the ability of consumers to sue a product maker; specifically, insulating mattress manufacturers from liability in fire cases when their products adhere to federal design standards regarding flammability. The National Highway Traffic Safety Administration considered a proposal that would preempt state tort actions based on allegedly defective car roofs that comply with federal standards.

Even in non-preemption cases, most states allow defendants to introduce evidence that a product was in compliance with applicable statutory or administrative safety regulations. While such evidence is not conclusive on the issue of defectiveness, several states have statutes creating a rebuttable presumption that products complying with applicable government safety regulations are not defective in design. Such statutes give potentially powerful effect to legislative and regulatory product safety standards.

Statutes also are the direct source of some products liability claims. As discussed below, one of the claims in our hypothetical lawsuit will be for breach of the implied warranty of merchantability. The implied warranty of merchantability, although originally a creature of the common law, is now provided for by statute in forty-nine states as part of the states' adoption of article 2 of the Uniform Commercial Code (UCC). Only the mixed civil-common law state of Louisiana, which still follows remnants of the French Commercial Code it inherited, has not adopted article 2. Note that the UCC is, as the name indicates, a "code," a systematized effort to regulate the law in a particular area, much like commercial codes in civil law countries.

Moreover, consumer protection and trade practices statutes are being relied on increasingly as the basis for claims in U.S. products liability actions, as in well-publicized litigation against the tobacco, firearms, fast-food, and sunscreen industries, where plaintiffs have asserted that the manufacturers deceived consumers in marketing their products. In civil law countries, consumer protection laws often are a primary source of products liability claims. This is the case, for example, in Argentina and many other Latin American countries.

Meanwhile, the common law of U.S. products liability is assuming a more code-like appearance with the advent of the *Restatement (Third) of Torts: Products Liability (Products Liability Restatement)*. Released by the ALI in 1998, the *Products Liability Restatement* resembles a code in that it contains twenty-one organized, cross-referenced sections setting forth the basic principles addressing most major products liability issues. While no state has adopted the *Products Liability Restatement* in its entirety, portions of the influential project have been cited in hundreds of judicial opinions.

In short, while the U.S. products liability system remains predominantly a creature of common law precedent created by state judges, it is becoming much more systematized than in the past. Most of this systematization is occurring through the adoption of legislation and regulations governing the area, just as in civil law countries.

Germany

In contrast to U.S. law, substantive products liability law in Germany, as is true in all civil law countries, emanates from statutory law. The German Civil Code (*Bürgerliches Gesetzbuch*) (GCC) and a more specific products liability act provide three bases for products liability.

The GCC governs the whole of German private law. It originally consisted of 2,385 sections spread among five "books": General Part, Law of Obligations, Law of Property, Family Law, and Law of Succession. Today, the GCC still ends at section 2,385, but the precise number of current sections is unclear because many sections have been dropped and added over the years, yet there has been no renumbering of the entire code. The civil code is essentially a large book of acts, and, in fact, the German word for code—*Gesetzbuch*—translates literally to "act book." One noteworthy aspect of the GCC that distinguishes it from many other civil codes is the inclusion of the beginning General Part, which defines terms and basic principles that apply throughout the code. This requires continual cross-referencing, making the code more difficult to use than, for example, the French Code.

The GCC came into force in 1900. Prior to the GCC, there were several different regional legal codifications in Germany, the roots of which can be traced back to Roman law as early as 500 B.C. Until 1871, Germany was a confederation of states which maintained their own sovereignty and codes. In 1871, Germany became a unified nation and began moving toward the harmonization of private civil law. The foundation for that harmonization was the GCC, which was officially promulgated in 1896 and took effect on January 1, 1900.

Thirty sections of the GCC are devoted to tort law. They are part of the law of obligations and are found in the twenty-seventh title of chapter eight of Book Two, a chapter called *Unerlaubte Handlungen*, which translates roughly to "Tortious Acts." The crucial provision is section 823, which is the matrix of general tort law in Germany. It applies to all types of tort claims, including products liability claims. This fault-based provision provides in subsection (1) that "[a]nyone who unlawfully injures the life, body, health, liberty, property or any other right of another, either willfully or negligently, is liable to such other person to compensate for any such damages resulting therefrom."

Detailed discussion of the substantive theories of products liability that have developed under section 823 is reserved for chapter eight. The provision is quoted here to make a critical point about the nature of civil law. It has been discussed how in civil law countries the role of a judge is only to apply law, not make law. But as you can see, the provision for fault-based tort liability under the GCC is quite broad. Words such as "negligent" (*fahrlässig*) are no more self-defining in Germany, simply because they are included as part of a code, than they are in the U.S. common law system. Indeed, nearly every word and phrase in section 823(1) requires interpretation to give it understandable and practically applicable meaning. What do "unlawfully" and "willfully" mean? What constitutes a cognizable injury to "the life, body, health, liberty, property or any other right of another"? "[R]esulting therefrom" encapsulates the complex concept of causation in two words.

Thus, even though judges are not authorized to legislate or change legislative provisions, there is a practical interplay between codified law and judge-made law of interpretation. The result in the area of products liability has been that *most* of the relevant law has been developed by judges interpreting section 823 and other relevant code provisions. This judge-made law was necessitated not only by the vagaries in the code, but also because fast-paced changes in the sphere of commerce made it impossible for any legislation to keep up with all the new legal questions these changes create on an almost daily basis.

Much of this case law developed when the Federal Supreme Court (*Bundesgerichtshof*) was first urged to deal with products liability cases in the 1950s and 1960s. Until then, products liability was largely ignored in Germany. Markesinis and Unberath recount a 1956 Federal Supreme Court decision in which the plaintiff was injured when his bicycle collapsed under him due to a manufacturing defect. The Court showed little sympathy for the plaintiff, rejecting liability based on a view that evokes images of a certain popular U.S. bumper sticker and tee-shirt slogan: that the event was just one of those unfortunate things that happen in life. BASIL S. MARKESINIS & HANNES UNBERATH, THE GERMAN LAW OF TORTS: A COMPARATIVE TREATISE 92 (4th ed. 2002).

In the early 1960s, Professor Werner Lorenz published an influential comparative article introducing German lawyers to products liability developments in the U.S. *Id.* The article coincided with a rise in product-related accidents that drew public attention. In this period, recognizing that the general tort law code provision was too indefinite to answer many of the questions arising in cases, judges took it on themselves to interpret the provision against the backdrop of changes wrought by modern industrial production processes, the division of labor and responsibilities within the production process, and, in particular, the long distribution chain for mass-produced consumer products.

German courts have interpreted section 823 to create a variety of important legal principles applicable to products liability cases, including the imposition of certain general duties on manufacturers to maintain safety (*Verkehrssicherungspflichten*), recognition of the three different types of product defects (manufacturing, design, and informational defects), and rules reversing the burden of proof from the plaintiff to the defendant in certain cases. This discussion highlights that judge-made law plays a much larger role in civil law systems than is commonly believed. Through their interpretations of section 823, German judges have greatly enhanced the ability of consumers to sue manufacturers for product-related injuries.

The second source of substantive law for products liability is not a code provision, but an act; specifically, the Product Liability Act (*Produkthaftungsgesetz*) (PLA). The PLA, which consists of nineteen rather tersely written sections, provides for strict liability when defective products cause injury to persons or property. The PLA is a young act, having come into force in 1990. Strict liability under the PLA stands independent from products liability under the civil code or other statutes. The PLA specifically provides in section 15(2) that "[a]ny liability under other legal provisions remains unaffected."

Germany passed the PLA to implement the European Union Product Liability Directive (Directive 85/374/ECC, July 25, 1985, formally known as the Directive for the Approximation of the Laws, Regulations, and Administrative Provisions of the Member States Concerning Liability for Defective Products) (EU Product Liability Directive) into national law. The EU Product Liability Directive is a statement of basic products liability principles built on a regime of strict liability adopted in 1985 by the Council of European Communities. The measure was intended to harmonize strict liability for defective products across the European Union by mandating that all member states enact legislation in accordance with its provisions. Because the EU Product Liability Directive has now been implemented into domestic law by all EU member states (France and Spain were the last holdouts), there is widespread uniformity of strict liability principles for defective products throughout the EU.

A third source of liability for defective products is contract liability under a theory similar to breach of warranty. Contract liability emanates from the original GCC of 1900. As discussed in chapter eight, German contract law in the area of products liability is more restrictive than in the U.S., particularly in requiring privity of contract between the injured person and the defendant. It does not play a large role in most products liability cases.

In conclusion, in Germany, substantive products liability law is statute-based as is typical of civil law systems, with theories of liability arising under both the civil code and a separate products liability act, supplemented by an extensive and important body of interpretative case law.

Argentina

Argentina, like Germany, is a civil law country. The nation has been a melt-ing pot of legal developments and a fertile field for comparative law in itself. Argentine law can be viewed as the result of a comparative experiment that has not always worked well in practice. In many respects, Argentine law is a crossroad between European law and Latin American culture and practices, with a strong added influence from U.S. law (e.g., the Argentine Constitution was initially modeled after the U.S. Constitution). It is somewhat common to hear Argentineans say that Argentina is "part of Europe in Latin America." This is not surprising given that most Argentine citizens are of Italian and Spanish ancestry.

Although "civil law country" is a comfortable label, as has been noted, it is inaccurate to characterize legal systems in simplistic categorical terms. It is true that the most important source of Argentine law is legislation. But it is also true that judicial decisions, although not binding on lower courts, are crucial in the development of the law. It seems that judges work much the same way everywhere. They first come up with what they believe to be a fair decision in the particular case and then "fill in the gaps" with the applicable law. To fill those gaps, they sometimes shrink or stretch the law. Things cer-tainly work this way in Argentina.

Argentine products liability law may be the paradigm of this judicial law-making process. Code and other statutory provisions, by themselves, offer a very incomplete picture of Argentine products liability law. In many instances, current law resulted from landmark cases establishing principles that only af-terwards were statutorily recognized. These cases, in turn, often were inspired by scholarly theories articulated by legal commentators, a point that bears em-phasis. The opinions of legal commentators carry tremendous weight in the development of the law in civil law nations, much more so than in the U.S. In part because there is no system of binding precedent in civil law countries, courts frequently turn to doctrinal opinions by legal scholars (referred to simply as "doctrine") for solutions. Whereas a U.S. court may cite to a law review article as secondary authority to support a position, in Argentina, doctrine serves more as a kind of primary authority.

Products liability law under the Argentine Civil Code (ACC) recognizes the same three types of claims already discussed for the U.S. and Germany: negligence, strict liability, and a strict liability contract theory. These theories are analyzed in chapter eight. Additionally, the Consumer Protection Law, as amended in 1998, imposes strict liability on those who sell defective products that injure consumers. A brief history will help give some perspective on these claims.

The ACC was enacted by Congress in 1869 and took effect in 1871. It was based on a variety of sources. The French Civil Code of 1804 (the "Napoleonic Code") was particularly influential, as were the civil codes of Spain, Chile, and even Louisiana. One of the greatest direct influences was the Brazilian Civil Code, from which some 1,200 of the ACC's 4,051 articles were borrowed. *See* CIVIL CODE OF ARGENTINA (including amendments reflected by Argentine online updating services as of January 28, 2001), at i (Julio Romanach, Jr., trans. 2001) (making this observation).

The ACC is made up of two preliminary sections and four books: Of Persons, Of Personal Rights in Civil Relations, Of Real Rights, and Of Real and Personal Rights. Tort law, including products liability law, is governed by the provisions of Book Two, Of Personal Rights in Civil Relations, which sets forth the law of obligations. The law of obligations encompasses both contractual and extracontractual liability, both of which play a role in products liability. Extracontractual liability is the source of tort law in Argentina. In fact, the best translation of the term "tort law" in Spanish would be *responsabilidad aquiliana*, or "extracontractual liability."

While early Argentine products liability law emanated from the code, it originated in the courts. Until the late 1950s, products liability did not exist as a practical matter in Argentina. The first period in products liability cases can be roughly designated as from 1950 to 1970, where the predominant legal theories rested in negligence and contract law, coupled with a not-yet fully developed res ipsa loquitur-type inference-drawing process. Very few cases were decided during this period.

As in Anglo-American law, many of the early cases imposing liability for defective products in Argentina involved bad food. These cases reflect a tension in products liability cases between tort and contract law (i.e., extracontractual and contractual liability) similar to that in U.S. products liability law.

Also as in the U.S., these cases lying at the intersection of tort and contract law mark the first inroads toward strict liability.

In *Sánchez v. Club Italiano*, a 1956 landmark case, the plaintiff took his wife and minor son to "Club Thursday," a weekly entertainment show organized by the defendant at a restaurant in Buenos Aires. Although the defendant organized the dinner show, the food was prepared and supplied by a third party with whom the defendant had contracted. Plaintiff alleged that after dining on a meal of "vitel tonné, rice with clams, roast beef with beans and seasoned with pastry cream and coffee," the three family members returned home and became seriously ill. Other guests attending the show also became ill. The plaintiff and his son recovered, but the wife died eighty days later. An autopsy revealed acute liver damage.

The club's principal defense was that there was insufficient proof that the food caused the wife's illness and death. The defendant noted that several food samples were sent to a laboratory for testing two weeks after the event, "which yielded no results whatsoever." The trial court rejected the defense after extensive consideration of conflicting expert medical testimony concerning possible causes of the wife's liver failure, stating: "They can conjecture upon conjecture as much as they like, but the attention will always return to the most likely probability," which, according to the court, was that the plaintiff's wife died due to food poisoning. Thus, though not saying so directly, the court drew a res ipsa loquitur-type inference from the circumstantial evidence that the death was attributable to the defendant.

On appeal to the National Civil Court of Appeals in Buenos Aires, the judgment was affirmed, although the court disagreed with the trial court's decision to base liability on the contract between the defendant and the food preparer, to which the plaintiffs were not in privity. Rather, the court said the defendant had a duty under the general negligence provision of the civil code (article 1109), to ensure the quality of the food it served. Cámara Nacional de Apelaciones en lo Civil, Sala C [CNCiv.], 4/26/56, "Sánchez Cesáreo R. y otro c. Club Italiano," La Ley [L.L.] (1956-83-410).

Sánchez was followed by another landmark case decided by the Supreme Court of Buenos Aires (the high court of the province of Buenos Aires) in 1965, which also involved a bad food claim against a restaurant. In *Demaría v. Restaurante Abruzzese*, the plaintiffs' son, a doctor, died of botulism after eating peppers at the defendant's restaurant. The court imposed liability against the restaurant despite evidence showing that the peppers, bought by the restaurant in sealed cans, were toxic on arrival. Noting that the case evinced both contractual and extracontractual obligations, the court upheld liability in reliance on a code provision imposing a duty of care with respect to objects that one uses or controls (currently codified as amended in 1968 as article 1113 of the ACC). Suprema Corte de Buenos Aires [SC Buenos Aires], 6/22/1965, "Demaría, Angel M. c. Restaurante Abruzzese y otro," La Ley [L.L.] (1965-119-383). As a side point of interest, both of these landmark cases cited judicial precedent, as is commonly done in Argentine judicial opinions, even though precedent is not binding or, theoretically, even relevant in a civil law system.

The second phase of Argentine products liability was spurred by changes to the ACC. In 1968, after nearly one hundred years of existence without change, the ACC underwent major revision. The broad purpose of the revision was to incorporate interpretations of existing code provisions by courts and scholars. Among the changes were additions to article 1113, which, as we analyze in chapter eight, became a critical linchpin for the introduction of strict liability for defective (as well as non-defective but "risky") products, although it took two more decades for these changes to blossom into full use. In the 1980s, several scholarly conferences addressed issues in products liability. Most of the theories that are currently applied in deciding products liability cases in Argentina were derived from the conclusions drawn at those conferences and the scholarly articles that followed.

As in both the U.S. and Germany, part of the "explosion" in products liability law in Argentina occurred in a series of cases involving exploding soda bottles, mostly in the 1980s. Although judicial opinions rendered during that time were somewhat erratic, they helped lay the foundation for the adoption of non-contractual strict liability as the dominant theory in products liability cases. In 1985, a Buenos Aires appellate court, in a case involving allegedly defective bovine vaccine, adopted a theory that, in effect, resulted in an implied warranty of product quality being assigned down the commercial chain from the manufacturer to the consumer, eliminating the need for the consumer to be in privity with the manufacturer in order to recover. See Cámara Nacional de Apelaciones en lo Comercial, Sala B [CNCom.], 9/25/85, "Rincón de Avila, Soc. en Com. Por Accs. c. Cooper Argentina S.A. y otros," La Ley [L.L.] (1986-C-6). This theory soon gave way to non-contractual strict liability without the need to resort to a complex assignment of warranties down the commercial chain. Modern manufacturers can be held liable based simply on their distribution of a defective or "risky" product.

The final phase of Argentine products liability law began with the adoption of the Consumer Protection Law (CPL), passed by the Argentine Congress in 1993. Law No. 24.240, Sept. 22, 1993, as amended, [LIII-D] A.D.L.A. 4125. The CPL constitutes the primary modern source of liability for injuries caused by defective products. Argentina's CPL is part of a broader movement in South America to adopt comprehensive consumer protection laws to promote a stable free market economy in consumer goods. Brazil began the movement by adopting a sweeping consumer protection law in 1990. Several other South American countries have followed suit. Argentina's CPL applies to a wide range of consumer transactions including the sale and leasing of goods, the provision of non-professional services, and even some real property transactions.

The CPL regulates contract terms for consumer goods in a number of ways that benefit consumers, including a prohibition on terms that disclaim liability, limit damages, or otherwise waive consumer rights. Article 2 provides that if there is any doubt concerning the disposition of the act, the interpretation adopted must benefit the consumer. The CPL provides for both administrative and judicial enforcement. Most importantly for our hypothetical plaintiff, Silvia Winter, and other products liability plaintiffs, the CPL contained a provision—article 40—imposing strict liability and joint and several liability on entities in product distribution chains that furnish defective products.

Unfortunately, it took five more years for the benefits of the CPL to consumers to be fully realized because article 40 was the subject of a presidential veto. Executive Decree 2089/93. The primary arguments in support of the veto mirrored those often heard in the U.S. from business interests and other advocates of restricting products liability litigation: that subjecting product sellers to broad strict liability and joint and several liability would impair the ability of Argentina to compete in the worldwide marketplace and result in increased prices for goods. *See* FEDERICO C. TALLONE, DAÑOS CAUSADOS POR PRODUCTOS ELABORADOS 156–57 (2002). In 1998, amendments to the CPL reinstated the provisions of article 40, fully implementing strict liability for sellers of defective products. Law No. 24.999, July 30, 1998, [LVIII-C] A.D.L.A. 2929.

CHAPTER 4

THE CASE FACTS:
SILVIA WINTER V.
VALUE-STORE, INC. ET AL.

Armed with background about our three countries of study and a survey of the sources of law generally and products liability law in particular in those countries, we're finally prepared to begin our comparative case study. A broken jar of peanuts serves as the vehicle on this journey into the convergence and divergence of tort litigation and products liability law in the U.S., Germany, and Argentina.

For as long as sellers of food and beverage products have been packaging products in glass containers, consumers have been getting injured by broken glass. Unlike some products, glass food and beverage containers exist throughout the world, glass breaks throughout the world, and, unfortunately, consumers get injured by broken glass throughout the world. "[N]o eyeball [or in our case, hand and wrist] resists well a flying splinter of broken glass." Craig Spangenberg, *Exploding Bottles*, 24 OHIO ST. L.J. 516, 516 (1963).

Broken glass container cases, most of them involving exploding beverage bottles, are among the oldest and most common type of U.S. products liability lawsuits. *See, e.g.*, Hudgins v. Coca Cola Bottling Co., 50 S.E. 974 (Ga. 1905) (exploding soda bottle); Glaser v. Seitz, 71 N.Y.S. 942 (Sup. Ct. 1901) (exploding bottle of seltzer water). As one veteran trial lawyer said, "When Coke was sold in bottles, anyone who claimed competence as a personal injury lawyer had to be able to say he had tried a Coca-Cola exploding bottle case." Jacob A. Stein, *Bottled Water*, 18 WASH. LAW. 48 (2004). These cases have been influential in the development of U.S. products liability law, highlighted by Justice Traynor's famous concurring opinion in *Escola v. Coca-Cola Bottling Co.*, 150 P.2d 436 (Cal. 1944), an exploding bottle case in which Traynor became the first U.S. judge to expressly argue for strict liability in tort for injuries caused by defective products. Broken glass container cases also have played a prominent role in the development of products liability law in Germany and Argentina.

We purposely chose an ordinary fact pattern. A student reader commenting on a pre-publication draft wrote that "a more exciting case, possibly with an explosion or death, might help the reader get behind the plaintiff a little more." No doubt, but that wasn't the goal. We wanted to use a simple, realistic fact situation to which consumers everywhere can relate, a case in which there are no clear heroes or villains. The legally relevant broken jar facts in our hypothetical case are patterned loosely after those in *Welge v. Planters Lifesavers Co.*, 17 F.3d 209 (7th Cir. 1994) (Posner, J.). Most of the facts, however, and all of the participants and narrative, are fiction.

Every personal injury case is a human story. Here is Silvia Winter's story:

Case Facts

Silvia Winter was a thirty-year-old student at the local university pursuing a degree in physical therapy. She was nearing graduation after what seemed like an eternity as a student. She chose physical therapy as a field of study because she liked working with and helping people. Also, as an older student with a lot of debt, she needed a degree with which she could actually earn a living. Silvia and her two younger brothers grew up in a family of modest means. Their father worked at a small jewelry store doing watch and other jewelry repairs. Their mother cleaned rooms in a hotel until poor health forced her to retire. Silvia worked as a waitress for several years following high school to help support her family after her mother became ill, which is why she started college so late. In her humble opinion, she had been living off low-wage jobs and student loans for too long.

At an on-campus job fair two years ago, she learned that physical therapists are in demand and earn decent salaries. She loved music and had taken piano lessons since she was a child, but had come to an early realization that music degrees aren't very marketable in the real world. Nevertheless, her piano remained one of her prized, and only, possessions.

Silvia lived in a small two-bedroom townhouse apartment near the university with another student, Norah. To help pay the bills, Silvia worked twenty hours a week at a local health club, checking in members at the front desk. After work on a Thursday evening, Silvia stopped at the Value-Store, a large supermarket near her apartment, to pick up a few groceries. She had started the morning with a difficult chemistry exam and worked all afternoon at the health club, so decided to treat herself to a sundae. She bought strawberry ice cream, marshmallow syrup, and a glass jar of Penelope Peanuts. She

specifically picked the Penelope brand after seeing an offer for a one-dollar rebate on the label.

"That's one less dollar I'll have to pay back in student loans," she joked to
herself as she set the jar in the shopping cart.

When she arrived home, Norah was in the living room with her longtime
boyfriend, Marco. Marco spent almost as much time at the apartment as
Norah. Silvia didn't mind. Marco was fun, and he absolutely adored Norah.

"We're going to The Onion," Norah said. "Come with us." The Onion was
a local bar and restaurant popular with older college students and young professionals. Silvia said she was exhausted, but Norah was persistent. "Come on,
sleep is overrated," she said. "Besides, Marco's new coworker is going to meet
us there, and I think you'll like him. He's *soooo* cute."

Silvia gave in, but said she'd need a few minutes to put away her groceries
and get cleaned up. Unpacking the groceries in the kitchen, she decided to remove the rebate coupon on the peanuts jar before she forgot about it. Using
an Exacto knife, a pencil-shaped instrument with a small razor blade at the
end, she cut out the rebate label and placed the jar in the cabinet.

They had fun at The Onion, but stayed out too late. Marco's friend was
cute, as advertised, but also a bit of a bore. He was a good dancer though,
and Silvia loved to dance. Fortunately, her Friday class didn't start until noon,
so she was able to sleep in. At 10:30 am, she got out of bed and began rush-
ing to get ready for class. She was hungry, but didn't have time to make
breakfast. Scanning the cabinets, she saw the peanuts. She removed the plastic seal from around the lid and twisted open the vacuum-sealed jar. She
poured out a handful of peanuts, replaced the top, and returned the jar to
the cabinet.

When she got home from work that evening, Norah and Marco were in the
living room, watching a movie on television. Her jar of peanuts was on the
floor between them, open and nearly empty.

"Hey, you're eating all my peanuts. Those were for my sundae." Like a lot
of college roommates, Silvia and Norah often ate each other's food. It usually
didn't bother her, but she did want to save enough peanuts for a sundae after
going through the trouble of buying the ingredients.

"Sorry, roomie," Norah said, handing her the jar and top. "We were starv-
ing. Look at the bright side. I kept Marco from eating your ice cream."

Silvia took the jar into the kitchen. She placed the lid on top, but as she
pushed it down the jar shattered. The glass severely cut her right wrist. She
dropped what was left of the jar, where it broke into even more pieces on the
tile floor.

Silvia's cry and the sound of breaking glass brought Norah and Marco running to the kitchen, where they found Silvia gripping her right hand and wrist with her left hand. Blood was already dripping on the floor.

"What happened?" Norah said in shock.

"The peanut jar! It just fell apart when I was trying to put the lid on. It cut me."

Norah wrapped a towel tightly around Silvia's wrist and Marco drove them to the emergency room at the university hospital. The emergency room doctor determined the cut was too severe for simple suturing and called in Dr. Sandra Schmitt, an orthopedic surgeon specializing in hand and wrist injuries. Dr. Schmitt told Silvia that several of her flexor tendons had been severed. She explained that flexor tendons connect the muscles to bone so that one can bend and close the joints of the fingers. No doubt there was nerve damage as well, since Silvia reported numbness in her hand.

Dr. Schmitt recommended immediate surgery to sew the tendons back together and attempt repair of the nerves. The longer the delay in surgery, the greater the likelihood of permanent damage. She explained the risks, adding that while the surgery usually was quite effective, there was no guarantee Silvia would regain full use of her hand and wrist. Silvia consented and Dr. Schmitt proceeded with the complex surgery, which she performed skillfully.

Silvia spent the night in the hospital. It was well past midnight when Norah and Marco arrived back at the apartment. Marco offered to clean up the mess in the kitchen while Norah called the hospital to check on Silvia's status.

Marco was scrubbing the kitchen floor when Norah returned.

"How is she?" Marco asked.

"She's resting, but the nurse said she was pretty traumatized. I don't feel so good myself and I didn't even get cut. That was a lot of blood," she said, looking at the rag in Marco's hand. "What did you do with the glass?"

"What do you think I did with it? I threw it in the trash."

"Maybe we should keep it."

"For what? Some kind of horror-show souvenir?"

"I mean it. She's really hurt. I heard that doctor telling the nurse that she was probably going to have permanent damage. Jars aren't supposed to break like that."

"They're glass. Glass breaks all the time."

Norah sighed. "I guess you're right." They left the broken peanuts jar in the trash, where it was picked up the next day by sanitation workers.

Silvia spent three months receiving physical therapy for her dominant right hand and wrist. During recovery, she had to quit her job at the health club. While she made progress, her hand still didn't feel right. Two fingers remained stiff and her range of movement was restricted. She also continued to experience pain in her wrist and numbness in part of her hand. She had tried to play her piano a couple of times, but had been unable to use her right hand. It reminded her of taking piano lessons in the fourth grade, when her teacher made her sit on one hand and use the other to play scales.

Just two weeks before graduation, Dr. Schmitt broke the bad news during an afternoon visit. The cut had caused permanent injury. While some improvement was still possible, she estimated Silvia had suffered a permanent disability in her right hand and wrist in the range of 20–25%. Her overall body disability was estimated to be 5%.

By that point, Silvia's medical expenses totaled $26,000 in 2006 U.S. dollars, including: $20,000 for the emergency room visit, surgery, anesthesia, other medication, and follow-up visits with Dr. Schmitt; and $6,000 for physical therapy. (The estimated total cost for the same treatment in Germany is $7,200 and in Argentina $8,150, but as explained in chapter ten, Silvia most likely would not be responsible for her medical bills in either of those countries.)

Meanwhile, Silvia had attended a couple of job interviews for physical therapist positions, with her wrist in a splint, but did not get the jobs. One interviewer told her the uncertain nature of her injury was "a concern."

On her last day as a college student, Silvia stayed after class to talk to one of her professors about her predicament. The professor was candid. She said it could be difficult to function in some, although not all, physical therapy jobs without the use of both hands and wrists.

"It doesn't seem fair," Silvia said absently as she gathered up her books. "All because of a jar of peanuts."

She was halfway to the door when the professor said, "Silvia, have you thought about talking to a lawyer?"

She had, but only because Norah had suggested it several times. The professor jotted a name and number on a piece of paper. "This guy is my neighbor. He's a lawyer who handles personal injury cases. Give him a call and say I gave you his name. I'm sure he'd be glad to talk to you."

Silvia met with the lawyer the next week and he agreed to take Silvia's case.

Preliminary investigation determined that the jar was manufactured by Levington, Inc. (Levington), a domestic glass container maker. Levington sold and transported the jars to Penelope Peanuts, Inc. (Penelope), which filled them with peanuts and marketed them under the Penelope brand name. A nationwide food chain, Penelope distributes its products through an independent wholesale food supplier, Charter Food Distributors, Inc. (Charter), which delivers Penelope's products to retailers such as Value-Store, Inc. (Value-Store).

Three Countries, Three Lawsuits

Hypothetical Silvia, we are assuming, lives in three incarnations in Miami, Florida, United States, Cologne, Germany, and Buenos Aires, Argentina. Accordingly, her hypothetical case will be filed simultaneously in the following three courts:

U.S. case. In the U.S., as a citizen and resident of Miami-Dade County, Florida, Silvia's case will be filed in the U.S. District Court for the Southern District of Florida, where we will reasonably assume she would demand a jury trial. As noted earlier, plaintiffs' personal injury lawyers generally prefer to litigate in state court, rather than federal court, and Silvia would have that option. She could file her case in state court in the Eleventh Judicial Circuit of Florida. However, where diversity of citizenship exists between the plaintiff and defendants and the amount in controversy exceeds $75,000, a tort plaintiff has the option of filing in federal court. 28 U.S.C. § 1332.

Here, the amount in controversy exceeds the jurisdictional amount and we will assume that diversity of citizenship exists; i.e., that Silvia is a citizen and resident of Florida and that all of the defendants are incorporated and have their principal places of business in states other than Florida. Opting to have Silvia file her case in federal court allows us to apply procedural and evidentiary rules of national application, rather than those applicable in just one state.

Even if Silvia's lawyer followed conventional wisdom and filed her case in a Florida state court, there is a reasonable likelihood the defendants would remove the case to federal court. U.S. Department of Justice statistics show that 24% of federal tort trials in fiscal 2002–03 originated in state court and made their way to federal court by way of removal. Were Silvia's case to proceed to the appellate level, her appeal would be filed in the United States Court of Appeals for the Eleventh Circuit, which has jurisdiction over federal cases arising in the states of Florida, Alabama, and Georgia.

German case. Silvia's German alter ego is a citizen and resident of Cologne, Germany, which is in the German state of North Rhine-Westphalia. As the amount in controversy in her case exceeds the minimum jurisdictional amount of 5000 euros ($6,000) for the State District Courts, she will file her case in the *Landgericht Köln*. If her case proceeded to appeal, the appeal would be filed in the State Appeals Court for Köln (*Oberlandesgericht Köln*).

Argentine case. "Argentine Silvia" will file her case in the national courts of Buenos Aires, where she resides. Jurisdiction over consumer protection and products liability lawsuits has been subject to controversy among the courts of Buenos Aires. As explained in chapter two, the national courts sitting in Buenos Aires are organized in a series of specialized courts. Civil and commercial courts are the two specializations in which most cases in Buenos Aires are filed each year. As many cases often present both general civil and commercial aspects, it is sometimes difficult to know which court has jurisdiction. No clear-cut criteria exist for making the determination.

Products liability cases frequently generate confusion in this regard. Some of them end up in civil courts of general jurisdiction and some of them end up in commercial courts, and it is not uncommon to see products liability cases removed from civil to commercial courts and vice versa. The Argentine Supreme Court has attempted to settle this jurisdictional dispute in two leading cases: Corte Suprema de Justicia [CSJN], 3/31/1999, "Safar Retamar, María Elena v. Moño Azul S.A./daños y perjuicios sumario," Fallos (1999-322-596); Corte Suprema de Justicia [CSJN], 08/08/2002, "Quidi, María Adelina v. Nobleza Piccardo S.A.," Jurisprudencia Argentina [J.A.] (2002-II-108). In both cases, the Supreme Court ruled that civil, not commercial, courts have jurisdiction over products liability cases when a consumer not in privity of contract with the manufacturer claims damages for personal injury.

Notwithstanding this doctrine, and keeping in mind that even Supreme Court decisions are not binding on lower courts in civil law countries, jurisdictional disputes remain a fertile ground for controversy in products liability cases. Nevertheless, we will assume Silvia files her case in a national first instance civil court of general jurisdiction for the federal capital of Buenos Aires. Any appeal would be taken to the National Civil Court of Appeals.

A unique aspect of Argentine law is the requirement that, pursuant to a 1996 act of Congress, a potential litigant must participate in mediation *prior* to filing a lawsuit. Law No. 24.573, 10/27/1995, [LV-E] A.D.L.A. 5894. In most legal systems where mediation is mandatory, it occurs subsequent to the filing of the suit. For example, in the U.S. District Court for the Southern District of Florida, the forum for Silvia's U.S. case, the local rules mandate that the parties participate in mediation within sixty days prior to trial, a time frame which may not arrive until years after a case is filed. USDC S.D. Fla. L.R. 16.2 (2005). Statistics compiled by the Argentine Ministry of Justice show that roughly one-third of mediations end in agreement. In many cases, however, pre-filing mandatory mediation is complied with in a perfunctory way intended to fulfill the letter of the law, rather than its spirit. In other words, the parties do it because they have to do it, but without a real intention to attempt to resolve the case through mediation.

CHAPTER 5

FACT GATHERING AND PRESENTATION

The manner in which evidence is gathered and presented in the U.S. common law system versus civil law systems such as Germany and Argentina could affect the outcome of Silvia's case as much or more than differences in substantive law. The reality of litigation practice is that the best case in the world becomes the worst case if it can't be proved. Paraphrasing Blackstone, experience shows that for every case arising from a dispute of law, more than one hundred spring from disputes of fact. Law school courses and textbooks emphasize rules of law, but "[p]roblems involved in proving facts in tort cases, as any trial lawyer will affirm, are often more challenging than developing the relevant rules of law." VICTOR E. SCHWARTZ ET AL., PROSSER, WADE AND SCHWARTZ'S TORTS: CASES AND MATERIALS 237 (11th ed. 2005). Certainly this is true in Silvia's case.

We take an excursion into the procedural world in this chapter by providing an overview of how facts are developed and presented to the court in the U.S., Germany, and Argentina. It would be simpler and tidier for readers if this chapter were divided into two chapters, one covering pretrial procedures and one covering trial procedures, but such a division does not work when discussing fact development and presentation in civil law systems. In civil law countries, no definite demarcation exists between the pretrial and trial phases of a case. Fact collecting and presentation in civil law systems occur simultaneously in a procedural world unknown to students of the common law: a world with no juries or pretrial discovery, where judges rather than lawyers question witnesses, where no verbatim transcripts are compiled, and where judges sometimes decide fully litigated cases without ever seeing the witnesses. Because there is no single unified trial event in civil law countries, Silvia would not get her "day in court," but rather her *days* in court in the form of an episodic series of hearings over an extended period that could be continued with no definite ending point in sight. It is in this procedural realm that some of the most dramatic and important collisions are found between the common and civil law worlds.

Remember that entire law school courses are taught on the matters surveyed below. Each "country section" begins with some insights into the relative roles of lawyers and judges, followed by a discussion of how evidence is collected and presented.

United States

Roles of Lawyers and Judges

Under the U.S. adversarial system of civil litigation, the parties and their lawyers bear exclusive responsibility both for uncovering the facts necessary to support their claims and defenses and presenting those facts to the court. Judges play no role in the fact development process, except to the extent they are called on to resolve discovery disputes during the pretrial phase of the proceedings. Even then, the judge's role is simply to resolve the dispute, not to become actively involved in eliciting the facts.

In terms of the trial, we have assumed that Silvia's lawyer demanded a jury trial, as is done in 90% of personal injury cases. In a jury trial, U.S. judges serve as neutral referees, not as active participants. The parties determine which evidence to present, how much evidence to present, and in what order to present it. Lawyers conduct all questioning of witnesses. A lawyer who calls a witness conducts direct examination of the witness, after which opposing lawyers are permitted to cross-examine the witness. Although judges have the power to ask questions of witnesses, they rarely exercise that power in jury trials or even in bench trials, which comprise the majority of U.S. civil trials.

The judge's primary role during a jury trial is to act as gatekeeper with regard to what evidence the jury will be permitted to hear. Unlike in civil law countries where few evidentiary rules exist, evidence-taking in the U.S. is regulated by detailed rules of evidence governing both the content and elicitation of evidence. *See* Fed. R. Evid. 101–1103 (2005) (the rules of evidence in federal court). This set of rules, which is in essence an organized, systematic "code" of evidence, has been intricately refined in a large body of case law. U.S. evidentiary rules stem in large part from a perceived need to prevent juries from hearing evidence that is unreliable or irrelevant, although the same rules apply to bench trials.

The rules of evidence are not self-executing. If a particular item of evidence is improper (e.g., hearsay) or a question is framed improperly (e.g., a leading question of a witness on direct examination or a question that calls for speculation), it is up to the opposing attorney to raise a timely, properly articulated objection. The judge usually will not do the lawyers' job for them. So, for example, suppose Silvia's lawyer had Norah on the witness stand and asked her what Silvia said to her the night of the accident. This question, calling for hearsay evidence, would be objectionable (subject to more than two dozen exceptions), but unless the defendants' lawyers objected at that moment, Norah would be permitted to answer the question and the objection would be deemed waived.

In short, in the U.S. common law system, the parties and their lawyers control virtually every aspect of fact development and presentation. The judge's role is essentially a passive one.

Fact Gathering and Presentation

Pretrial Informal Fact Investigation and Discovery

In the U.S., facts are gathered and developed during a clearly defined "pretrial" phase of the proceeding. Lawyers develop facts in two ways: investigation conducted without the aid of formal legal procedures and "discovery" conducted through mechanisms provided for by the rules of civil procedure; in Silvia's case, the Federal Rules of Civil Procedure.

Informal fact investigation includes interviewing clients and cooperative witnesses and reviewing documents in their possession, retaining experts to furnish opinions on technical matters, conducting Internet and other records research, and sometimes even hiring private investigators to locate witnesses or track down other information. In Silvia's case, Silvia herself would be the most important witness. Her testimony detailing the events involving the jar, from the moment she removed it from the supermarket shelf until the moment it shattered, would be crucial to the liability issues. Her testimony regarding her injuries would be similarly important to determining the extent of her damages. Testimony in U.S. courts is almost always received orally, so Silvia's demeanor, appearance and overall "likeability" would all play crucial, if intangible, roles in persuading the jury. This is particularly true in a case such as Silvia's in which physical evidence is lacking due to the destruction of the jar.

Given the importance of her testimony, her lawyer would carefully review her testimony with her prior to her pretrial discovery deposition (discussed below) and court appearance. This is one criticism of the U.S. system of truthfinding. By the time a party or other key witness appears at a deposition or in court, she will have "gone over her story" with lawyers perhaps several times. Within proper bounds, there is nothing unethical about a lawyer "preparing" a witness to testify. Indeed, it could be viewed as malpractice not to do so. An unprepared witness might not know to emphasize important facts, or might state a fact in an unfavorable way rather than in a more favorable, but equally truthful way. For example, an unprepared Silvia might testify that she "cut into the jar" with the Exacto knife to remove the rebate label, when, in fact, she may have used the knife only to "scratch off the label." Psychological studies show that differences in descriptive word choices can have a potent impact on how an event is perceived by an audience.

A competent plaintiff's lawyer also would interview Norah, Marco, and Dr. Schmitt. Since Norah and Marco were the last ones using the jar before it shattered, they would be important witnesses since the defendants no doubt would raise the possibility that one of them damaged the jar. Other informal fact investigation would include a search for records or reports of other breakage incidents involving glass containers manufactured or handled by the defendants.

With regard to formal discovery, the Federal Rules of Civil Procedure, and similar rules in every state, provide a variety of tools that parties can use to unearth facts, including oral depositions, written interrogatories, requests for the production of documents and other tangible things, physical and mental examinations of persons, and requests for admission. *See* FED. R. CIV. PRO. 26–37 (2005) (rules regulating discovery and discovery procedure in federal courts). This is contrary to civil law countries, where pretrial discovery does not exist.

On the upside, the liberal U.S. discovery system facilitates in-depth fact-finding. Since discovery is controlled by the parties, who have financial and other motivations to uncover any fact that might help their cases, the system carries built-in incentives to be thorough. In civil law systems, where judges run the fact-development process, this incentive is missing. Faced with a heavy caseload, a busy judge in a civil law system does not have an incentive to turn over every possible evidentiary stone and the parties have no power to do it on their own. The U.S. discovery system also largely eliminates "trial by ambush." If the parties have taken advantage of available discovery opportunities, very few surprises are left by the time the trial rolls around.

The other side is that the U.S. discovery system can be inefficient and add enormously to the transactional costs of litigation. It may not be necessary to turn over every stone in a case, and every additional stone that is turned over through a formal discovery mechanism adds more cost, although it should be noted that the most intensive and expensive discovery occurs in complex litigation, which comprises only a small portion of U.S. cases. *See* Linda S. Mullenix, *The Pervasive Myth of Pervasive Discovery*, 39 B.C. L. REV. 683, 684 (1998) (citing studies from the Rand Institute of Civil Justice and the Federal Judicial Center showing that no discovery is pursued in 38–50% of civil cases).

The system is also susceptible to abuse. Vexatious discovery can wear out opposing parties, financially and otherwise. Truth-finding can be obstructed by failures to respond promptly and candidly to discovery requests. Unfortunately, lawyers and their clients who play by the rules sometimes end up at a disadvantage compared to those determined to thwart the rules. While remedies exist for abusive discovery in the form of motions to compel discovery, motions for protective orders, and motions for sanctions for frivolous or abusive tactics, pursuing such remedies is itself expensive and can result in further delay.

With that introduction, let us take a look at the discovery phase of Silvia's case. Silvia's lawyer faces the unenviable task of trying to reconstruct the history of the peanuts jar from the time it was manufactured until the moment it came apart in her hands. Such an investigation could require a substantial investment of both time and money. Lawyers vary in the thoroughness in which they engage in pretrial discovery, depending on the nature and facts of the case, as well as how much money the lawyer is willing to invest in the case. One successful veteran personal injury lawyer in Florida (where Silvia's U.S. case is filed) said he would try to keep the out-of-pocket costs, not including attorney time, in a case like Silvia's under $50,000. One could spend more or less. Another Florida lawyer pointed out that a solo practitioner (which he is) would try to "cut corners" on the costs, bringing them down somewhat. As examples, he mentioned that a high-end firm would be more likely to take more depositions, conduct video depositions, and have all depositions, rather than just selected ones, transcribed. Nevertheless, we'll use the $50,000 figure as a rough cost estimate.

No attempt is made to map out the precise discovery that would be conducted in Silvia's U.S. case. Rather, an overview is presented of the basic discovery avenues available to her.

Mandatory disclosures. In 2000, the Federal Rules of Civil Procedure were amended to mandate disclosure of a variety of categories of evidence without the need to make a formal discovery request. Fed. R. Civ. P. 26(a)(1) (2005). The amendment was intended to reduce discovery and, hence, shorten proceedings and reduce litigation costs. Rule 26(a)(1) requires that all parties, without awaiting a discovery request, disclose the following: (1) name and contact information of any person likely to have discoverable information; (2) a copy or description of all documents in the party's possession that may be used to support the party's claims or defenses; (3) a computation of any category of damages claimed by the party; and (4) any insurance agreement that may provide coverage in the matter. Early evidence suggests that the laudatory purposes of the mandatory disclosure provision are not yet being fulfilled. Lawyers appear to be spending as many hours on discovery as before. *See* Mullenix, at 686–87. Anecdotally, a federal district court judge told McClurg he has seen little "motion practice" arising from disputes over the mandatory disclosure rule and no noticeable reduction in motion practice regarding other discovery disputes, suggesting to him that the rule has not had much effect.

Interrogatories. Both sides would serve interrogatories (written questions) on the other, and the defendants might serve interrogatories among themselves if they are not pursuing a united defense. Rule 33 allows a party to serve up to twenty-five written interrogatories, including all subparts, on any party. FED. R. CIV. P. 33 (2005). Additional interrogatories can be filed with the permission of the court. Each side is required to provide written answers to each interrogatory under oath, or make objection to it, stating the reasons for the objection. Interrogatories are much less expensive than oral depositions, but also less effective at uncovering information. Skilled lawyers have elevated answering interrogatories and document requests in noncommittal or evasive ways to an art form.

Silvia's lawyer would serve interrogatories on the defendants seeking, *inter alia*, information identifying all persons who may have handled the jar; technical data regarding the jar's raw materials and production specifications; information about quality control and safety procedures; and any complaints or reports of breakage in the relevant line of containers or time frame. The defendants' lawyers would serve interrogatories seeking information about the accident events, identification of witnesses, including who has possession of the jar fragments (no one in this case), Silvia's medical treatment, lost wages, and any preexisting medical problems.

Depositions. Rule 30 allows a party to take the sworn testimony of any person, including a nonparty, upon oral examination and to compel attendance by way of subpoena. FED. R. CIV. P. 30 (2005). Depositions can be an extremely effective way to develop facts and size up witnesses because they involve face-to-face encounters and the opportunity to doggedly pursue lines of questioning. Unlike written interrogatories, it is much more difficult for an oral deponent to evade answering questions about key issues.

Depositions work to pin down a witness's story and are a vital tool for impeaching witness testimony at trial. When witnesses say something different (or say it differently) on the witness stand from what they said (or how they said it) in their depositions, opposing lawyers are permitted to use their depositions to impeach their testimony.

Unfortunately, oral depositions, while effective, are costly. They not only consume many hours of attorney time, but require substantial out-of-pocket costs for court reporter and transcription fees (which can run several dollars per page), as well as travel costs for attorneys and witnesses. The costs of a single day of deposition-taking can run into thousands of dollars.

In Silvia's case, a thorough attempt to reconstruct the history of the jar would require identifying and taking the deposition of each person who handled the jar along the way, including employees of Levington (the jar maker), Penelope (the peanut seller), Charter (the wholesale distributor), and Value-Store (the retailer). It also would entail taking the depositions of designated corporate representatives for each defendant regarding their quality control procedures and other incidents of broken containers. *See* Fed. R. Civ. P. 30(b)(6) (2005) (authorizing a party to take the deposition of a corporation and to describe the matters on which information is sought, and requiring the corporation to designate one or more representatives to testify as to such matters). In reality, because of the high costs involved, Silvia's lawyer might be more selective in choosing deponents, despite her ostensible responsibility to reconstruct the journey of the jar.

It is difficult to predict exactly whom Silvia's lawyer would opt to depose, in part because discovery decisions of all types are affected by other developments in the case. For example, Silvia's lawyer might be disinclined to depose employees or officers of Levington because of a cost-benefit decision to focus on entities lower in the distribution chain. However, that decision would change if facts came to light showing prior similar incidents involving broken glass containers manufactured by Levington.

One deposition in the case that would be certain to take place would be Silvia's. Silvia is the key witness and the defendants no doubt would depose her. A good lawyer would conduct Silvia's deposition thoroughly, so that there would be no room for her to add or change any fact when she testified at trial. It is also probable that the defendants would take the depositions of Norah, Marco, Dr. Schmitt, and any other expert witness Silvia intended to call.

Requests for production of documents. Rule 34 allows any party to request the production of relevant documents from any party or nonparty. Fed. R. Civ. P. 34 (2005). The request must specify the type of documents sought, but it does not have to identify the precise documents. Silvia would be likely to serve broad document requests on the defendants pertaining to all the matters described in the interrogatory discussion above.

Document requests under U.S. discovery rules are a good example highlighting the alternative universes of fact gathering in U.S. litigation as compared to Germany, Argentina, and other civil law countries. U.S. plaintiffs routinely file broad document requests with the hope, not infrequently realized, of finding a "smoking gun" internal memorandum or other document that proves to be dispositive of the case. For example, Silvia's lawyer might serve a request for Levington to produce "any and all documents in any form relating to complaints, studies, reports, memoranda or other communications regarding the breakage of glass containers manufactured by the defendant" in this particular batch or in the relevant time frame.

Suppose it turned out that Silvia's jar came from a batch that had a higher than normal breakage rate and that Levington was in possession of documents showing that fact. Such documents literally could win the case for Silvia. In a civil law country, however, it is quite possible that such documents would never see the light of day because of rules limiting document requests to specifically identifiable documents whose existence is already known to the requesting party. "Fishing expeditions" for incriminating documents do not exist in Germany or Argentina. Other structural mechanisms can work to help offset these limitations. For example, in Germany, manufacturers are subject to stricter reporting requirements regarding product defects, and in Argentina, plaintiffs sometimes first file criminal claims in the hope that the criminal prosecutor, with broad inquisitorial powers, will uncover hidden information. Nevertheless, there can be no doubt that the ability to make broad document requests is an enormous advantage to U.S. plaintiffs. *See, e.g.*, Michael V. Ciresi et al., *Decades of Deceit: Document Discovery in the Minnesota Tobacco Litigation*, 25 WM. MITCHELL L. REV. 477, 493–94 (1999) (discussing how the nationwide settlement in 1998 between forty-six states and the tobacco industry resulted in large part from the state of Minnesota's successful battle to obtain the production through discovery of approximately thirty-five million industry documents).

Request for physical examination. Rule 35 authorizes the court, upon request by a party, to order a physical or mental examination of a party when the party's condition is in issue. FED. R. CIV. P. 35 (2005). Because Silvia's injuries are likely to be in dispute, the defendants might make a motion to have a specialist examine Silvia's hand and wrist.

Requests for admissions. Rule 36 authorizes a party to serve on another party written requests to admit facts, including the authenticity of documents. FED. R. CIV. P. 36 (2005). The matter will be deemed admitted unless the recipient responds to the request within thirty days. The response must admit the fact, object to the request on a lawful ground, specifically deny the matter, or detail the reasons why the party cannot truthfully admit or deny the matter. Any matter admitted within the rule is deemed to be conclusively established in the proceedings.

Not surprisingly, parties resist admitting critical facts, even when they're true, and strain to find ways to avoid doing so. But the procedure can be helpful in nailing down certain matters. Silvia's lawyer might, for example, serve requests for admission seeking to establish that Levington manufactured the jar that injured Silvia or that Silvia's receipt showing purchase of the jar from Value-Store is authentic.

Despite the impressive arsenal of discovery tools available to Silvia and her lawyer, it is entirely possible, if not likely, that no one will ever really know what caused this particular jar to shatter.

Fact Presentation (i.e., "The Trial")

U.S. litigated case resolution is profoundly shaped by the existence of juries, which in modern times are unique to the U.S. in civil cases even among common law countries. In England, jury trials have been eliminated in most types of civil cases. Almost by necessity, the presence of juries converts the trial court adjudication of a case into a clearly defined, sometimes dramatic "event." *See* MERRYMAN, at 112. The necessity of bringing together a group of citizens from disparate walks of life at one time and in one place to hear all of the evidence, receive instruction on the law, and resolve the case imposes consolidating pressures not present in civil law countries, where courts usually receive evidence and hear argument during a series of hearings that can stretch over many months or even years. *See id.* Trial by jury is one of the defining features of the U.S. common law system, but do not lose sight of the fact that only a small number of cases ever make it to trial (only 2% of tort cases). Most cases are resolved by settlement. Moreover, outside of the realm of tort cases, most U.S. trials are bench trials.

At U.S. trials, as during pretrial, lawyers run the show. The lawyers, in consultation with the client, decide on the overall trial strategy and on the particulars for implementing it, including: which potential jurors to strike with peremptory (discretionary) challenges, which witnesses to call, in what order to call them, what questions to ask them, which documents to admit into evidence, and when to object to the other side's evidence. As noted, the judge sits more or less as a neutral referee. Here are the basic steps in the trial process:

Jury selection. The first step in a jury trial, not surprisingly, is selecting a jury. In federal court, where Silvia's U.S. case is filed, federal districts have the option of setting the number of jurors in civil trials at any even number from six to twelve. Most federal districts have opted for six-member civil juries. Most judges allow lawyers to participate in jury selection through a process known as *voir dire*, in which the lawyers are permitted to question potential jurors (or submit requested questions to the judge) with the goal of identifying jurors favorably or unfavorably disposed to their client's case.

Any party can move to strike a juror "for cause" (e.g., the juror is related to a party, lawyer or witness in the case), but each party also gets a certain number of what are called "peremptory challenges" that can be used to strike a juror for any non-discriminatory reason. In fact, no reason need be given. The lawyer would simply tell the court, "The [plaintiff or defendant] strikes

Juror No. 4." Although it wouldn't happen in Silvia's case, in big cases, lawyers sometimes hire expert psychological jury consultants to help them make these choices.

Opening statements. The lawyers for each party make an opening statement laying out their respective cases for the jury; that is, the lawyers tell the jury what they think the evidence will show. In a case like Silvia's involving several defendants, each defendant's lawyer would have the right to present an opening statement. Each probably would exercise that right, although it would be common for a group of defendants linked as closely as these defendants are linked to select one lawyer, probably either Levington's or Penelope's, to play the leading role in the opening statement and other phases of the trial.

The plaintiff's case. After the opening statements, Silvia's lawyer would present all of her evidence, both oral and documentary, to the jury. Each defendant's lawyer would have the opportunity to cross-examine each witness called by Silvia. Again, one defense lawyer probably would take the lead, with lawyers for the other defendants asking briefer follow-up questions. When Silvia finished presenting her evidence, her lawyer would inform the court that "the plaintiff rests."

Motion for judgment as a matter of law. It is standard practice after the plaintiff has finished presenting her evidence for the defendant to make a "motion for a directed verdict," as it is most commonly referred to, on the basis that the evidence is insufficient to support the plaintiff's case. In federal court, it's called a "motion for judgment as a matter of law." *See* Fed. R. Civ. Pro 50(a) (2005). To grant such a motion, the judge must believe that, viewing the evidence in the light most favorable to the plaintiff, no reasonable juror could find that the plaintiff has proved the facts supporting her claims by a preponderance of the evidence (or "more likely than not") standard.

The defendants' case. Assuming the judge denied or reserved ruling on the defendants' motion for judgment as a matter of law, which would usually be the case, the defendants would present their evidence. Silvia's lawyer would have the opportunity to cross-examine each defense witness. When the defendants finished, they too would "rest."

Rebuttal. After the defendants rested, Silvia would have the opportunity to present rebuttal evidence generally limited to issues raised by the defendants' evidence. This right of rebuttal is exercised sparingly and, when used, sparsely. The defendants would be able to cross-examine any witnesses presented by Silvia in this rebuttal stage. If Silvia's rebuttal witnesses opened new doors of inquiry, defendants would be permitted to present additional testimony as "surrebuttal."

Renewed motion for judgment as a matter of law. After the defendants finished presenting their case, they would renew their motion for judgment as a matter of law. In all but the clearest cases, such motions are denied because judges face a higher risk of getting overturned on appeal when they usurp the role of the jury.

Closing arguments. At the close of all the evidence, each side presents a closing argument to the jury. Because the plaintiff bears the burden of proof, the plaintiff gets two bites at the apple. The plaintiff argues first, followed by the defendant, after which the plaintiff gets one more shot to rebut the defendant's arguments. Unlike in the opening statements, in which lawyers are restricted to stating what they believe the evidence will show, the closing argument is just that: an attempt to assemble a persuasive *argument* combining facts and law, using just about any rhetorical method the lawyer thinks will be most effective.

Because the jury instructions on the law are decided on prior to the closing argument, lawyers commonly use those instructions to argue that the law commands a verdict in favor of their respective client under the evidence as presented. Such arguments often assume this form: "Ladies and gentlemen, the judge is going to tell you that [quoting the instruction]." Often, lawyers project excerpts from the instructions on a screen or display them on poster boards to clarify and reinforce the legal principles to the jury. It might seem odd to students of the civil law tradition, but in jury trials, untrained laypersons are the ones who apply the law to the facts to resolve the case.

Jury instructions. After the closing arguments (or in some jurisdictions, before the closing arguments), the judge instructs the jury on the law. Even here, the lawyers have substantial input. Each side submits requested jury instructions to the court. The judge then holds a "charge conference" (jury instructions are also called the "jury charge") with the lawyers at which they argue their positions for or against the inclusion of particular instructions. Once the instructions have been decided on, the judge reads them one time to the jury. Most judges allow the jury to take a copy of the instructions with them into the jury room.

Jury deliberations. After the closing arguments and jury instructions, the jurors retire to select a foreperson and deliberate their verdict.

Verdict. The jury must return a verdict by unanimous agreement in federal court, although many states have dispensed with the unanimity requirement in civil cases. If the jury is unable to agree on a verdict, a mistrial is declared. Juries do not explain the reasons for their verdicts. Nor do they make specific findings of fact, except that the modern trend is to use verdict forms that ask questions regarding matters such as the basis for finding a defendant liable, relative percentages of fault among multiple defendants and the plaintiff, and damages amounts for different categories.

All trial testimony is recorded verbatim by a court reporter, which is different from Germany, where witness testimony is only summarized by the judge or, in Argentina, by a clerk of the court. It is not uncommon for U.S.

appellate courts to seize on particular statements made by parties or other witnesses as support for affirming or reversing a decision.

Justice Department statistics show that the median time frame for tort cases disposed of by trial in the U.S. district courts (where Silvia's case is filed) in 2002–03 was twenty months from the filing of the complaint to the verdict. Two-thirds of tort cases were completed within two years, although 5% lingered for more than five years until completion.

Germany

Roles of Lawyers and Judges

The roles occupied by lawyers and judges in civil law countries, including Germany, are very different than in the U.S., although the overall tenor of the process is similar. One of the most frequently uttered distinctions between common and civil law systems is that common law systems are "adversarial" while civil law systems are "inquisitorial." From this distinction comes the belief that lawyers control most aspects of the proceedings in common law systems, while judges control most aspects of the proceedings in civil law countries. While the first half of the statement is fairly accurate, the second half is only partly accurate as applied to civil, as distinct from criminal, litigation. Civil litigation in Germany is quite adversarial. *See* John M. Langbein, *The German Advantage in Civil Procedure*, 52 U. Chi. L. Rev. 823, 841 (1985) (commenting that outside of the realm of fact-gathering, German civil procedure is as adversarial as in the U.S.).

Parties and their lawyers control most aspects of civil litigation in Germany. The principal of "party control" over civil proceedings even has a name: *Dispositionsmaxime*. The lawyers frame the claims and defenses in their pleadings and have the power to terminate proceedings by settlement or withdrawal of the action. The lawyers identify the witnesses and other relevant evidence. They make partisan arguments from the beginning of the case, starting with the initial pleadings, through the end of the case in their final arguments.

The starkest difference in the relative roles of lawyers and judges between the U.S. and Germany is that in Germany the function of lawyers in developing and eliciting evidence is much more restricted once the case has been filed. Because German procedure does not provide instruments for pretrial discovery like the U.S. system, the lawyers must investigate the case facts and accessible evidence with great care before recommending that the plaintiff file an action. As elaborated on below, the parties' initial pleadings must identify all witnesses and documentary evidence. Once the case gets to court, however, the judge will decide what evidence is legally relevant and will conduct the bulk of the questioning. Another way to put it is to say that the parties control the initial trajectory of the lawsuit and its destiny in terms of whether and when to terminate it, but the judge manages the case once it gets going.

"Hints and Feedback"

The overall role of a German trial judge is much more active than in the U.S., and, in fact, more active than in many other civil law countries. It goes far beyond controlling compliance with the formal strictures of evidence and procedure. The judge manages and directs the proceedings with a very hands-on approach. Nowhere is this method of case management more dramatically reflected than in the judge's duty to give "hints and feedback" to the parties as the case progresses.

To facilitate efficient proceedings and eliminate the danger of unfair surprise, a German civil trial judge has a continuing duty to alert the parties and their lawyers as to what he or she is thinking about the case as it proceeds. This includes, per section 139 of the German Code of Civil Procedure (*Zivilprozessordnung*) (GCCP), a duty: (1) to discuss with the parties the relevant facts and legal issues as the judge sees them; (2) to inform the parties of the court's concerns regarding the issues; and (3) to communicate these hints and feedback and document them in the record as early as possible. Further, a court may base its decision on an aspect of an issue which a party has overlooked or an aspect which the court views differently from both parties only if the court has first called attention to the matter and given the party or parties an opportunity to comment on it.

The duty to give hints and feedback would be the equivalent, in the U.S. system, of stopping at various points in a trial and soliciting input from the jury about which way it is leaning with regard to various issues. Not surprisingly, the duty to give hints and feedback can play a prominent role in facilitating settlement. If the judge's hints and feedback indicate the court is leaning one way or the other on a critical issue, this handwriting on the wall, so to speak, may prompt a party to pursue a settlement.

It is not unusual for lawyers to ask the judge for a statement on "how the court sees the case for the time being." The judge's responses give the lawyers an opportunity to continually reassess both their chances of winning and the potential costs of continuing the lawsuit. This type of case development regularly occurs in products liability cases as they are often complex and present several uncertainties. Hints from the judge are one reason so many products liability cases end with party settlements. Even though settled cases do not end with definitive court judgments, it will be clear in many cases to all involved that it was the judge's legal or factual assessment expressed in a hint that played the decisive role in the parties reaching settlement. This is why in German legal practice these hints are also called *prozessleitender richterlicher Hinweis*, which translates to "action-leading judicial hint." The hints can be combined with specific suggestions regarding what kind of settlement the court could consider reasonable.

The following example provides elucidation. Imagine that Silvia's case, which it has been assumed is filed in the State District Court in Cologne (the *Landgericht Köln*), has progressed to the first hearing of the plenary phase, where the court hears testimony and argument. The lawyers and judges are debating in the courtroom. When they are finished with this "first sitting," the lawyers ask the court for an action-leading judicial hint. The judge's response might assume the following style. Necessarily, this hint incorporates references to German legal rules that are discussed in later chapters:

> The court has the following view on this case: I am still not in the position to make a definite judgment as several relevant points remain unclear. And as you know, in this type of products liability case the specific judicature regarding the burden of proof poses additional uncertainties.
>
> Apart from these general remarks, in this particular case there are several specific ambiguities on both sides. First, the court sees the points the plaintiff has raised regarding the issue of defectiveness. I can imagine, and based on the *Anscheinsbeweis* doctrine [see chapter eight] justify, an assertion that the jar was defective *unless* the plaintiff had not treated the jar properly with the Exacto knife. From my point of view this situation requires further evidence.
>
> On the other hand, when I look to you on the defendants' side, I must make clear that I have not seen enough evidence and substantiation to be convinced that the defendants and their staffs did all they were able to do to ensure the quality of their jars or at least to document their final status before supplying them to customers. As you and the plaintiff have both referred to in writing, I may need to consider the Federal Supreme Court's doctrine on the violation of the *Befundsicherungspflicht* and the related rules of evidence which provide for a shifting of the burden of proof with respect to the product's defectiveness [see chapter eight].
>
> And also, on the one hand, I see your argument that the treatment of the jar with the Exacto knife might lead to a finding of the plain-

tiff's comparative negligence. But on the other hand, you bear the burden of proof for this negligence and, in addition, the court is contemplating whether this superficial usage of a knife was a foreseeable and, thus, not unusual usage from a reasonable consumer's perspective. A jar so fragile could establish the defectiveness of the jar for normal use. I am trying to imagine what would be the case if a consumer after shopping happened to hit the bag containing the jar against another hard object, such as a door or the floor, or simply another hard container in the same shopping bag.

For additional substantiation, the defendants need to consider these open points when preparing the next written submission. Depending on the outcome of these factual points, we would next need to answer the questions of whether all damages can be attributed to the injurious event, as well as the appropriate amount of such damages. So far we only have medical reports of the treating physician. We will definitely need to have at least one follow-up examination of the plaintiff to assess the course of her injuries and their impact on her capacity to earn an income. So, in summary, I see a number of points needing further clarification.

As the court has been asked to provide the parties with a view of what a potential settlement could look like at this stage, I will close today with this final remark. Considering the statements above, the potential duration of this case in this court of first instance, and the uncertainties and procedural risks for both sides, I would think it might make sense for you to consider a settlement of the case on a 50–50% basis. You might discuss this with your clients.

It is easy to see from the above example how action-leading hints can be very effective tools for judges to steer lawsuits toward settlement, especially in situations where the case is complex and the legal and factual issues are not sufficiently clarified.

Action-leading hints underscore the power of a German judge over the proceedings, and the dependence of the parties on the judge. Often, case resolution will depend on the skill of a judge in using hints and feedback to influence and convince the parties to settle. As the parties themselves (e.g., a defendant's corporate representatives) often do not attend the court sittings, lawyers regularly ask the court to provide the hint in writing so that they can forward it to the client. Particularly for defense lawyers, such a written hint is very helpful in convincing clients that a settlement makes sense.

Fact Gathering and Presentation

As already noted, there are no separate pretrial and trial phases in civil law countries such as Germany. Rather, fact investigation and presentation merges together in a continuous sequence that begins with the initial attorney-client interview and ends in the final judgment. Facts asserted in pleadings that are not specifically contested may be taken as true, and relied on throughout the proceedings, without the need for further proof. A rough demarcation can be made, however, among three stages.

The first stage comprises the time between the initial attorney-client interview and the filing of the lawsuit and can be called the *pre-judicial stage*. The second phase is the *preliminary proceedings stage*, which are the proceedings that begin with the filing of the complaint and wrap up before the start of the oral plenary hearings in court. The third and most crucial stage consists of the *plenary hearing stage* where evidence is formally received in court and oral argument is heard.

Pre-Judicial Stage

The pre-filing stage of a lawsuit is critical in German law. Any experienced German litigator would agree that a lawsuit "can already be lost" at this early stage of the case. The structuring and clarification of the factual issues at this stage will serve as the foundation for the rest of the proceedings.

As there is no discovery under German law, the pre-judicial stage is where Silvia's lawyer would seek to gather and marshal all of the main case facts that Silvia intends to rely on in the proceeding. This will include identifying, preserving, and assembling into an overall picture of the case all relevant evidence (e.g., witness names, documents, and physical objects). The plaintiff bears the brunt of the fact gathering in German civil proceedings.

Another important aspect of the pre-judicial stage is the correspondence between the plaintiff's lawyer and the defense lawyers. The plaintiff's lawyer must contact the prospective defendants and confront them with the plaintiff's claims. This pre-judicial contact is mandated by section 93 of the GCCP, which, as interpreted by courts, provides that if the plaintiff does not make a demand on the defendant prior to filing the lawsuit, the plaintiff must bear the attorneys' fees and costs of the litigation if the defendant acknowledges the claim at the beginning of the trial. Thus, Silvia's lawyer would need to identify all relevant tortfeasors and contact them through a demand letter. As it would be hard to put a precise figure on her claims early in the litigation, her lawyer would seek simply an admission of liability. Should one or more of the defendants concede liability, the time pressures of the statute of limitations would be relieved and Silvia would have time to finalize her medical treatment and specific monetary claims before having to implement litigation.

Because this pretrial correspondence will regularly be the subject of court filings, available for evaluation by the judge at a later point, the content and wording of the correspondence is critical. Much like the discussion of oral testimony in the U.S. section above, every word choice must be carefully considered. Each choice can have crucial implications when evaluated at a later stage.

Preliminary Proceedings Stage

The next stage in Silvia's case would be the preliminary proceedings. The preliminary proceedings consist primarily of a series of written exchanges among the parties and court, including the all-critical initial pleadings. Traditionally, after the initial pleadings were filed, the judge would schedule a preliminary oral hearing. That practice has changed dramatically in recent decades. The GCCP now allows preliminary proceedings to be conducted in writing. *See* GCCP §§ 272(2), 276. Today, it is standard practice for the preliminary phase of most cases, including the vast majority of tort cases such as Silvia's, to be handled for a long period of time solely in writing. After receiving and reviewing the initial pleadings, the court will enter what is usually a series of orders seeking to clarify and pin down the issues, elicit additional facts, and extract legal arguments from the parties. These orders and the parties' responses will go back and forth until the issues become clear. The court will continuously narrow the focus of the case to those key questions which need to be answered to decide it. The preliminary proceedings set up the case for the plenary hearing, where testimony and argument are orally heard by the court.

Initial Pleadings

Although the initial pleadings in German litigation carry the same titles as their American counterparts, i.e., "complaint" and "answer," their content and impact on the litigation are much greater. The U.S. Federal Rules of Civil Procedure require only "notice pleading"; that is, pleadings sufficient to put the other parties on notice of the claims and defenses. *See* FED. R. CIV. PRO. 8 (2005) (requiring the complaint to contain "a short and plain statement of the claim" and an answer to contain a statement of defenses in "short and plain terms"). Development of the detailed facts supporting claims and defenses is left for pretrial discovery.

Not so in Germany. The complaint is, both formally and substantively, the crucial blueprint on which the entire lawsuit will depend. The requirements for the content and form of the complaint are laid down in section 253 of the GCCP, titled *Klageschrift*, which translates to "Complaint." Section 253 requires the plaintiff to identify each defendant and the competent court and to give a clear statement of the matter in dispute and the basis for her claims.

To comply with the latter requirement, the complaint must set forth with particularity the factual support for the plaintiff's claims. This generally will include a statement of each essential fact, along with the anticipated source of support for the fact. If that source is a witness, the witness's name and address will be included. If the source is a document, the specific document will be identified and often included as part of the complaint.

As a result, complaints in German civil litigation can resemble lengthy case files. Silvia's complaint in Germany would be many pages longer than its American counterpart. It would specifically identify witnesses such as Norah, Marco, and Dr. Schmitt and include document attachments such as her purchase receipt for the jar of peanuts and all of her relevant medical records. If new facts emerge, it is possible for a plaintiff to amend the complaint.

German civil procedure law only expects the parties and their lawyers to provide the court with the *facts* forming the basis for their allegations. They are not expected to include legal statements or evaluations. It is up to the judge to draw the legal conclusions from the facts presented. This constellation is based on the Roman law principles of *da mihi factum, dabo tibi ius* ("give me the facts, I give you the law") and *iura novit curia* ("the court knows the law"). Nevertheless, in practice, initial pleadings do frequently contain legal elucidation, particularly when the legal subject is complex, which is usually the case in products liability litigation.

As with the pre-judicial correspondence, it is important for the lawyers on both sides to think carefully about the best way to present crucial case facts in the pleadings. Often much time is spent in drafting initial pleadings in search of the best wording to support the claim and defenses from both a legal and a psychological perspective. Consider, for example, Silvia's use of the Exacto knife to remove the rebate label. If the knife were mentioned by the plaintiff's lawyer (which it probably would not be), careful thought would be given to every word written regarding this delicate subject.

Similar rules and practices apply to the defendant's answer. Each defendant would be expected to set forth both factual assertions and the sources of support for them. Defenses must be explained in some detail. Legal arguments addressing the sufficiency of the complaint or merits of the plaintiff's claims, which would be the subject of separate pleadings in the U.S. (such as a motion to dismiss or motion for summary judgment), also would be included.

Fact Investigation

In Germany, as in most civil law countries, there is no pretrial discovery. Silvia would have no interrogatories, discovery depositions, broad requests for production of documents, or other tools to help her lawyer ferret out facts relevant to her case. Moreover, informal discovery is hindered by the fact that lawyers generally do not interview most witnesses prior to their appearance in court. While there is no direct ethical prohibition on interviewing witnesses, the practice traditionally has not been looked on favorably by judges as it can be seen as "causing partiality." Judges will tend to discount the testimony of witnesses who have been prepped or coached by counsel. Both judges and lawyers will frequently ask witnesses whether they have had any contact with any of the lawyers. If the answer is affirmative, the lawyer for the other side will try to denounce the witness as partial and attack his or her credibility.

In practice, however, lawyers by necessity must interview some witnesses to determine the state of the case, and in the plaintiff's situation, to determine whether a valid claim exists. So long as the interview is conducted in accordance with "good practice rules," the witness's testimony will be accepted by the court. Good practice rules mean documenting the interview in a written memorandum, including documentation that the lawyer identified himself as a representative for a particular party and informed the witness there was no obligation to speak to the lawyer. Thus, Silvia's lawyer would be permitted to contact witnesses such as Norah, Marco, and Dr. Schmitt (after obtaining a waiver from Silvia of the confidentiality of her medical records). Even without conducting witness interviews, as a practical matter, lawyers usually can learn the substance of the testimony of friendly witnesses from talking to the client.

Students of the U.S. common law system probably find the absence of pretrial discovery to be somewhat shocking. How are the lawyers supposed to find out what happened, they may ask, without discovery? There can be no doubt: the absence of discovery inhibits the ability of lawyers in civil law countries to dig out hidden information. German lawyers have been heard to state that they "dream" of having pretrial discovery as it exists in the U.S.

Consider Silvia's use of the Exacto knife to remove the rebate label. The plaintiff's lawyer would not volunteer this important information to the defendants. The lawyer regularly would keep quiet about such a matter in both the pre-judicial demand letter and the complaint. Such nondisclosure would not be considered unethical. A plaintiff is not obligated to bring forth facts that contradict her claim. In Germany, it is said, based on an ancient Roman procedural principle, *nemo tenetur edere contra se* ("nobody is held to plead against himself").

As a result, because there is no adversarial fact development through discovery, it is quite possible that such a potentially critical piece of evidence could remain hidden throughout the litigation. Similarly, if the defendant Levington had information showing a breakdown in its quality control with respect to the line of jars from which Silvia's jar came, that important fact also could remain undisclosed. Each side has extremely restricted access to matters within the other side's sphere. On the other hand, such matters often do come to light, even if only accidentally, as through a witness admission or hearsay reference or even careless blabbing by the lawyer. The parties themselves, especially plaintiffs, sometimes become nervous and make admissions when being questioned by the judge or the other side's lawyers. And, of course, criminal penalties exist for false answers to direct questions. Nevertheless, there is a very real chance that the defendants would never find out about the Exacto knife, particularly since the glass shards are not available for expert examination.

The absence of discovery tools makes it much more important for the plaintiff and her lawyer to investigate the case facts on their own. Silvia's lawyer would count on her to assemble all available evidence and to identify all potential sources for further evidence. Because substantiating the jar's defectiveness is so crucial, Silvia's lawyer would search outside of her personal sphere for more to go on. This could include calling in an external expert, researching press reports, searching for prior similar cases, and contacting regulatory authorities and local and federal consumer councils, which are very strong in Germany. The plaintiff also would normally receive information from the pre-judicial correspondence with the producer and the other members of the distribution chain. Together, these methods could lead to a significant additional amount of information that would help Silvia assemble a complete picture of the case.

The parties are also helped immensely in terms of fact gathering by the pleadings. As stated, each side must set forth the specific factual allegations on which they intend to rely in their initial pleadings and in clarifying responses called for by the court. Sources for these facts also must be disclosed, including witness names and the identification of specific documents. If a party relies on a particular document, the other side is entitled to review the document. *See* GCCP §§ 134, 135. Moreover, the parties may request the court to order another party to produce specific, identified documents. Under civil justice reforms adopted in 2001, the court also can order a nonparty to produce documents, a power previously unknown to German law.

While fact investigation is not likely to be as thorough as in the U.S., particularly with regard to sweeping document examinations, in the end, the results of fact development in the U.S. and in Germany probably come out quite similar in most cases.

Plenary Hearing Stage

There is no conception of a trial as a single unitary event in civil law countries. In Germany, the closest thing to a trial for Silvia would be the plenary proceeding (*Haupttermin*). The plenary proceeding is the oral hearing, or series of hearings, at which the court hears the argument of counsel and takes evidence. The trend has been toward trying to consolidate the plenary hearing into a single event, a trend spurred by a 1976 amendment to the GCCP providing that "[a]s a general rule, the litigation shall be completed in one oral hearing which shall be comprehensively prepared by all parties." GCCP § 272(1). The goal is to accelerate the lawsuit. Nevertheless, while conceptually the plenary proceeding is considered to be a single event, in practice it is still common for the hearing to be adjourned and resumed, often on several occasions. *See* PETER L. MURRAY & ROLF STÜRNER, GERMAN CIVIL JUSTICE 249 (2004). Products liability actions regularly require several hearings. In Silvia's case, we could anticipate a general hearing, followed by at least two hearings to take witness testimony, and one or more hearings to hear the expert reports.

By the time the plenary hearing arrives, the court will have refined the critical factual and legal issues in the case through the preliminary proceedings. The plenary hearing will be limited to a trial of those issues. In this way, the German system is more efficient than the U.S. system. In the U.S., all evidence from both sides must be both discovered and presented to the jury in every case, even if 90% of it turns out to be irrelevant to the jury's ultimate decision.

To the contrary, German judges can and usually do "cut to the chase" by focusing only on the most salient evidentiary inquiries and legal issues. By way of example, let's assume hypothetically that the judge in Silvia's case determined that the dispositive issue was whether Silvia damaged the jar when she used the Exacto knife to cut out the rebate label. The judge would be able to proceed directly to that issue, without the necessity of hearing evidence about other issues that the judge considered to be unimportant in resolving the case.

The plenary hearing is conducted quite informally, which is very different from the rigidly structured U.S. trial process. The steps at the hearing do not occur in a fixed sequence. The judge functions as a kind of moderator and there is a lot of "back and forth" among the judge and the lawyers throughout the hearing. With that caveat, the following general steps can be identified.

Plenary hearings begin with the judge calling the case, followed by the parties' lawyers delivering an oral statement of their positions. *See* GCCP § 137(1) ("The oral hearing is to be opened with the parties presenting their claims."). The plaintiff's lawyer goes first. In the past, the lawyers would read the claims and defenses aloud from the pleadings, sometimes in a lengthy recital, but the modern practice is for the lawyers to offer just brief oral summaries and make reference to their written submissions.

Next, the court sometimes engages in a colloquy with the parties—the actual parties, not their lawyers—in an effort to clarify facts and assertions, although like most hearing events, there is no formally prescribed sequence for these exchanges. They can occur at any point during a hearing at the judge's discretion. It is important to understand that, unlike in the U.S., parties are precluded from testifying as "witnesses" because of their interest in the litigation. As such, their words are not considered as formal evidence. This usually would be true even in a case such as Silvia's where she is the person with the most knowledge about what happened to the jar. The GCCP does provide a limited exception for "party interrogation" in circumstances where a party makes a motion for such interrogation of an opposing party (GCCP § 445), where a party (such as Silvia) requests to be examined and the other parties and the court agree (GCCP § 447), or where the court decides *sua sponte* that such interrogation is necessary with respect to a particular fact. GCCP § 448. However, this happens only in exceptional situations. In most cases, no party interrogation will occur and the statements of parties will not be considered evidence.

Often, the next step is for the lawyers to present oral argument regarding the factual and legal issues. It might seem backwards to common law students to hold oral arguments before the presentation of the evidence, but it is not unusual for the court to listen to several rounds of argument from counsel during the proceedings. German litigation is motivated in part by a desire for economy and efficiency and many cases can be disposed of without the necessity of taking evidence. Moreover, as in all systems, settlement is deemed to be the most favorable outcome of litigation in Germany. Thus, judges usually will explore settlement possibilities early in the plenary hearing and, as highlighted above, provide the parties with hints and feedback with the goal of moving them toward settlement.

Taking of Evidence

If the parties do not settle the case, the next stage is the taking of evidence. As indicated, by this point, the court, working with the parties, will have narrowed the focus of the case to the key issues. Evidence taking will be limited to those issues. The judge decides which witnesses, among those identified by the parties, will be heard and in what order they will be heard. The court has no power to summon witnesses who have not been named as witnesses by the parties. At the most, by giving hints and feedback, the court might suggest that a particular question needs to be addressed by evidence (e.g., by witnesses, documents or other material). Thus, even though judges control the elicitation of evidence, the parties control the overall content of the evidence by the sources they identify.

The court will not seek to help a party by nominating a particular witness that the party has not named. If a judge supports a party by doing so, the other party might file a motion for recusal of the judge because of partiality. *See* GCCP §42 (providing for recusal of judges for reasons causing distrust). In Germany, judges rarely take chances to support a party even if the party or her lawyer has obviously overlooked a critical point. This is a consequence of the design of German civil procedure as an "adversarial party procedure" where each party has to take care of its own interests and concerns. *See* BGH, NJW 2000, 1108 (1109). The approach is rooted in the overarching German legal principle of the private autonomy of legal subjects. *See* ADEM KOYUNCU, DAS HAFTUNGSDREIECK PHARMAUNTERNEHMEN—ARZT—PATIENT 208 (2004).

German civil procedure provides for five means of proof: the inspection of an object (GCCP §371 et seq.); testimony from nonparty lay witnesses (GCCP §373 et seq.); expert testimony and reports (GCCP §402 et seq.); documentary evidence (GCCP §415 et seq.); and party interrogation (GCCP §445 et seq.).

If it is clear prior to the plenary hearing that evidence-taking will be necessary, the judge usually will have issued a "proof order" setting forth the factual issues to be addressed and the witness testimony and documentary evidence that will be received. Unlike U.S. practice, witnesses in Germany testify first in a narrative form, telling their story in their own words. *See* GCCP §396.

After the witness has told his or her story, the court will follow up with questions. It is usual for the judge, rather than the lawyers, to pose most of the questions to a witness. After the court has finished, the parties are called on to ask further questions, if any, directly to the witness. The party who named the witness is allowed to go first, followed by the opposing parties. The latter is the German equivalent of cross-examination. U.S.-style cross-examination, which consists of incisive and sometimes aggressive questioning made up almost solely of leading questions with "yes" or "no" answers, is unknown to German practice. The German practice of opposing parties asking follow up questions could be described as "cross-examination lite." The questioning takes place under the guidance of the court. In the course of this questioning, the judge may intercede and ask additional questions for clarification. Also, the judge will "carpet" a lawyer who gets too impertinent or aggressive in his or her questioning.

Given the absence of juries, there are few strict rules of evidence. No rules, for example, prohibit hearsay evidence. Questions that go to the *admissibility* of evidence in the U.S. go to the *weight* of the evidence in Germany. Langbein, at 829. Thus, in Silvia's case, the judge would have wide discretion to consider whatever facts the judge believed were relevant.

Traditionally, civil law systems relied much more on written submissions of testimony than common law systems. In Germany, however, that is no longer the case. Nearly all witness testimony in Silvia's case would be heard orally by the court in the presence of the parties, or at least their lawyers. One of the basic principles of German procedural law translates to the "principle of speech." In effect, this means that the spoken word of a witness is the decisive evidence. The only major exception involves expert witnesses, who often submit written reports to the court (see chapter six).

Unlike in the U.S., German trial proceedings are not the subject of complete verbatim transcripts. Section 159 of the GCCP requires that a record be made of oral evidentiary proceedings, including the statements of witnesses or experts, but the evidence can be and usually is summarized, not written down word for word. Commonly, the judge will stop periodically during the proceeding to dictate relevant portions of the proceedings into a recording machine. If a party regards certain statements of a witness to be extraordinarily relevant, the party can request that the particular statements be quoted in the record. GCCP § 160(4). The record must be read to or otherwise presented for scrutiny to the witness or interested party (GCCP § 162(1)), who must approve it or note objections. However, this requirement is obviated if the record was composed in their presence or, as often happens, the right to playback is waived. GCCP § 162(2). A primary purpose of the record is for use in the event of an appeal. Unlike in the U.S., appellate courts do not have access to a witness's precise words when reviewing a case.

After the evidence is received at one or, more likely, several sessions, the lawyers present more oral argument. The plenary proceeding ends when the judge declares it to be closed. The judge then takes the case under advisement and renders a decision.

From initial pleading to final judgment in the trial court, Silvia could expect a wait of approximately twenty-four months.

Argentina

Roles of Lawyers and Judges

As is usually the case in Latin American countries, Argentine civil procedure is quite adversarial. Pursuant to the so-called "dispositive principle," the parties have full control of the dispute they bring to the court. The parties decide which facts will be presented in the complaint and response thereto, and which evidence will support those facts. The parties define the scope of the proceeding and have the power to terminate it through settlement or abandonment.

However, major exceptions have found their way into the dispositive principle in the form of amendments to the National Code of Civil Procedure (NCCP). The NCCP controls all civil proceedings in federal court and in the "national" courts in the federal capital of Buenos Aires (Silvia's forum). Each of the twenty-three provincial court systems has its own code of civil procedure, although most of them parallel the NCCP. The amendments, the most important of which occurred in 1968, 1981, and 2002, grant broad powers to judges to take charge of judicial proceedings. As law professors teach Argentine law students, it is now more accurate to describe the principle of party control as the "attenuated dispositive principle." The core system remains adversarial but with many inquisitorial features built into it. Judges in the 1960s and 1970s used to be impartial, mute umpires whose purpose was to "keep track of the score." Now they are somewhat more likely to step onto the playing field and score for one of the parties, but it is still the case that most judges do not actively take charge of ordinary litigation.

Instead, the biggest point of differentiation of Argentine law—one likely to astound fact-focused U.S. common law lawyers—is how small a role most judges play at all in either fact gathering *or* fact presentation to the court. Most judicial proceedings take place in writing, and even when oral testimony is heard it usually happens in front of a low-ranking court employee—not the judge. More to follow on that point.

Fact Gathering and Presentation

Fact Gathering

Pretrial discovery is not available in Argentina, which, as in most other civil law countries, makes the lawyer's job of assembling a case an unenviable one. Quite simply, it is very difficult to unearth relevant facts under the current system. The result, it is fair to say, is that the Argentine system of fact development often leads to case conclusions in which a judicial "formal truth" prevails over an objective "real truth." Some time ago, Argentine scholars discussed, but did not vigorously pursue, the possibility of adopting U.S.-style discovery rules. The advocates of discovery cited the flaws of the system now in force. Those opposed to discovery expressed concern that implementing discovery rules could lead to a worse overall situation due to the lack of sound, hands-on case management by judges. The fear was that turning discovery over to the parties without active judicial involvement could lead to abuse. Aggravating the problems caused by the absence of discovery is the fact that the initial complaint, which controls the shape and destiny of the entire lawsuit much more than in the U.S., can seldom be amended after filing.

Silvia's lawsuit would begin with the filing of a complaint in which she must: (1) identify herself and each defendant by name and address; (2) explicitly describe the relief sought; (3) clearly explain the facts supporting her claim; (4) elaborate on the law that applies to the claim; and (5) set forth her claim "clearly and positively." NCCP Art. 330. The plaintiff will seldom be permitted to amend the complaint after it has been served on the defendant. If new facts are discovered, there is a potential for expanding the claim, but only if the new facts are discovered prior to the preliminary hearing. *See* NCCP Art. 365. Further, unlike U.S. practice where appellate courts are limited to considering facts in the trial record, new facts that occurred or were discovered after the trial court hearings can be introduced when the case reaches the court of appeals, although that happens only rarely. *See* NCCP Art. 260(5)(a).

Making the lawyer's job even more difficult, all documents supporting the claim must, at least in principle, be attached to or duly identified in the complaint. Likewise, a complete list of the evidence to be produced during the lawsuit must also be part of the complaint. The whole complaint process is a one-shot game: say it once and say it right.

The ability of lawyers to successfully accomplish the challenging feat of constructing a comprehensive pleading is generally tied to their years of experience working within the system. Argentine law schools concentrate for the most part on teaching the law. Little is offered to students in the way of practical experience, which is perhaps a complaint shared by law students everywhere. Students are not taught how to prepare a complaint. New graduates set off on a sometimes painful trek of becoming real lawyers. Although more seasoned lawyers often assist in this endeavor, no formal coaching or mentoring system is in place.

Because it is so critical to get it right the first time, before even thinking about beginning to draft a complaint, Silvia's lawyer typically would engage in several interviews with her until feeling he or she had mastered the facts. The lawyer also would identify possible nonparty witnesses and meet with them or discuss the facts over the phone. In this way, Argentine practice more closely resembles U.S. practice than German practice. No negative light is cast on the fact that a witness has spoken to a lawyer for one or more of the parties. To the contrary, a recent court of appeals decision held that a plaintiff's lawyer has a pre-filing duty to evaluate the viability of the claim in light of the evidence expected to be presented in the lawsuit. Cámara Nacional de Apelaciones lo Civil, Sala H [CNCiv.], 8/9/05, "Marengo, Raúl A. v. A., D. L.," Semanarios de Jurisprudencia Argentina [S.J.A.] (10/19/2005). There is no realistic way to evaluate a claim without interviewing the witnesses.

Consultant experts also would be retained, first, to give an impartial account of the chances for success in the case, and then to help draft a favorable explanation of the facts in light of the consultant's specialty. Further, the plaintiff's lawyer might discuss the case with colleagues who have represented clients in similar cases. The lawyer might also visit public consumer protection agencies and/or private consumer protection associations to learn more about similar cases.

Thus, in Silvia's case, prior to drafting the complaint, her lawyer would interview Silvia thoroughly; examine her medical records; call Dr. Schmitt, Silvia's treating physician, both to discuss the case generally and also to enlist the doctor as a possible witness; and interview Norah and Marco, who other than Silvia are the primary witnesses to the event, as well as possible culprits since they were using the jar immediately before Silvia's injury. The lawyer also would refer the matter to a doctor with whom the lawyer has a working relationship to examine Silvia's medical records and perhaps Silvia herself. A responsible and determined plaintiff's lawyer also would search the records of federal and provincial consumer protection agencies for reports of prior similar incidents involving any of the parties that comprised part of the distribution chain of the Penelope Peanuts jar.

Of course, even with all of this extrajudicial preliminary work, the plaintiff's lawyer could still be ignorant of relevant facts. To protect the client and him/herself, the lawyer would sue all possible defendants (in this case, the entire distribution chain: Levington, Penelope, Charter, and Value Store) and list all possible items of evidence in the complaint, even the most trivial ones. Remember, the plaintiff's lawyer only has one bullet.

Coming back to judges, as mentioned, the dispositive principle—i.e., the principle of party control—has become more attenuated due to amendments to the NCCP. No attempt is made to exhaust all such attenuations here. The overall gist of them, at least on paper, is that Argentine judges now have the duty and broad powers to order all measures they deem necessary or appropriate to unearth the truth. Some of the more important specific manifestations of this transformation are found in article 36 of the NCCP. Titled "Instructive and Imperative Powers," article 36 provides that "even without the request of the parties," the judge may: (1) summon the parties at any time and request them to explain their claims or defenses in greater detail, and also propose conciliatory measures; (2) summon witnesses, experts or expert consultants at any time to interrogate them about the case; and (3) order the production of documents from parties or nonparties. As to witnesses, judges can depose any person that has been mentioned in the lawsuit even if the person has not been listed as a witness by the parties. *See* NCCP Art. 452.

Here, readers can see just one of innumerable examples showing why it is impossible to simply categorize legal traditions as civil law or common law systems and expect them to be the same. In Germany, the judge is limited to calling witnesses named by the parties. In Argentina, a judge can summon any person as a witness who has been simply mentioned in the course of the litigation, whether or not the person has been listed as a witness. This is a potentially significant procedural distinction.

But then, life does not always imitate codes of procedure. In practice, Argentine judges rarely exercise these strong truth-finding powers. Most cases do not justify such a radically active judicial approach, and even in cases that do, heavy caseloads and backlogged dockets deter judges from forging inquisitorial paths that may lead nowhere. On the other hand, in fairness, it must be noted that a small but growing number of dedicated judges do depart from the blind umpire role. Experience shows that when they do, the effort pays and justice is better served.

Fact Presentation

Once the written complaint and answer have been filed, preliminary motions, also in writing, sometimes follow. After they have been addressed by the court, which again will occur in writing only, the court summons the parties to a preliminary hearing. A judge presides over this hearing, invites the parties to reach a settlement, and, if settlement is not possible, rules on which evidence will be admissible during the evidentiary stage.

At this point, the case is ready to enter the evidentiary phase. Before addressing the specific types of evidence available under Argentine law, let us get an overall picture of how proof is received. Readers looking for profound distinctions among the three legal systems selected for study will find one here. In Argentina, the judge's participation in evidence-taking in a case such as Silvia's typically would be extremely minimal. Usually, a low-ranking court employee presides over evidence-taking proceedings. Such proceedings take the form of witness "depositions" where the witnesses travel to the courthouse to give their testimony. These are not discovery depositions as in the U.S., but the taking of the person's testimony as evidence. Different witnesses usually give their testimony on different days. As in other civil law countries, there is no single unified "trial" event.

The court employee will ask questions prepared by the parties. If the lawyers raise objections during the questioning, the clerk of court, who serves as a primary aide to the judge, is called into the room to rule on the dispute. Although judges ultimately sign off on orders ruling on any objections, they very rarely participate in the evidentiary hearings. They usually do not meet or even see the witnesses in the case. Thus, in Silvia's case, the judge who decides her case probably would never hear the testimony of Silvia or any other witness so as to be in a position to assess their credibility. Lest readers write this procedure off as some quirk of Argentine law, it should be noted that the traditional norm in civil law proceedings, the development of which were heavily influenced by medieval canon law, was for the clerk to take the evidence and summarize it for the judge for use in rendering a decision. MERRYMAN, at 113. The transition to oral testimony before the judge or judges who will decide the case is of relatively recent origin in most civil law countries.

When all the evidence has been produced the judge formally closes the evidentiary stage by means of a written order and invites the parties to file briefs with their closing arguments. After the briefs are filed the judge announces, also through a written order, that the case is ready for a decision on the merits. If no party opposes the declaration within five days, the term begins for the judge to take the case under consideration and render a decision.

With that overview, let us look more carefully at the types of evidence that may be received.

The NCCP articulates the different "means of evidence" that the parties may produce in a lawsuit, although the list is not exclusive. Means of evidence not directly governed by the rules can still be admissible and will be governed by the rules applicable to the closest parallel type of evidence. For instance, the NCCP has no provision governing email as evidence, but it is nevertheless admissible under the rules applicable to documents in general.

The specifically listed means of proof are: (1) documents; (2) written interrogatories; (3) party "confession"; (4) witness depositions; (5) neutral expert reports and opinions; and (6) judicial inspection of things and places.

Documents. In general, both parties and persons or entities alien to the litigation that possess documents "essential to the litigation" are legally obliged to file those documents with the court or indicate the archive in which those documents are kept. *See* NCCP Art. 387. In practice, however, this is not always done. Moreover, there is no discovery power to request documents unless the existence of a specific document is already known. This limitation is a substantial hindrance to gathering documentary evidence and means that many relevant documents are never produced in litigation. For example, continuing the hypothesis posed earlier, were Levington to have in its possession documents showing a high failure rate for the production batch from which Silvia's jar came, it is doubtful that anyone would ever learn of the existence of those documents. On the other hand, failure to produce a known, identified document leads to "a presumption that the document and its contents do indeed exist." NCCP Art. 388. The parties can also ask the court to order the production of specifically identified documents in the possession of a third party unrelated to the lawsuit, although the third party can resist disclosure on a showing that it would be harmful. NCCP Art. 389.

Written interrogatories. For the sake of clarity we have translated as "written interrogatory" what the NCCP names as "*prueba informativa.*" *Prueba informativa* is composed of reports that the parties request, through the court, from public agencies, *escribanos* (sort of a mix between a notary public and a lawyer), or private entities. The request must refer to specific, clearly identified facts that are relevant to the matter in controversy. The response from the addressee is limited to information contained in records (archives, registries or ledgers) of the individual or entity answering the request. NCCP Art. 396.

In short, *prueba informativa* is a request for specific data kept in the registries of a public agency or private legal entity. We translated the term to "written interrogatory" because this evidence-taking procedure usually takes the form of a questionnaire drafted by the requesting party and sent out through the court. For example, Silvia's lawyer might prepare such a questionnaire to be sent to the hospital where Silvia received her emergency treatment, requesting information about the treatment that is contained in the hospital's records. The parties have the right to challenge the truthfulness and accuracy of the answers to this questionnaire, in which case the court can request the responding agency or entity to produce the actual records on which its answers are based. NCCP Art. 403.

Party "confession." Argentine law provides for a procedure in civil cases known as "confession." This is the only opportunity for a party's statements to be heard. As in Germany, parties are precluded from testifying as witnesses given their interest in the outcome of the litigation. Thus, despite the fact that Silvia has the most in-depth knowledge of what happened to her and to the jar, her "story" would not be considered reliable or given much weight.

The law requires that judges hear confession evidence, but, as with other evidence, they routinely delegate the task to the clerk of court or even a lower-level employee. The procedure for confessional hearings is governed by a series of articles in the procedural code. *See* NCCP 409–414.

Each party has the right to ask the court to summon the adverse party to a hearing at which the deposed party will be required to answer questions regarding the matter in controversy. Nonparty witnesses are not subject to confessional hearings. Questions are submitted to the court by the requesting party. Each question must pertain to a single fact. The judge may *sua sponte* alter the order or form of the questions, but may not alter their substance. The person being interrogated must answer "true" or "not true" to the question, although the code permits follow-up explanations as necessary. *See* NCCP Art. 413. Failing to appear at a confessional hearing or refusing to answer questions will result in the facts being construed as admitted. NCCP Art. 417.

While the procedure sounds rather dramatic, in practice, confessional hearings, while common, are perfunctory and usually useless. The party required to answer the questions is not placed under oath. Customarily, the party will deny all important facts and simply offer his or her position regarding the matter in dispute. In part because of these deficiencies in the process, many have called for the abolition of confessional hearing.

A confessional hearing almost certainly would take place in Silvia's case. If Silvia were summoned for such a hearing, attorneys for the defendants would ask her to acknowledge or deny the facts that the defendants had set forth in their answers to the complaint. Likewise, Silvia's lawyer would request each of the defendants' representatives to acknowledge or deny the facts that Silvia described in her complaint. For instance, Silvia's lawyer would pose to the defendants' representatives questions such as the following: (1) Tell the court whether it is true that Silvia sustained injury as a result of a peanuts jar shattering; (2) Tell the court whether it is true that the peanuts jar shattered due to its defective condition; (3) Tell the court whether it is true that your company (manufactured, distributed, sold) said peanuts jar; and so on. The party deposed would answer "true" or "not true" to each question, after which the party would have the opportunity to add clarifying statements.

Witnesses. Each party is entitled to propose up to eight witnesses. If a party offers more than eight witnesses the judge has the discretion to summon more than eight, but only after hearing the first eight and upon a determination that exceeding the limit is "strictly necessary" for deciding the case. NCCP Art. 430. Judges rarely summon more than eight witnesses per party, and in Silvia's case, given the fairly simple nature of the facts, the eight-witness limitation should not present an obstacle. Witnesses give testimony under sworn oath to tell the truth and must be informed of the criminal penalty for perjury. NCCP Art. 440.

The NCCP provides for a "preliminary interrogation" of every witness in which a court official asks the witness for basic data such as name, age, marital status, and occupation, as well as information pertaining to whether the witness has any relationship to the parties or interest in the dispute.

Witness examination usually proceeds as follows. The lawyers prepare a questionnaire for the witness before the hearing and give it to the court employee presiding over the taking of the testimony. The court employee reads the questions to the witness and elicits answers. Although not routine, it is not unusual for the court employee to ask additional questions. After the questionnaire is completed, the lawyer offering the witness usually asks follow-up questions, after which the opposing party's lawyer is permitted to cross-examine the witness.

The NCCP contains several articles regulating the form and manner of questioning. *See* NCCP Arts. 442–50. Interesting provisions include an authorization for a witness to refuse to answer a question if the answer would expose him to criminal prosecution or "compromise his honor" (NCCP Art. 444(1)), and an article providing that one who interrupts a witness may be fined an amount not to exceed $14.67 (NCCP Art. 446), although neither of these provisions play much of a role in real life.

As noted above, a judge is not obliged to hear witness testimony in person, and usually delegates the questioning of witnesses to the clerk of court. *See* NCCP Art. 442 ("Witnesses shall be liberally questioned by the judge or whomever legally replaces him.") The clerk of court is a judicial officer whose job description is much broader than that of an American clerk of court, whose functions are primarily ministerial in nature (accepting filings, issuing summonses, maintaining records, etc.). A closer analogy would be to a judicial law clerk under the American system, but even that job description would be too narrow. In Argentina, the clerk of court functions more like an assistant judge. The clerk has a broad range of job functions, including questioning witnesses and summarizing their testimony for later review by the judge, drafting opinions, and performing administrative tasks such as overseeing the work of court personnel. A law degree is a prerequisite to hold the position of clerk of court.

Although the taking of witness testimony is a job usually assigned to clerks of court, these officers commonly delegate the task to subordinates. It is now awkwardly common to have low-ranking court employees, frequently law students, presiding over evidentiary hearings. They then draft a sort of transcript summarizing the witness's testimony. Only rarely do these summaries fairly and completely represent what the witness actually said.

Judges simply read these summaries when reviewing the record, then draft the decision on the merits. Sometimes, judicial participation is even more limited. In some cases, the clerk of court drafts the decision, in which case the judge never sees even the written summary of the witness testimony. The clerk's opinion will be based on the summary drafted by the law student and the judge will just receive a brief oral account from the clerk.

This procedure diminishes the importance of witness testimony far below its importance in the U.S. or even Germany. This helps explain why witness testimony carries so much less weight in Argentine practice and why judges rely so heavily on the conclusions of court-appointed experts, where available.

Neutral experts and technical consultants. The court can appoint one or more experts to render opinions on technical matters and the parties may retain expert "technical consultants" to assist them and the court's expert. Experts are separately addressed in chapter six.

Judicial inspection. The parties can request, or the court can decide *sua sponte*, that an inspection be conducted of premises or things. NCCP Art. 497(1). As these cumbersome measures usually entail scheduling a meeting among the judge and the parties outside the court building, judges are somewhat reluctant to grant such requests. Judicial inspections are rarely conducted.

Given the above, one can see that fact presentation in Argentina, as is true of other judicial procedures, is more "loose" than in the U.S. or Germany. Justice also takes somewhat longer in Argentina. Although no statistical information is available, with so many defendants involved, thirty-six to forty months would be a reasonable estimate for the time frame between the filing of the complaint and final judgment in the trial court, with an extra year added for the inevitable appeal.

Summary Chart — Fact Gathering and Presentation

	United States	Germany	Argentina
Core principles of civil litigation are adversarial in nature.	Yes	Yes	Yes
Parties have primary control over fact development.	Yes	Judges play dominant role, but parties set overall boundaries.	Judges have broad fact gathering powers, but in practice parties exercise substantial control.
Judges play a significant role in developing facts.	No	Yes	In theory, but not in practice.
Pretrial discovery is available.	Yes	No	No
Juries serve as fact-finders.	Yes, except in bench trials.	No juries. Judge is always the fact-finder.	No juries. Judge is always the fact-finder.

Fact presentation is governed by extensive rules of evidence.	Yes	No	No
Testimony is almost always received orally in open court.	Yes	Yes	No. Usually heard by court clerk or subordinate.
Lawyers conduct examination of witnesses.	Yes	No, except for follow-up questions.	No, except for follow-up questions.
Parties are permitted to testify as "witnesses."	Yes	Only in rare instances.	No
All witness testimony is recorded verbatim.	Yes	No. Mostly summarized.	No. Summarized only.
Court gives hints and feedback to parties as case progresses.	No	Yes	No
Judges have the power to summon witnesses in civil cases who have not been named as witnesses by the parties.	No	No	Judges have this power, but rarely exercise it.
Estimated time frame for Silvia's case from filing of complaint to final judgment in trial court.	20–24 months.	24 months.	36–40 months.

CHAPTER 6

EXPERTS

The topic of expert witnesses would have fit comfortably in the previous chapter, but is important enough, particularly in tort litigation, to warrant separate treatment. Expert witnesses are used pervasively in all three countries, but are handled very differently, in ways that can affect the outcome of litigation.

In Silvia's case, expert testimony could have been the single most critical item of evidence—*if* the broken jar fragments had been retained. Expert examination of broken glass containers can sometimes determine what caused the glass to break. Experts may be able to offer an opinion, for example, as to whether the break occurred because of a nick or bump to the outside of the container, which could be inflicted anywhere along the distribution chain, or from an original defect in the glass. *See* Spangenberg, at 523 (stating about exploding carbonated soft drink bottles that "[a] very great deal can be told from the fracture pattern, and if all the particles of glass can be recaptured, then almost the whole story can be told"). On the other hand, expert examination of a broken glass container is not necessarily a foolproof key to unlocking the defect puzzle. In *Welge v. Planters Lifesavers Co.*, the case on which Silvia's fact pattern is loosely based, the jar of peanuts was preserved and examined by experts for both sides, but they could not find the fracture that precipitated the shattering of the jar or figure out when the defect that caused the fracture came into being. 17 F.3d at 212.

Unfortunately, the shattering jar that injured Silvia was destroyed. Although Norah thought about saving the broken glass, Marco's observation that "glass breaks all the time" persuaded her that there was no point in preserving the remnants. This is an extremely common problem in products liability cases. When consumers get injured by a defective product, they often don't think to "save the pieces." When an accident occurs, injured persons are focused on getting medical treatment. They are not contemplating litigation or future proof problems. *See, e.g.*, Embs v. Pepsi-Cola Bottling Co., 528 S.W.2d 703, 705–06 (Ky. 1975) (exploding Seven-Up bottle swept up and disposed of by retailer; plaintiff allowed to recover); Bredberg v. Pepsico, Inc., 551 N.W.2d 321, 324 (Iowa 1996) (shattering bottle of Diet Mountain Dew "swept up and thrown away after the accident"; plaintiff prevailed on appeal).

But even without expert testimony regarding the condition of the particular jar that injured Silvia, experts would play a key role in Silvia's case in all three countries.

United States

Experts are a standard feature of U.S. civil litigation. Certainly, this is true of products liability litigation, which often requires technical engineering or other scientific testimony. A dated, but still oft-cited Rand study of 529 California civil trials in 1985–86 found that experts were used in 86% of all trials (with an average of 3.3 experts per trial), including 100% of products liability cases (average of 4.7 experts per trial).

Experts are just as common in civil law systems, but are appointed by the court rather than retained by the parties. Langbein observed that European jurists who visit the U.S. express amazement at the U.S. expert witness practice, an amazement he said "turns to something bordering disbelief when he discovers that we extend the sphere of partisan control to the selection and preparation of experts." Langbein, at 835. Although Federal Rule of Evidence 706 authorizes federal trial judges to appoint experts, they rarely exercise that authority. The parties choose and pay for their own experts, creating the perception that many experts are "hired guns." There is some truth in the perception. While lawyers attempt to create an aura of objectivity surrounding their experts, the reality is that expert witnesses are anything but impartial. As flamboyant personal injury lawyer Melvin Belli once said famously: "If I got myself an impartial [expert] witness, I'd think I was wasting my money."

This does not mean there are no independent experts who render objective opinions. Quite the contrary is true. It just means that lawyers are not going to retain or keep paying them once they learn those opinions do not support their clients' positions. Even highly qualified, fair-minded experts retained and paid by partisans experience pressure to "join the team—to shade one's views, to conceal doubt, to overstate nuance, to downplay weak aspects of the case that one has been hired to bolster." Langbein, at 835. As far back as 1884, a New York court commented that the opinions of hired experts "cannot fail generally to be warped by a desire to promote the cause in which they are enlisted." Ferguson v. Hubbell, 97 N.Y. 507, 514 (1884).

Experts are in abundant supply in the U.S., in part because serving as an expert witness can be lucrative. Legal newspapers and magazines are filled with advertisements by experts. Numerous corporate services exist. One large referral service, the TASA Group, boasts a global roster of experts in more than 10,000 categories. *See* http://www.tasanet.com/.

Expert testimony has long been a controversial issue in the U.S., with critics accusing experts of filling courtrooms with "junk science." *See generally* Peter Huber, Galileo's Revenge: Junk Science in the Courtroom (Basic Books 1993). In 1993, the landscape for expert testimony changed dramatically in the U.S. when the Supreme Court decided *Daubert v. Merrell Dow Pharmaceuticals, Inc.*, 509 U.S. 579 (1993), a products liability case involving the morning-sickness drug Bendectin, which allegedly caused birth defects in the children of some mothers who ingested it.

In *Daubert*, the Court mandated that federal trial judges police the admissibility of scientific expert testimony to ensure that the fact-finder hears only testimony that is grounded in valid scientific knowledge and method. The Court set forth four factors for trial judges to consider: whether the expert's theory or technique can be or has been tested; whether it has been subjected to peer review; the known or potential error rate in the expert's methodology; and whether it has attracted widespread acceptance within the relevant scientific community. The previous test—known as the "*Frye* test" after a 1923 case of the same name—judged the admissibility of expert testimony solely by whether it was "generally accepted" by other experts in the field. While *Daubert* applied only to scientific expert testimony, the Court extended the *Daubert* rules to all technical expert testimony in a later products liability case. *See* Kumho Tire Co. v. Carmichael, 526 U.S. 137 (1997). Rule 702 of the Federal Rules of Evidence, governing the admissibility of expert testimony, was amended in 2000 to incorporate the principles of *Daubert*. *See* Fed. R. Evid. 702 (2005) (authorizing an expert to offer opinion testimony if the testimony is based on sufficient facts or data, is the product of reliable principles and methods, and the expert has applied the principles and methods reliably to the facts of the case). A majority of states also have adopted the reasoning of *Daubert*, although some have rejected it.

Daubert's strictures place judges in an uncomfortable role. As U.S. Court of Appeals Judge Alex Kozinski commented when *Daubert* was remanded to his court, judges "are largely untrained in science and certainly no match for any of the witnesses whose testimony we are reviewing," yet it is a judge's job under *Daubert* to determine whether an expert's proposed testimony constitutes "good science." Daubert v. Merrell Dow Pharmaceuticals, Inc., 43 F.3d 1311, 1315 (9th Cir. 1995). One view of *Daubert* is that it was intended to make it easier to admit expert testimony by eliminating the requirement that the expert's methodology be generally accepted in the relevant scientific community in favor of a multifactor analysis. Empirical studies, however, have shown that, post-*Daubert*, more challenges have been made to the admissibility of expert testimony with the result that a greater proportion of expert testimony is being excluded as evidence by judges. *See* A. Leah Vickers, Daubert, *Critique and Interpretation: What Empirical Studies Tell Us About the Application of Daubert*, 40 U.S.F. L. Rev. 109, 126–36 (2005) (summarizing empirical studies supporting these conclusions).

Addressing experts in Silvia's U.S. case, Silvia would be likely to hire a materials expert to testify that a normal jar would not have shattered, despite the use of an Exacto knife to remove the label, in the absence of a preexisting defect. She also would call Dr. Schmitt, her treating physician, as both a fact witness and an expert witness. Her lawyer would want to avoid hiring a separate medical expert, if possible, as a way to keep costs down. Unlike in civil law countries, expert fees are not taxed against the loser in the U.S. Thus, even if Silvia were to prevail on the merits, she would have to bear the costs of her experts. Recall the observation from the veteran Florida personal injury lawyer that he would try to keep the out-of-pocket costs in a case like Silvia's below $50,000. The same lawyer estimated the cost of a materials expert for Silvia's case at roughly $10,000, so it is easy to see how quickly $50,000 can evaporate. Finally, Silvia might have to retain an expert in physical or vocational therapy to testify about her reduced job opportunities in the physical therapy field due to her injury.

In the U.S. system, experts can be like Newton's Third Law of Motion. For every expert called by one side, the other side seeks an expert of opposite and equal (or superior) force to rebut the testimony. The result is the much-denunciated "battle of the experts," in which the lay jury must sort out conflicting testimony on technical matters and decide which expert is more persuasive. The defendants in Silvia's case most likely would present combined fact and expert testimony from in-house experts regarding glass jar construction, quality control, and handling procedures in an attempt to rebut any inference that the jar was defective while it was within their respective spheres. *But see* Pulley v. Pacific Coca-Cola Bottling Co., 415 P.2d 636 (Wash. 1996) (holding that quality control evidence was not admissible where plaintiff claimed she found a cigarette butt in a soft drink bottle because the proffered testimony risked converting a strict liability case into a negligence case). They also would present medical testimony disputing Silvia's injuries, and possibly a vocational rehabilitation expert to testify about Silvia's job opportunities.

Germany

In civil law systems, including Germany, experts are appointed by the court and serve, at least in theory, as neutral and objective officers of the court. In Germany, court-appointed experts (*Sachverständige*) are routinely used, so often that one criticism of the German expert system is that overworked judges may be tempted to delegate too much fact-finding and analysis to the expert, in effect, allowing the expert to decide the case. *See* Murray & Stürner, at 290 (making this point); *id.* at 280–90 (detailed discussion of German expert procedure).

The German Code of Civil Procedure (GCCP) contains several sections addressing expert witnesses, including sections pertaining to the selection of experts, challenges to experts, and payment of experts. *See generally* GCCP §§402–14. Experts may be appointed at the request of a party or at the judge's own insistence. In selecting an expert, the judge will often base the decision on having had a positive experience with the expert in a prior case. Courts also select experts from lists prepared by governmental licensing authorities in particular professions.

From a U.S. perspective, experts in Germany more closely resemble court-appointed special masters than regular witnesses. They are appointed to serve as aides to the court in an order that will designate the specific factual or legal issues that the expert is to address. Judges can and often do communicate with appointed experts ex parte, although these communications are regularly disclosed to the parties at oral hearings.

No *Daubert*-type rules exist regulating what expert evidence the judge is permitted to consider, but since *Daubert* and its progeny were designed primarily to prevent juries from hearing unreliable expert evidence, there is less need for such rules in a civil law system where juries do not exist. While *Daubert* applies to U.S. bench trials as well as jury trials, the procedures for determining reliability are more flexible in the former. A judge in a U.S. bench trial can hear expert testimony without a prescreening hearing, but can rely on the testimony only if it is ultimately determined to be scientifically valid and reliable under *Daubert*'s principles. While Germany lacks specific rules and procedures on the issue, German judges similarly are expected to rely on expert evidence only if it is deemed to be reliable.

As in the U.S., it is possible for a witness to be both a fact witness and an expert witness, as in the case of Dr. Schmitt, Silvia's treating physician. GCCP §414 (providing that when testifying as to facts, an expert witness is subject to "the provisions concerning evidence by witnesses").

Although the expert is appointed by the court, the parties remain actively involved in the process. Before appointing an expert, the court asks the parties whether they have objections or comments regarding the proposed expert. At this stage parties are entitled to request the expert's recusal. Not infrequently, lawyers seek to recuse an expert because of a bad experience with the expert in other litigation, such as where intensive quarreling occurred at the hearing or where the lawyer was dissatisfied with the expert's opinion.

The parties often propose experts to the court who they regard as qualified to evaluate the case facts. Sometimes, judges ask the parties to recommend experts, which they are allowed to do under the procedure code. GCCP § 404(3). If the parties can agree on an expert, the court is *required* to appoint that expert. GCCP § 404(4). This practice is quite common, especially in highly technical cases in which only a limited number of well-known experts are available. Similarly, it is common for the parties and the court to agree on an expert that was proposed by only one party where the expert is a well-regarded specialist in the field at issue. This happens frequently in personal injury cases with regard to professors of medicine at university hospitals. Agreement by the parties serves not only the interests of the parties, but of the court, because searching for an appropriate expert can be time consuming.

Usually, the expert will be expected to file a written report with the court, copies of which are forwarded by the court to the parties. The parties then are asked by the judge to lodge objections, submit follow-up questions for the expert, or ask the expert to clarify certain points. Based on the parties' comments the court may ask the expert to furnish additional information in writing or may schedule an oral hearing at which the parties and their counsel may appear. These hearings proceed like other evidentiary hearings, with the judge first asking questions before allowing the lawyers to follow up with their own questions. Often, the parties supplement the court-appointed expert's report with reports prepared by their own experts. The opinion of the court-appointed expert, however, typically is given great weight and it is unusual for a court to depart from it.

Experts are paid by the party who bears the burden of proof on the issue for which the expert has been appointed, although expert fees, like other costs, ultimately will be levied against the losing party under the loser pays rule for attorneys' fees and costs (see chapter ten). Expert remuneration is governed by the Judiciary Remuneration and Reimbursement Act (*Justizvergütungs-und-entschädigungsgesetz*), which sets forth hourly rates for different types of experts. The hourly rate for a medical expert, for example, generally varies between 50–70 euros ($60–84), with a maximum of 85 euros ($102). There is no separate category for experts on the issue of glass container breakage, but compensation for such an expert probably would range from 60–80 euros ($72–96) per hour. These amounts are relatively low compared to the fees charged by experts in the U.S., which frequently run hundreds of dollars per hour.

In Silvia's case, she would be likely to request the court to appoint experts to present reports as to: (1) the defectiveness of the jar; and (2) her physical injuries, including the degree of her disability and an evaluation of how it would affect her present and future ability to work. Prior to filing the lawsuit, however, Silvia would be well advised to obtain reports from her own consulting experts on both of these issues to include as part of her complaint. Silvia is an unemployed college student with no financial resources. As discussed in chapter ten, contingency fee arrangements with lawyers are prohibited in Germany. Thus, to bring her lawsuit, Silvia most likely would apply to the court for legal aid. However, to obtain government-paid legal aid, she would first have to convince the court that she has a reasonably good chance of succeeding on the merits. To obtain a favorable legal-aid ruling in her case, she would have to set forth a plausible case in her complaint that the jar was defective and also document her injuries.

Thus, Silvia would be advised by her lawyer to enlist a competent technical expert to prepare a report regarding the probable defectiveness of the jar. Usually, this would entail examining the shards of glass, but since that won't be possible, she would seek an expert able to report that a preexisting defect is the most likely reason for a jar to shatter like the Penelope Peanuts jar did. The expert also would conduct research regarding whether similar jar defects have been reported in public sources or by consumer support and advice organizations, which are widespread in Germany. As for the medical report, Silvia could rely on a report prepared by her treating physician, Dr. Schmitt, which would be much less expensive than having to hire an external expert.

Retaining these experts prior to filing the case would not be required as a matter of law, but a competent German trial lawyer definitely would recommend them. German lawyers are quite cautious as they can be held liable for professional negligence if they do not follow the "securest-way principle," a principle developed by the Federal Supreme Court that essentially means the lawyer must choose or recommend the most secure means of achieving the client's goal. Normally, the costs of pre-filing experts are not covered by legal aid, but an exception exists if the plaintiff can show that obtaining an expert or experts prior to filing the case was necessary for the plaintiff to assert her rights. In Silvia's case, there is a fair chance that given the technical nature of the defect issue and her medical condition, the court would conclude that it was necessary for her to retain a technical expert and a report from Dr. Schmitt prior to filing the lawsuit.

As discussed above, for the plenary or "trial" phase of the case, the court would appoint its own independent experts on the issues of defect and Silvia's medical injuries. As proof of defectiveness is one of the essential components of Silvia's claim, the technical expert would be authorized first and, depending on his findings and evaluation, medical experts then would be appointed to clarify Silvia's injuries. Regarding the medical examination and prognosis, it would not be unusual for the court to appoint several experts in a single order to take evidence, in succession, on the factual issues for which each expert has been nominated. Thus, it is likely that a medical practitioner would be appointed to examine Silvia and to document and assess her injuries. Afterwards, the court file would be forwarded to the second expert to prepare a report on Silvia's prognosis, ability to work, and degree of disability. The file might then be forwarded to a third expert, such as a rehabilitation expert. It is usual that the court would appoint one of these experts, perhaps the last one, to act as the so-called "main expert" (*Hauptgutachter*). The main expert would examine Silvia as to the specific factual issues for which he or she was nominated, and then assess the previous expert reports for the purpose of offering a complete medical overview of Silvia's situation.

Argentina

In Argentina, experts are handled in a manner very close to that described for Germany. Expert evidence (*prueba pericial*) gets its own chapter of the National Code of Civil Procedure (NCCP), with twenty-two articles devoted to the subject. *See* NCCP Arts. 457–78. These articles address virtually all aspects of expert evidence, including the appointment, competence, payment, and recusal of experts.

Parties are entitled to request the appointment of neutral experts in cases requiring special knowledge in some field of "science, art, industry or other specialized or technical activity." NCCP Art. 457. Experts are always appointed by the court, but the parties are authorized to retain their own expert "technical consultants." NCCP Art. 458. Each court of appeals administers lists of experts who have expressed interest in working with the courts. These lists are renewed annually. They include experts in all the professions recognized in major universities and by the Ministry of Education. Examples include specialists in medicine, engineering, and architecture.

The only formal requirement to testify as an expert is that the person holds a university degree. Persons not holding a degree are rarely accepted as experts, although the procedure code provides that in a situation where no expert with a "valid title" is available, the court may appoint any person with knowledge of the subject area. NCCP Art. 464. Substantial experience in the particular specialty or other credentials are not required. Local rules provide for the appointment by lottery among the professionals included on a given list, although judges sometimes disregard this lottery method and directly appoint experts with whom they have had a good experience in past cases.

Each party has the right to hire its own consulting expert (*consultor técnico*), whose main job is to "supervise" the work of the court-appointed expert and translate the expert's technical reports and opinions for the parties and their lawyers. The consulting experts for both parties usually meet with the court-appointed expert, often informally, for the purpose of suggesting studies for consideration or to discuss the expert's conclusions. *See* NCCP Art. 471 (providing that the parties' technical consultants may attend "technical proceedings" conducted by the expert).

The court-appointed expert should file a written report with the court (NCCP Art. 472). This report should address the specific questions (*puntos de pericia*) that each party posed at the time of requesting the appointment of the expert. The parties' consulting experts can file their own reports. They also can request clarification or directly challenge the court-appointed expert's report. In reality, however, judges almost never depart from the conclusions of the court-appointed expert. Thus, a neutral expert's report often constitutes the principal basis for the judge's decision on the merits. As in Germany, there are no *Daubert*-type rules regulating which expert opinions the court is permitted to consider. As with other evidentiary matters in civil law countries, questions regarding the validity of expert opinions go to the weight to be given the opinions, not to their admissibility. *See* NCCP Art. 77 (stating that "[t]he evidentiary value of the expert opinion shall be estimated by the judge").

Apart from a small sum that the party requesting appointment of an expert should deposit to cover an expert's expenses, no payment of an expert is required until a final decision has been entered. The loser pays rule (see chapter ten) applies with some exceptions. In general, the losing party should pay the court-appointed expert's fees, which often amount to 3–5% of the award. However, when the losing party is insolvent, court-appointed experts can collect up to 50% of their fees from the prevailing party. In all cases, experts' fees are calculated by the court at the time of entering the decision on the merits or enforcing the final award. Statutes set the fees for a few professions such as architects and engineers. For others, courts look to case precedent in calculating expert fees.

Now that the "cold" system for experts in Argentina has been explained, it is time to point out that the way expert evidence works in reality can sometimes lead to poorly administered justice. Highly reputed professionals rarely apply to be listed as court experts. Usually, those who apply are unemployed or poorly paid professionals, people who have never practiced in their professions or people whose only employment is serving as a court-appointed expert. Thus, an individual with a medical degree can be appointed as a neutral expert even if he or she has never practiced medicine or, more commonly, has never been exposed to the particular practice area involved in the case. Some good professionals are also listed, but they represent only a small portion of the total number of experts on the lists. Local judicial rules often limit the availability of these good experts by restricting the appointment of any given expert on a list to two cases per court per year. The result is that weak professionals too often end up being appointed in complex cases involving matters that are far beyond their expertise and experience.

This shortcoming is particularly visible in products liability cases, which often depend on technical medical or scientific evidence such as that relating to the "state of the art." Although the consulting experts retained by the parties can try to counter-balance the court-appointed expert's inexperience with their own reports, once a wrong conclusion has found its way in to the neutral expert's report, it is very difficult to convince a judge to disregard it. It also is worth noting that defendants often are the only parties who can afford to hire qualified consulting experts.

Because she has a decent case on the merits, "Argentine Silvia" would likely seek appointment of as many experts as possible. One reason for this is purely strategic. Silvia would not have to put up much money in requesting the experts, yet each expert would cost the losing party an amount equal to 3–5% of the award. Thus, appointing many experts can raise the cost of the lawsuit significantly. It is not uncommon to see cases in which four or five neutral experts have opined, thus, increasing litigation costs by 15–25% of the award.

Facing this possibility, defendants confronted with reasonably good claims often are pressured into settling on or before the preliminary hearing. After the preliminary hearing the evidentiary stage would be opened, the experts would be appointed, and the taxed-costs clock would begin ticking. Of course, the court is supposed to appoint only those experts that are really needed, but there is a real risk of having a case heard by a judge who is not paying active attention to such matters or a judge who prefers to appoint all requested experts in order not to diminish the plaintiff's right to due process. Judges in the latter category sometimes adhere to a questionable, but commonly applied principle known as the "ample evidence" doctrine, which is essentially a position that more evidence is better than less evidence.

Even assuming that Silvia and her lawyers would not get the benefit of the ample evidence doctrine, the court would likely appoint: (1) an industrial engineer to explain, even in absence of the broken pieces, whether the jar could have shattered as Silvia alleges; (2) a physician to examine Silvia and determine the origin, nature, and extent of her injuries and incapacity; and (3) a psychiatrist to opine on whether Silvia suffered any psychological damage.

Criticisms of the Different Approaches to Expert Witnesses

Which model of expert selection is preferable? Several commentators have argued for a system of court-appointed experts in the U.S. and, in fact, early in the U.S. common law, experts were appointed by the court, as they still are in England. Significant thoughtful analysis has been made of the current system. Here we just quote a list of some of the frequent criticisms:

> Critics of expert witness testimony [in the U.S.] attack many aspects of the system: the supposed objectivity of science; the unquestioned legitimacy of scientific data; gender differences in the use of expert witnesses; the "battle of the experts"; and instances where expert witnesses are ceded excessive power and leeway in the courtroom. Other legal writers fear that juries rely on experts to do their thinking for them; question whether judges are equipped to fulfill their gate-keeping obligation to determine the quality of the scientific reasoning used by the expert; are dismayed that experts' ethos and testifying skill are more influential than the quality of their technical expertise; and decry that junk science often finds its way into the courtroom. Other scholars focus on the recognition that paying experts creates a moral hazard. Finally, critical scholars fear that courts sanction expert testimony by treating experts with an aura of infallibility and telling jurors that experts merely report their objective findings and opinions.

M. Neil Browne et al., *The Perspectival Nature of Expert Testimony in the United States, England, Korea, and France*, 18 Conn. J. Int'l L. 55, 68–70 (2002) (citing other sources). To these objections, inefficiency and extravagant expense can be added.

Other legal scholars, however, have questioned whether any expert, even a court-appointed expert, can be truly neutral and objective. Here are some commonly raised criticisms:

> First and foremost, critics will question whether any neutral, inde-
> pendent, or objective expert actually exists, as "every expert comes to
> the court with an axe to grind." Individual experts' education, cul-
> ture, and the agenda of research funding sources could possibly in-
> fluence ... [court-appointed] experts, even further limiting their
> "neutrality." Finally some will argue that these court-appointed ex-
> perts undermine the adversarial process. Decision-makers may give
> undue deference to disinterested conclusions made by "objective" ex-
> perts, thereby ignoring their duty to sort out the evidence and wit-
> nesses as presented and contested by the opposing parties.

Justin P. Murphy, *Expert Witnesses at Trial: Where are the Ethics?*, 14 Geo. J. Legal Ethics 217, 238 (2000) (citing other sources).

With regard to the criticism that experts carry undue influence in U.S. liti-gation, note from the country summaries that the influence of experts appears to be greater in Germany and Argentina, where courts usually adopt the con-clusions of the court-appointed expert. In the U.S., while some experts no doubt hold great sway with jurors, it's a misconception to think that all juries are held spellbound by expert opinions. One reason is that U.S. lawyers have consider-able latitude in cross-examining experts regarding matters such as how much they are being paid, how many times they have testified as an expert, whether they testify primarily for plaintiffs or defendants, etc. Such cross-examination is effective at raising questions about the partiality of expert witnesses.

A few years ago, McClurg was surprised when he was picked to serve on a federal jury in an automobile accident case, counter to the conventional wisdom that the last person a lawyer wants on a jury is another lawyer (and certainly not a law professor!). The defendant had conceded liability. The only issue was the extent of the plaintiff's back injury. Her case turned in part on the credibility of a well-credentialed and highly paid expert witness who flew in on a private plane the morning of trial to testify, facts that came out in cross-examination. The expert testified articulately and, McClurg thought, persuasively that the plaintiff had suffered a serious back injury. Upon retiring to the jury room to deliberate, one of the first comments ut-tered by a fellow juror was that the plaintiff's "fancy" expert in the private plane was simply a hired gun who was not to be believed. The other jurors muttered their concurrence and disdain for the expert. His testimony did not come up again during the deliberations.

Summary Chart—Expert Witnesses

	United States	Germany	Argentina
Experts are widely used in tort litigation.	Yes	Yes	Yes
Expert witnesses are retained by the parties.	Yes	No. Court appoints experts.	No. Court appoints experts.
Parties may hire consulting experts.	Yes	Yes	Yes
Expert testimony is subject to reliability prescreening (i.e., *Daubert*) prior to being accepted as evidence.	Yes	No	No
Expert fees are generally taxed against the losing party.	No	Yes	Yes
Expert remuneration is set by statute.	No	Yes	Only for some professions (e.g., architects and engineers).
Courts usually follow court-appointed expert's opinion.	Not applicable.	Yes	Yes

CHAPTER 7

GENERAL BURDENS OF PROOF (AND A WORD ABOUT CAUSATION)

Although broken bottle and jar cases involve simple fact patterns, they present difficult proof issues. A glass food container travels down a long and winding distribution chain in which it passes through the hands, machinery, and vehicles of many persons and entities, presenting several opportunities for a defect to be created. Glass containers can break due to an original defect or damage inflicted on the container after manufacture. Silvia's case, reduced to its essence, is a "whodunit?" A glass jar shouldn't shatter in a consumer's hands while she's simply placing the lid on it. But who and what put the jar in the condition allowing that to happen? Possible defect-inducing suspects in Silvia's case include Levington (the jar maker), Penelope (which cleaned, labeled, filled, and topped the jars), Charter (the food distributor), Value-Store (the retailer), Silvia, and even Norah or Marco. Making matters more complicated is the fact that the key piece of evidence—the jar—has been destroyed.

In the final analysis, the most important question in Silvia's case may not be the factual one of whodunit?, which might never be known, but the legal question of who would bear the burden of proving whodunit? The inability of either side to persuasively establish when and where the defect in the jar arose could render the burden of proof an outcome determinative issue.

How legal systems respond to the often insurmountable proof obstacles in broken glass container cases, whether they fashion rules that benefit plaintiffs or defendants, itself says something about those systems. Most plaintiffs in cases such as Silvia's would lose if held to their traditional burdens of proof. As we'll see in chapter eight, judges in all three countries have responded to this proof obstacle by fashioning crucial burden-shifting procedural mechanisms favorable to plaintiffs like Silvia. This chapter lays a framework within which to process those mechanisms by addressing the general burdens and standards of proof applicable to tort litigation in the three nations. But first, we take a timeout for this important:

Word about Causation

All tort systems require that there be a causal connection between the defendant's conduct and the plaintiff's injury as a predicate to holding the defendant liable to pay compensation. *See* Jaap Spier & Olav A. Haazen, *Comparative Conclusions on Causation, in* Unification of Tort Law: Causation 127 (J. Spier ed., 2000) (stating in a text analyzing causation requirements in ten nations that "[a]ll jurisdictions recognize causation as a requirement of tortious liability"). Causation has consumed perhaps more than its fair share of judicial and academic attention in the legal systems of all three of our subject countries. Markesinis and Unberath quote a joke among French lawyers who, paraphrasing Voltaire's comment on the existence of God, tease their German colleagues "by saying that if causation did not exist as a subject, it would have to be invented so that German lawyers would have something to exercise their minds." Markesinis & Unberath, at 103. Certainly, the same preoccupation with the subject can be found in judicial decisions and scholarly commentary in the U.S. and Argentina.

Around the world, including in the U.S., Germany, and Argentina, proving causation is a two-step process that requires the plaintiff to show that the defendant was a "factual cause" of the injury, as well as a "legal cause," usually called "proximate cause" in the U.S. Factual cause encompasses the *sine qua non* ("without which not") or "but for" principle. The plaintiff must show that but for the defendant's wrongful conduct (or in the case of strict products liability, but for a defect in the defendant's product) the plaintiff's injury would not have occurred. Legal cause, once one cuts through the mostly illusory "rules" and confusing verbiage, is simply a tool courts use to determine a fair stopping point for liability in cases involving unusual chains of events or when policy considerations influence a court to deny or approve liability in a particular class of cases.

Studying texts on German and Argentine law, one is struck by the similarities in discussions of causation to U.S. law. The same issues that make the study of causation the bane of every first-year Torts student's existence in the U.S. apparently bedevil students of the law everywhere. An Argentine text poses the age-old question of how far to extend the inquiry into the relationship of cause and effect (i.e., factual causation) in colorful fashion, suggesting that, taken to its extreme, "everyone is guilty of everything" and "that it would follow to punish not only the man and woman that commit adultery, but also the carpenter who made their bed." Tallone, at 66.

And look at this statement about legal cause that sounds like it could have come straight out of a U.S. torts treatise, but which, in fact, describes German law: "Causation is lacking if an act results in a very unexpected, unforeseeable consequence that nobody had to reckon with." Ulrich Magnus, *Causation in German Tort Law, in* UNIFICATION OF TORT LAW: CAUSATION, at 65. Every U.S. law student and lawyer remembers the bizarre sequence of events in *Palsgraf v. Long Island R.R. Co.*, 162 N.E. 99 (N.Y. Ct. App. 1928), but apparently every legal system has its "Mrs. Palsgraf." Consider a well-known German case where a tortfeasor negligently caused the plaintiff's husband to lose his leg in 1937 in an automobile accident. Eight years later, he was killed in World War II during an artillery barrage. The plaintiff filed suit against the original tortfeasor, alleging that the decedent was killed because he could not run from the artillery fire quickly enough due to the lost leg. The court rejected liability based on a lack of "adequate cause" (the term used in Germany for legal or proximate cause), which the court candidly characterized as simply "a way of limiting liability" in situations involving improbable circumstances. BGH, NJW 1952, 1010. These parallels impart an important comparative insight. Many of the legal rules people tend to think of as unique to one system or another are, in fact, simply naturalistic reflections of fundamental, universal non-legal phenomena. Ubiquitous notions of fairness and common sense more than country-specific legal rules dictate that any tribunal, wherever found, would consider the degree to which an actor's conduct contributed to an injury to be an important factor in imposing liability.

In Silvia's case, depending on how the issue is framed, causation is either one of the simplest issues or the single most difficult issue with which Silvia would have to contend. If framed in terms of whether a defect in the jar caused Silvia's injuries, the answer is clearly yes. The jar shattered during normal use as Silvia was attempting to put the top on it. That the broken glass caused her injuries is a given in our case facts. Factual causation is clear and there is no issue of legal or proximate cause in the sense of questions of liability for remote or unforeseeable consequences. Silvia's injuries were a direct, immediate consequence of the breaking glass. Compare the case facts to a different set of hypothesized facts where legal cause would be an issue: a splinter of glass flies out and hits Silvia's pet cat, prompting the cat to run out the front door and trip the mail carrier walking on the sidewalk.

However, if causation is analyzed in terms of *attribution*—that is, in terms of *who* caused the defect in the jar that resulted in its breaking—causation becomes the great riddle on which the entire case hinges because, as discussed above, many actors could have "caused" the defect. In all three countries, the attribution issue in cases such as Silvia's is not usually the subject to an independent causation analysis. Although attribution clearly is an issue of factual causation, analysis of the issue in cases like Silvia's usually is subsumed within the broader issues of proof, burdens of proof, and the cognitive process of drawing factual inferences, including causal inferences, from other facts. Thus, for example, in U.S. casebooks and torts treatises, the doctrine of res ipsa loquitur, highly relevant to Silvia's case, is analyzed separately from causation, even though attribution of an inferred negligent act to a particular defendant is a critical component of the doctrine.

The happy result is that readers will be spared extensive discussion of causation as an independent, free-standing element. The issue of attribution of the defect in the jar is analyzed as part of the larger issues of proof and burdens of proof.

General Burdens and Standards of Proof in Tort Litigation

United States

The burden of proof applicable to nearly all issues of both liability and damages in U.S. tort litigation is straightforward. U.S. civil plaintiffs bear the burden of proving the facts necessary to support each element of their claims by a preponderance of the evidence. Civil defendants bear an identical burden of proof with respect to any affirmative defenses they raise. Preponderance of the evidence means the greater weight of the evidence. Using a scale metaphor, it is evidence that tips the balance of the scale in favor of the plaintiff, even if just slightly, such as 51% to 49%. A fact is established by a preponderance of the evidence if the fact-finder believes the existence of the fact is more likely than not.

A U.S. tort plaintiff such as Silvia must satisfy two different evidentiary burdens to prevail. First, the plaintiff must meet the "burden of going forward with the evidence" in order to get her case past a motion for directed verdict and to the jury. To meet this burden, the plaintiff must produce sufficient evidence to persuade the trial judge that reasonable jurors, viewing the evidence in the light most favorable to the plaintiff, could (not necessarily would) find that she has proved each element of her case by a preponderance, or more likely than not, standard. If the judge finds the plaintiff has failed to meet this burden, the judge will grant a directed verdict to the defendant and the case will be over. If the judge finds the plaintiff has satisfied the burden of going forward with the evidence, the case will go to the jury, where plaintiff must meet her second burden: the ultimate "burden of persuasion." The plaintiff must persuade the jury that under all the evidence, the facts necessary to support her claims have been established by a preponderance of the evidence.

As suggested above, if Silvia were held tightly to the preponderance of the evidence standard as to each element of her claims, she would face a steep upward climb on the liability front. Unless she were to stumble on a "smoking gun" document during discovery, such as an internal memorandum showing unusually high rates of breakage in the batch of peanuts jars from which hers came, she really has no way to prove the existence of a specific defect or its origins. However, as elaborated in the discussion of Silvia's substantive theories of recovery (chapter eight), she might receive the benefit of the negligence doctrine of res ipsa loquitur and a similar inference-drawing advantage with regard to her strict liability claims in both tort and contract that would have the practical effect of shifting the burden of going forward with the evidence to the defendants.

Germany

As in the U.S., tort plaintiffs bear the burden of proof as to the elements of their claims, although major exceptions to this principle may apply to a case like Silvia's. Germany has specific code provisions addressing the measure and intensity of evidence needed to satisfy the burden of proof. Unlike the U.S. and Argentina, the burdens differ depending on whether the issue is liability or damages. The leading principle for proving liability is embodied in section 286 of the German Code of Civil Procedure (GCCP). The "free conviction" principle, as it is known, grants trial judges a high range of discretion to determine whether an assertion or claim can be regarded as true or not true. The principle emanates from the fact that there are no juries in Germany, with the result that the trial judge is not only the law determiner but the fact-finder. Section 286(1) provides:

> The court shall render its decision by freely evaluating the entire substance of the proceedings and the results of any evidence that was taken to decide whether a factual allegation is to be considered as true or not true. The judgment shall contain the reasons that were instrumental for the court's final conclusion.

While this provision gives the judge broad discretion in determining facts, it does not leave the matter to whim or caprice. By requiring judges to set forth reasons in writing as to why they regard an assertion as true or not, section 286(1) ensures that a judge's "free conviction" can be checked by the court of appeal.

Furthermore, the Federal Supreme Court ruled in a famous case that section 286 requires that an assertion be regarded as true in "doubtful situations of fact" when the judge is "satisfied with a degree of certainty applying practical considerations which puts doubts aside without totally excluding them." BGHZ 53 (245). This case is widely known as "the *Anastasia* case" based on the plaintiff's claim that she was the Grand Duchess Anastasia Romanov, surviving daughter of the last Russian Tsar, which conflicted with historical accounts that the Tsar's family was murdered by revolutionaries in July 1918. It is not possible to define this burden of proof by a scale metaphor as has been discussed with regard to the U.S. preponderance of the evidence standard. In general terms, however, it is a very high and strict standard of proof. While section 286 does not require absolute certainty by the judge to find a fact established, it clearly requires much more than just a 51% probability. Remember, however, that this provision applies only to the liability aspects of the lawsuit.

If the defendant's liability has been established in accordance with the proof standard of section 286, another evidentiary provision of the GCCP, section 287, comes into play. Section 287 is the crucial provision for assessing the damages a plaintiff has suffered and for which she will be compensated. Section 287 also grants a judge "free discretion" in assessing damages, taking into account all the circumstances, but it has been construed by courts to impose a more lax burden of proof with respect to damages than is required to establish liability, one that approximates the U.S. preponderance standard. Although section 287 does not expressly set forth a "more likely than not" preponderance standard, case law has construed it to stand for the "conviction of preponderant probability." *See* BGH, NJW 1992, 3298 (holding that lower "more likely than not" proof standard applies under section 286 in showing causality relating to damages than applies under section 287 to show causality relating to liability).

Silvia is fortunate in at least one respect. The nature of her case could invoke some important judge-made doctrines of German law, analyzed in chapter eight, that can shift the burden of proof, both formally and informally, to the defendants on the critical issues in her case.

Argentina

As in the U.S. and Germany, traditionally, parties to a lawsuit in Argentina bore the burden of proving their respective allegations regarding both liability and damages. Article 377 of the National Code of Civil Procedure (NCCP) specifically requires each party to "prove the element or elements for his own claim." The last decade, however, has witnessed a relaxation of this burden via what is known as the doctrine of the dynamic burden of proof (*carga probatoria dinámica*), which originated as scholarly doctrine and then made its way into judicial decisions. The doctrine of the dynamic burden of proof essentially holds that the burden of proof rests on the party who is best situated to prove a given fact, regardless of whether the party would normally bear the burden of proof under article 377.

Originally developed in medical malpractice cases, the doctrine can apply to any type of tort case. It originated as a device to avoid unfair decisions in cases where defendants failed to cooperate in good faith during the fact-finding phase. Argentine judges have become increasingly intolerant of defendants who simply deny liability without advancing their own version of the facts and providing relevant, available evidence. For example, in a recent case against an automaker, the court invoked the doctrine against the defendant because it failed to cooperate in technical studies that could have helped determine the cause of the car's malfunctioning.

Arguably, in many products liability cases involving manufacturing defects, it is easier and fairer to require a manufacturer to prove how a given product was crafted than to require an injured consumer to supply evidence of a particular product defect. Although article 377 remains good law and is generally applied, in products liability cases such as Silvia's the defendant may be expected to advance and prove a sound version of the facts in dispute. The operative word is "may." There is no way for the parties to know in advance whether the doctrine will be invoked. Its application becomes known at the time of entering the decision on the merits, never before. When entering a judgment, the judge considers in light of the overall circumstances which party should have proved what and which party failed to do so.

As to the amount of evidence required to support a favorable decision on the merits, the goal of the parties' evidentiary activity is to convince the judge of the truth of their respective versions of the facts. Although judges enjoy ample discretion to investigate facts on their own in civil law systems, in Argentina they seldom do so in reality. Judges are not generally obliged to unearth the truth. They usually decide the case on the facts that the parties have proved in the course of the lawsuit. In this way, Argentina's civil law system functions not so differently from the U.S. litigation system.

On the other hand, judges are not permitted to turn a blind eye if clues in the record raise legitimate questions regarding the accuracy of the factual version presented in the suit. Per the landmark Federal Supreme Court case *Colalillo v. Compañía de Seguros España y Río de la Plata*, and its progeny, the goal of a court is to determine real truth, not merely formal truth in accordance with rules of procedure and evidence. Corte Suprema de Justicia [CSJN], 9/18/1957, "Domingo Colalillo v. Compañía de Seguros España y Río de la Plata," Fallos (1957-238-550). "[C]ivil procedure must not be conducted in strictly formalistic terms," the Court said, adding that the guiding principle of procedural law is the establishment of objective truth.

Procedural rules, including the rules of evidence, are construed to be a part of due process and cannot be used as a means to justify unfair decisions that would be tantamount to a conscious disregard for the truth. To use an extreme example, suppose that after the evidentiary stage in Silvia's case was formally closed, the defendants happened upon a diary entry showing Silvia tried to use the glass from the jar to commit suicide by slitting her wrist. The judge would be required to find for the defendants even if the duly admitted evidence supported a judgment for Silvia.

It has already been noted that the absence of juries in civil law countries results in a much less rigid approach to rules of evidence. *Colalillo* goes a step further in saying that when confronted with the possibility of reaching a clearly unjust decision, a judge has the authority to disregard formal evidentiary and other procedural rules. While justice no doubt carries the day over technical legal rules, at least *sub silentio*, in many individual cases in all legal systems, Argentine law may be unique in giving official imprimatur to judges to not follow certain procedural rules when their application would result in clear injustice. A rough U.S. equivalent of *Colalillo* would be for the U.S. Supreme Court to tell lower court judges they should not follow the Federal Rules of Evidence or Federal Rules of Civil Procedure in situations where the rules would allow entry of a judgment that was contrary to objective truth.

An irony of *Colalillo* is that a foundational axiom of the civil law tradition is that judges are to have no power to even interpret code or other statutory rules, much less to ignore them. Note also that *Colalillo* is another good example of case law imprinting an important legal principle in a civil law system, even though case law technically has no precedential power. Finally, so that a misleading impression is not left, be aware that the *Colalillo* principle, as grand as it sounds, often conflicts with real life. As discussed in chapter five, given the absence of discovery and limited fact investigation carried out by judges, objective truth often is not ascertained.

In reaching conclusions after hearing all the evidence, judges must apply the so-called *sana crítica* standard, analyzing, weighing and criticizing all the relevant pieces of evidence. This analysis and evidentiary weighing must be reduced to writing. A judgment that is not the result of a logical process reasonably explained in the opinion can be deemed arbitrary and violative of due process. Arbitrary decisions are cause for reversal by appellate courts.

In conclusion, in general principle Argentine tort plaintiffs are required to prove each element of their claims. However, in a case such as Silvia's, where the defendants may be found to be in a better position to ascertain relevant facts regarding the production and distribution of the peanuts jar, the traditional evidentiary burden could be relaxed. The defendants probably would be expected to come forward with their own version of the facts, either exclusively or at least concurrently with Silvia.

Summary Chart—Burdens of Proof and Causation

	United States	Germany	Argentina
Causation is a necessary predicate to tort liability.	Yes	Yes	Yes
Plaintiffs must show both "factual causation" and "legal causation."	Yes	Yes	Yes
Generally, plaintiffs bear burden of proving facts supporting their claims.	Yes	Yes	Yes
Procedural devices in the nature of res ipsa loquitur exist to ease plaintiff's proof burden in certain cases.	Yes	Yes	Yes
Different standards of proof apply to liability and to damages.	No	Yes. Required degree of conviction by judge is higher for liability than for damages.	No
Judges may disregard procedural and evidentiary rules if they interfere with determination of objective truth.	No	No	Yes (*Colalillo* principle).

CHAPTER 8

THEORIES OF RECOVERY

Silvia's case is a classic products liability case. The products liability systems of the United States, Germany, and Argentina, like most developed products liability systems throughout the world, recognize liability for three distinct types of product defects: manufacturing defects, design defects, and informational defects. Manufacturing defects occur when an individual product unit deviates from the seller's own performance standards and specifications. A product with a manufacturing defect is "the one that got away." In Germany, such a product is referred to as an "outlier" or *Ausreißer*. In Argentina, they're called "escapes" or *fugas*. Design defects involve products that are properly manufactured and come off the assembly line as intended, but which are nevertheless flawed due to an error in the design process, such as the omission of a safety device. Informational defects involve a failure to provide adequate warnings and instructions regarding product risks and how to avoid or reduce them.

Broken glass container cases almost always involve alleged manufacturing defects. The California Supreme Court once described a broken soda bottle case as "[t]he archetypal example" of a manufacturing defect. Brown v. Superior Court (Abbott Laboratories), 751 P.2d 470, 474 (Cal. 1988). The plaintiff in such a case asserts that the individual container that broke and caused her harm was flawed due to a defect arising during manufacturing, processing or distribution. Allegations of design or informational defects — "generic defects" that expose an entire product line to liability — are rare. As such, discussion of them is omitted. Thus, it is important to keep in mind that our hypothetical case study covers only one of the three types of product defect.

What is found below is remarkable convergence in the substantive products liability theories available in the U.S., Germany, and Argentina. All three nations recognize claims based on negligence, strict liability, and breach of contract, although in all three countries these separate claims blur together at the margins. Additionally, the law of all three nations takes cognizance of the difficulties a plaintiff would have in proving liability in a case such as Silvia's, and provide mechanisms for alleviating the plaintiff's proof burden either formally or informally. Although the law varies in details from country to country, the core liability theories show strong cohesiveness.

The convergence in doctrine discussed in this chapter came as a surprise to the authors. We had expected to find much more radical substantive law differences that would help explain the different perceptions of the U.S. tort system vis-à-vis countries in other parts of the world. Instead, this chapter in particular enlightened us that the most important differences in how tort systems function are not rooted in substantive legal rules as much as they are in procedural and institutional differences. John Fleming made this observation in his book, *The American Tort Process*, where he observed that "what makes American tort law so peculiarly different from that of other countries, those of the common law no less than the civil law, is not their substantive doctrinal content so much as the institutional framework in which it operates." "The dish," he said, "may consist of the same basic ingredients but is metamorphosed by the manner of its cooking." JOHN G. FLEMING, THE AMERICAN TORT PROCESS v (1988). The following exploration of the substantive theories of recovery for manufacturing defects in the U.S., Germany, and Argentina lends credence to these views.

United States

In most U.S. jurisdictions, Silvia would raise three distinct claims in her lawsuit: negligence, strict liability in tort, and breach of the implied warranty of merchantability. U.S. law permits a plaintiff to plead and attempt to prove multiple claims arising from the same event, although the plaintiff is entitled to only one recovery. Typically, a plaintiff such as Silvia would sue all entities in the distribution chain involving the broken jar, although financial and strategic considerations sometimes dictate a different decision. In this case, we'll assume Silvia has sued all possible defendants, including Levington (the jar maker), Penelope (the peanuts producer), Charter (the wholesale food distributor), and Value-Store (the retailer).

Negligence

Even though U.S. law provides for strict liability for manufacturing defects—i.e., liability without fault—Silvia's lawyer typically would include a negligence claim in the complaint. Why include a claim that requires proof of fault when a strict liability claim is available? As a strategic matter, showing that a defendant did something "wrong" has a more potent impact on juries than the more sterile, technical claim of strict liability. An empirical study of mock jurors showed that the use of negligence terminology, over the language of strict liability, resulted in more verdicts for plaintiffs and in higher amounts. *See* Richard L. Cupp & Danielle Polage, *The Rhetoric of Strict Products Liability Versus Negligence: An Empirical Analysis*, 77 N.Y.U. L. REV. 874 (2002).

A negligence claim would require Silvia to prove four elements: (1) that the defendants owed her a legal duty; (2) that one or more of them breached that duty by failing to exercise reasonable care; (3) that the breach was both a factual and legal cause of her harm; and (4) injury. The primary element at issue in Silvia's case would be the second one: the "breach" issue. Under U.S. law, product makers and sellers owe a duty to all persons who might foreseeably use or be affected by a defective product. While causation could be viewed as an issue, as explained in chapter seven, the question of attribution of a product defect in cases like Silvia's is usually not analyzed separately as a causation issue, but rather as part of the larger inquiry into whether the product contained a preexisting defect. As for injury, while the extent of Silvia's injury would be in issue, the fact of her injury is not.

Thus, Silvia's primary task in asserting a negligence claim would be to show that one of the defendants breached its duty to exercise reasonable care in creating or not discovering a defect in the jar. Proving negligence in a broken glass container case can be difficult and often impossible. With so many people handling the container from the top of the distribution chain all the way down to Silvia, Norah, and Marco, showing fault by any particular defendant could present an insurmountable hurdle, particularly since the product is not available for inspection.

Res ipsa loquitur. Silvia's best hope would be for the court to invoke res ipsa loquitur. Res ipsa loquitur, which translates from Latin to "the thing speaks for itself," is a procedural device that allows plaintiffs to get certain unexplained cases to a jury despite lacking proof of a specific negligent act by the defendant. It is not so much a separate legal doctrine as it is "a common sense appraisal of the probative value of circumstantial evidence." *Boykin v. Chase Bottling Works*, 222 S.W.2d 889, 896 (Tenn. Ct. App. 1949). The existence of some facts circumstantially supports an inference of other facts. For example, if it's dark outside, the most probable explanation is that it is nighttime, even though a possible explanation is that a solar eclipse is occurring.

Res ipsa loquitur applies to cases where the happening of the accident itself circumstantially supports an inference that negligence is the most likely explanation and an inference that the defendant is the most likely culprit. Thus, in the landmark case of *Byrne v. Boadle*, 159 Eng. Rep. 299 (1863), a barrel of flour fell from a second-floor window and landed on the plaintiff.

The flour business was held liable for damages despite the absence of any explanation as to how or why the event happened. As the court tersely explained: "A barrel could not roll out of a warehouse without some negligence." In other words, the event spoke for itself.

Normally, two elements must be satisfied to make out a case for applying res ipsa loquitur: (1) the event must be one that ordinarily does not occur in the absence of negligence; and (2) the instrumentality that caused the harm (in our case, the jar) was under the exclusive control of the defendant at the time any negligence was likely to have occurred. Some jurisdictions add as a third element that the plaintiff must exclude her own negligence as a cause, but most take the position that this requirement is subsumed within the control element.

The purpose of the control element is to attribute the inferred negligent act to the defendant. Because we are, by definition, dealing with unexplained events in res ipsa loquitur cases, plaintiffs usually seek to satisfy the control element by presenting evidence tending to exclude other causes, including the plaintiff's own negligence. Excluding explanations other than the defendant's negligence is, in fact, the purpose of the control element. Accordingly, some modern cases have supplanted the control element with section 328D(1)(b) of *Restatement (Second) of Torts*. Section 328D(1)(b) abandons the traditional control element language in favor of the requirement that the plaintiff show that "other responsible causes, including the conduct of the plaintiff and third persons, are sufficiently eliminated by the evidence...."

Absent an unlikely damning admission from one of the defendants (e.g., an employee of Value-Store testifies he dropped the carton containing Silvia's jar of peanuts during stocking) or a lucky break in discovering a quality control breakdown by Levington or Penelope, Silvia's "proof" of negligence would boil down to an attempt to exclude explanations other than negligence by one of the defendants as the most likely cause for the jar breaking. Specifically, Silvia would attempt to establish that she, Norah, and Marco each handled the jar carefully. Silvia would testify, for example, that she didn't drop the jar or knock it against a hard object when she placed the jar in or removed it from her shopping cart, her car, or the kitchen cabinet. Norah and Marco would testify that they also handled the jar carefully when they retrieved it from the cabinet, opened it, and ate peanuts from it in the living room.

An obstacle for Silvia is that, faithfully construed, res ispa loquitur usually does not apply to cases involving multiple defendants or multiple potential tortfeasors. When a barrel falls out of a flour-business window, the most likely explanation is that someone associated with the flour business was negligent. But when independent multiple actors are involved, there often is no basis for drawing an inference that they all were negligent or that any particular one of them was negligent. Nevertheless, several American courts have assisted plaintiffs asserting negligence claims in broken glass container cases by applying res ipsa loquitur, even when it requires some stretching to do so. Thus, in an early influential case, *Payne v. Rome Coca-Cola Bottling Co.*, 73 S.E. 1087 (Ga. Ct. App. 1912), the court allowed a plaintiff injured by an exploding bottle of cola to recover against the manufacturer even though the bottle had passed through the hands of another individual and two other business entities before reaching plaintiff. In Silvia's case, a court might be willing to shift the inference of negligence up the distribution ladder to, say, Penelope, if representatives of Value-Store and Charter presented evidence that they handled the jar with due care.

The defendants' strategy would be to deflate any inference of negligence on their part by raising the possibility that either Silvia or her friends damaged the jar after it was purchased from Value-Store. They might also point fingers at each other and argue that the defect originated somewhere else in the distribution chain and they weren't negligent in failing to discover it. All defendants would specifically focus on Silvia's use of the Exacto knife to cut out the rebate label as a possible explanation for why the jar broke. The Exacto-knife issue is discussed in chapter nine, addressing defenses.

In a majority of states, res ipsa loquitur creates a permissible inference of negligence that a jury may choose to draw or reject. It does not formally shift the burden of proof to the defendant, although it has that practical effect. Faced with the possibility of being found negligent, defendants usually will attempt to show they were not negligent. They often do this by pointing fingers at others, as well as by seeking to introduce evidence of reasonable quality control and inventory handling procedures. In a minority of states, res ipsa loquitur formally shifts the burden of going forward with the evidence, and in a few states, it shifts the ultimate burden of persuasion to the defendant.

Strict Liability in Tort

Silvia's lawyer also would bring a claim for strict liability in tort. In the 1960s, in part to ease the proof obstacles facing plaintiffs like Silvia, state courts, most of them relying on *Restatement (Second) of Torts* §402A, adopted strict liability, or liability without fault, for defective products in manufacturing defect cases.

It is common to characterize the entire U.S. products liability system as a system of strict liability, but that is not accurate. In manufacturing defect cases such as Silvia's, courts apply true strict liability. The plaintiff need not show fault to recover. In both design defect and informational defect cases, however, most courts apply a negligence-based analysis, even when they insist on calling it strict liability. Reverting to a negligence standard in design defect and informational defect litigation is necessitated by the fact that no objective standards exist for determining the existence of a defect in such cases. In design cases, plaintiffs assert that the defendant should have made the design "safer" in some way. But how safe is safe enough and where does one find a standard for making that determination?

Most courts apply a risk-utility test in design defect cases that requires the fact-finder to weigh the foreseeable risks of the product as designed against the utility of the product as designed. As part of this equation, most courts require plaintiffs to prove the existence of a reasonable alternative design, weighing factors such as technological feasibility, cost, and whether the alternative design would impair the usefulness of the product for its intended purpose or create other risks. Despite protestations to the contrary by some courts, there is no escaping that such a test requires the fact-finder to evaluate the reasonableness of the manufacturer's decision in choosing the challenged design over other designs and, hence, bespeaks negligence. Similarly, in informational defect cases asserting that the product maker furnished inadequate warnings, most courts impose a duty on product makers only to deliver reasonable warnings of foreseeable product risks. Again, this standard rings in negligence.

In manufacturing defect cases, however, true strict liability is imposed. The plaintiff is required to show only: (1) that the product contained a defect; (2) that the defect caused her injury; and (3) that the defect existed when the product left the particular entity which plaintiff seeks to hold responsible. There is no requirement to prove the defendant was at fault in creating the defect. The first case in which a U.S. judge explicitly argued for strict liability in tort for defective products was, coincidentally, an exploding bottle case. In *Escola v. Coca Cola Bottling Co.*, 150 P.2d 436 (Cal. 1944), a majority of the California Supreme Court stretched res ipsa loquitur to allow the plaintiff, a waitress injured by an exploding Coca-Cola bottle at a restaurant, to recover from the bottler. Justice Traynor concurred in the judgment, but argued that the time had come to impose "absolute liability" when a defective product causes physical injury. Traynor's position won out nineteen years later in *Greenman v. Yuba Power Products*, 377 P.2d 897 (Cal. 1963).

In Silvia's case, proving the jar had a defect and that the defect caused her injury would be easy. Non-defective jars do not shatter while being handled normally, and the shattering glass clearly caused Silvia's injury. Proving that the defect existed when the product left the various parties she would seek to hold responsible would be much harder. The higher up the distribution chain one travels, the more difficult this proof issue would become. Under strict liability, each entity in the distribution chain is liable for selling a defective product, but it remains a defense that the product wasn't defective when it left the particular entity. And, of course, Silvia would be faced with the argument that she caused the defect herself with the Exacto knife.

Inference-drawing à la res ipsa loquitur. Significantly, however, courts give plaintiffs asserting strict liability claims the benefit of an inference-drawing process virtually identical to res ipsa loquitur, which is technically applicable only as to negligence claims. The similarity in approach makes sense. Drawing logical factual inferences from other facts is a cognitive process more so than it is a legal concept. Whether the claim is grounded in negligence or strict liability should not make a difference. If the facts circumstantially support an inference that the product was defective and that the defect existed at the time the product left a particular defendant, plaintiff can prevail against that defendant despite lacking proof of a specific defect. This principle has been formally adopted as part of the *Products Liability Restatement*. Section 3 provides:

> It may be inferred that the harm sustained by the plaintiff was caused by a product defect existing at the time of sale or distribution, without proof of a specific defect, when the incident that harmed the plaintiff:
>
> (a) was of a kind that ordinarily occurs as a result of a product defect; and
>
> (b) was not, in the particular case, solely the result of causes other than product defect existing at the time of sale or distribution.

RESTATEMENT (THIRD) OF TORTS: PRODUCTS LIABILITY § 3 (1998).

The parallels to res ipsa loquitur are obvious. The major substantive difference is that, under strict liability, the evidence need not support an inference of *negligence* for the plaintiff to win. An inference of *defect* will suffice, combined with circumstantial evidence supporting an inference excluding other likely causes, which is virtually identical to the control element of res ipsa loquitur.

Strict liability for non-manufacturer sellers. In a majority of states, Silvia's most direct strict liability path would be against Value-Store because there are fewer proof gaps to fill. Since under strict liability a retailer is liable simply for selling a defective product, regardless of fault, Silvia would have to account only for what happened to the jar after it left the store, as compared to showing in a claim against Levington (the jar maker) what happened to the jar during its long journey, both in duration and geography, after the jar left Levington's control. Under established common and statutory law, retailers or wholesalers who pay products liability judgments are entitled to indemnity from the manufacturer, assuming the product was defective when it left the manufacturer's hands.

Importantly, however, a growing minority of states have passed legislation protecting retailers from strict liability in products liability cases, subject to some exceptions. Persons claiming against retailers in these states must prove negligence to recover unless one of the exceptions applies. Proving negligence against a retailer in a products liability case is rarely successful. A retailer's duty under negligence law is limited to performing a reasonable inspection of its goods. Such an inspection would not be likely to reveal a latent defect in a glass jar. As of this writing, Florida, where Silvia's U.S. case is filed, retains strict liability for retailers. *See* Samuel Friedland Family v. Amoroso, 630 So. 2d 1067, 1068 (Fla. 1994) ("Florida courts have expanded the doctrine of strict liability to others in the distributive chain including retailers, wholesalers, and distributors.")

From the above it can be seen that while strict liability would eliminate the burden on Silvia to prove fault, it would not alleviate her problem of proving when the defect in the jar arose.

Implied Warranty of Merchantability

Silvia's third claim would be for breach of the implied warranty of merchantability. Under section 2-314 of the Uniform Commercial Code (UCC), all products carry with them an implied warranty that they "are fit for the ordinary purposes for which such goods are used." UCC §2-314(2)(c) (1998). The UCC is a civil law-type code, comprehensively addressing the law of commercial transactions. Article 2, setting forth the law of sales, has been adopted in every U.S. state except Louisiana.

The law of implied warranty is technically rooted in the law of contracts, but bears many tort-like qualities, so many that the theory is sometimes referred to as "strict liability in contract." When Justice Traynor wrote his famous opinion in *Greenman v. Yuba Power Products, Inc.*, adopting strict liability in tort, he expressly noted that courts were already accomplishing the same thing under the guise of implied warranty. He opined that although products liability has "usually been based on the theory of an express or implied warranty running from the manufacturer to the plaintiff," expansive common law changes in the law of contracts made it "clear that the liability is not one governed by the law of contract warranties but by the law of strict liability in tort." *Greenman*, 377 P.2d at 901.

Four aspects serve to render the implied warranty claim virtually identical to a claim grounded in strict liability in tort: (1) the warranty is imposed by operation of law rather than by agreement of the parties; (2) privity of contract between buyer and seller is no longer required; (3) courts refuse to allow sellers to disclaim warranties of merchantability in personal injury cases; and (4) no fault need be shown. The overlap between the two theories is so complete that some states have opted to allow only one claim or the other and the *Products Liability Restatement* recommends that strict liability tort and warranty claims not be submitted to a jury in the same case. *See* RESTATEMENT (THIRD) OF TORTS: PRODUCTS LIABILITY § 2 cmt. n (1998). In most states, however, both claims remain available and are routinely asserted by plaintiffs.

Some differences between the two claims arise in particular cases. Tort and contract claims have different statutes of limitations. Certain types of economic damages, such as harm to the product itself, may be recoverable only under a contractual warranty theory. Disclaimers of warranties may be honored as a defense to breach of warranty claims in cases not involving physical injuries or used products. Lack of privity of contract can still be an obstacle in some states, particularly in commercial transactions.

A jar that shatters when the lid is placed on top is not fit for the ordinary purposes for which such products are used and the unfit aspect of the jar caused Silvia's injuries. But just as with her negligence and strict liability claims, Silvia would confront the issue of showing that the jar was unfit at the time it left the particular entity Silvia seeks to hold responsible. Just as under strict liability in tort, a product seller is responsible for a breach of warranty that renders a product unfit for use only if the defect existed at the time the product left the seller's possession and control.

Conclusion

In the U.S., Silvia would sue all defendants in the distribution chain. Her claims would include two common law tort claims (negligence and strict liability) and one contract-based statutory claim (breach of the implied warranty of merchantability). As to each claim, her principal obstacle would be showing that the defect that caused the jar to shatter existed while the jar was in the control of the particular defendant from which she sought to recover.

A fair chance exists that she would be aided by the procedural device of res ipsa loquitur as to her negligence claim and a similar circumstantial inference-drawing process as to her strict liability and implied warranty claims. Because res ipsa loquitur, if applied, allows the jury to infer negligence (i.e., fault), there really ends up being little substantive difference among Silvia's three claims in this type of case. If a judge determined that reasonable jurors, viewing the evidence in a light most favorable to the plaintiff, could find the elements of the plaintiff's claims to be supported by a preponderance of the evidence, the case would go to the jury.

Does the breaking of the Penelope Peanuts jar under the facts presented meet that standard? It's questionable, but, as the Iowa Supreme Court once observed, in actions "involving exploding containers of carbonated soft drinks and beer, juries and courts have generally resolved issues of liability in favor of the injured plaintiffs." Bredberg v. Pepsico, Inc., 551 N.W.2d 321, 327 n.5 (Iowa 1996). Judicial generosity toward plaintiffs in these types of cases no doubt stems from the recognition that holding victims of broken glass food and beverage containers strictly to their burden of proving when the defect arose in the distribution chain could result in injustice in many cases. In tracing the history of American products liability law, Fleming observed that res ipsa loquitur has been used as an instrument of judicial policy to extend liability to injured consumers, rather than merely as a rule for evaluating circumstantial evidence. FLEMING, at 10.

On the other hand, winning is never a sure bet in any legal system, including the U.S. One question is whether Silvia's case would be distinguished from the long line of cases involving carbonated beverage bottles, which are more dangerous because they are under internal pressure. Even if Silvia's peanuts jar received analogous treatment, plaintiffs have lost many exploding beverage bottle cases. See, e.g., Stewart v. Crystal Coca-Cola Bottling Co., 68 P.2d 952, 955 (Ariz. 1937) (defendant not liable because alternative explanations existed for why bottle exploded); Hutchins v. Rock Creek Ginger Ale Co., 194 A.2d 305, 307 (D.C. 1963) (defendant not liable where bottle stocked on grocery store shelf exploded because plaintiff made "no attempt to show what became of the bottle from the time it was delivered ... until the time it allegedly exploded"); Burkett v. Panama City Coca-Cola Bottling Co., 93 So. 2d 580, 582 (Fla. 1957) (defendant not liable where plaintiff dropped bottle on floor, exposing it to "extraneous harmful influences"); Joffre v. Canada Dry Ginger Ale, Inc., 158 A.2d 631, 635 (Md. 1960) (defendant not liable where evidence allowed numerous varying inferences); Cerepak v. Revlon, Inc., 200 N.W.2d 33, 36 (Minn. 1972) (judgment for defendant where plaintiff was injured by an exploding deodorant bottle which she had used on several prior occasions); Abernathy v. Coca-Cola Bottling Co., 370 S.W. 2d 175, 177 (Mo. Ct. App. 1963) (bottler not liable where evidence failed to show that an exploding soda bottle had not undergone unusual temperature changes, been damaged or otherwise handled negligently after the bottle passed from defendant's possession and control); Poulos v. Cock 'N Bull Beverage, Inc., 487 P.2d 1350, 1352 (N.M. Ct. App. 1971) (plaintiff, relying on res ipsa loquitur, failed to establish exclusive control of the product by any of the defendants); Curley v. Ruppert, 71 N.Y.S.2d 578, 580–81 (N.Y. App. Div. 1947) (defendant not liable where bottle was delivered three days before accident and there was no evidence that the bottle was defective).

In *Welge v. Planters Lifesavers Co.*, the case from which Silvia's jar facts were borrowed, the U.S. Court of Appeals for the Seventh Circuit reversed the trial court's grant of summary judgment to the defendants and remanded the case for trial. The plaintiff's roommate bought him a jar of peanuts. The roommate removed a rebate label using an Exacto knife, then placed the jar on top of the refrigerator. A week later, the plaintiff opened the jar, took some peanuts from it, and replaced the lid without incident. The next week, the plaintiff did the same thing, but when he replaced the lid on that occasion, the jar shattered, causing hand injuries.

In the ensuing products liability suit, the defendants moved for summary judgment on the ground the plaintiff had failed to exclude causes of the accident other than a preexisting defect in the jar. The trial court granted the summary judgment. In reversing, the appellate court, per Judge Richard Posner, invoked the principle of res ipsa loquitur, opining that the breaking of the jar under the facts presented constituted sufficient circumstantial evidence of a defect to get the case to a jury. Apart from the issue of the Exacto knife, which is covered in chapter nine on defenses, Judge Posner responded skeptically to the defendant's assertion that it was possible some other after-sale harm befell the jar:

> Elves may have played ninepins with the jar of peanuts while [plaintiff and his roommate] were sleeping.... The plaintiff in a products liability suit is not required to exclude every possibility, however fantastic or remote, that the defect which led to the accident was caused by someone other than one of the defendants.

17 F.3d at 211. He made this observation after pointing out, with tongue firmly in cheek, that Chicago, where the accident occurred, is not Los Angeles, ruling out earthquakes as an explanation, nor is it Amityville, eliminating "supernatural interventions" as a cause. *Id.* at 210. With regard to the distinction between glass jars of peanuts and carbonated beverage bottles, Judge Posner noted that, while it is true that the latter are under pressure, it is also true that the glass is strengthened accordingly. *Id.* at 213. *Welge*, however, is only one case. Moreover, it was not a final decision on the merits. The court simply held that there was enough evidence, viewing the facts in the light most favorable to the plaintiff, to avoid summary judgment.

Jury Verdict Research (JVR), a company that collects personal injury verdict and settlement data and uses it to make case evaluations, applied its database to our hypothetical case facts (supplemented with reasonable assumptions not specifically mentioned in the facts) to evaluate Silvia's U.S. case. A 2006 JVR case analysis estimated the probability of a plaintiff verdict in Silvia's case filed in Miami-Dade County, Florida to be only 26%. While it is not possible to gauge the accuracy of the JVR projection, it does offer one window of insight into Silvia's case. See chapter ten for more extensive discussion of JVR's analysis of Silvia's case.

Ultimately, Silvia's success would depend on how stringently or liberally the judge and jury handling her case were willing to construe the inferences that the jar had a defect and that one or more of the defendants was responsible for the defect. Because fewer proof gaps exist, Silvia's easiest target would be Value-Store, the entity at the bottom of the distribution chain. See Welge, 17 F.3d at 212 (stating that since the retail defendant was a large and solvent entity, "there would be no need for the plaintiff to look further for a tortfeasor"). However, a veteran Florida trial lawyer commenting on Silvia's case emphasized that juries are not impressed by technical doctrines such as strict liability. They want to be shown that someone did something "wrong." In his opinion, Silvia's best chance for success would be if her lawyer could locate other substantially similar incidents of product breakage involving either Levington or Penelope. In the last chapter, we offer our overall assessments of Silvia's case. At this point, we can simply note that while Silvia has a decent case, it carries no assurance of a happy ending.

Germany

German law grants Silvia three claims quite similar to those available under U.S. law: a negligence claim under the German Civil Code (GCC), a strict liability claim under the 1990 Product Liability Act, and a fairly weak contract claim derived from the GCC. As in the U.S., more than one claim can be brought in the same lawsuit. One important point to take note of up front is that German law is much more restrictive with respect to the liability of non-producing defendants such as wholesalers and retailers.

Negligence (i.e., General Tort Liability)

Section 823 of the Civil Code. With regard to general tort liability, section 823 of the GCC is the basic, most relevant provision in German private law. Section 823(1) provides: "Anyone who unlawfully injures the life, body, health, liberty, property or any other right of another, either willfully or negligently, is liable to such other person to compensate for any such damages resulting therefrom." As the wording indicates, section 823(1) is a fault-based provision. To be liable to pay damages, the defendant must have acted intentionally or negligently. A second paragraph, section 823(2), imposes liability for harm resulting from violations of duties imposed by statutes, somewhat similar to the U.S. common law doctrine of negligence per se for statutory violations.

Section 823 has been construed to impose duties of safety on persons whose conduct creates foreseeable risks of harm to others that are quite similar to tort duties recognized under U.S. law. In recent years, German courts, responding to the increased risks of living in a crowded, interdependent society, have applied an enhanced duty of safety—known as a *Verkehrssicherungspflicht*—to a variety of types of risk-creating conduct, including making and selling defective products.

Normally, fault under section 823 must be proved by the plaintiff. Since most products liability cases do not involve allegations of intentional fault, proving a products liability claim under section 823 resembles proving a basic negligence claim under U.S. law. For a successful claim under this provision, Silvia would need to prove a product defect, an injury, a causal association between the defect and injury, and fault by the manufacturer or seller.

The German code contains only a general definition of negligence. Section 276(1) of the GCC provides that an obligor is responsible for "intent" or "negligence." Section 276(2) adds that a person acts negligently if he ignores the due care that is necessary in common intercourse. As in the U.S., as interpreted by German courts, the standard for negligence in private civil law, as opposed to criminal law, is an objective one that does not take into account the subjective knowledge or abilities of the particular actor. The relevant question is: did the defendant behave as a reasonable person would have behaved under like conditions and circumstances? If not, he is liable, regardless of his personal shortcomings.

The *Anscheinsbeweis* doctrine. The difficulty of proving fault by one of the defendants in creating a defect (and the closely connected issue of attributing any defect to one of the defendants) has already been discussed. In Germany, Silvia may be assisted by some important procedural devices that have the effect of alleviating the plaintiff's burden of proof. One of them is the *Anscheinsbeweis* doctrine, or doctrine of prima facie proof. The *Anscheinsbeweis* principle is basically the German equivalent of res ipsa loquitur. Like res ipsa loquitur, the *Anscheinsbeweis* doctrine is a principle of general applicability not limited to products liability cases. A tort victim who cannot prove by specific evidence that a defendant's fault caused her injury can nevertheless prevail if the facts circumstantially, in light of everyday experience, support a finding that the defendant was at fault and that the fault caused the injury. *See*

WALTER VAN GERVEN ET AL., CASES, MATERIALS AND TEXT ON NATIONAL, SUPRANATIONAL AND INTERNATIONAL TORT LAW 345–46 (2000) (explaining that the *Anscheinsbeweis* principle does not effect a formal shifting in the burden of proof from plaintiff to defendant, but allows plaintiff to establish a prima facie case of defendant's fault by showing "facts which, in the light of general experience as to how events unfold, justify the conclusion that the defendant failed to exercise due care under the circumstances").

It is possible that the *Anscheinsbeweis* doctrine would apply to Silvia's case to support an inference that the product was defective and that one or more of the defendants were at fault in creating the defect or in placing the defective product on the market. On the other hand, there are other possible explanations for why Silvia's jar shattered that could prevent a court from drawing an inference that the most likely cause was a preexisting defect due to the fault of one of the defendants. Silvia could have damaged the jar with the Exacto knife or otherwise. Norah or Marco, the last ones to use the jar, could have dropped it or bumped it against a hard object.

Fortunately for Silvia, in addition to the *Anscheinsbeweis* doctrine, German case law provides other mechanisms for alleviating the plaintiff's burden of proof in certain types of products liability cases. These burden shifting procedures were developed by the Federal Supreme Court in several section 823 cases over the last decades involving a variety of consumer and industrial products, including exploding bottles.

The *Fowl Pest* case. In the landmark 1968 *Fowl Pest* case (BGHZ 51, 91), the Federal Supreme Court transformed German products liability law by moving it from the realm of contract law into the realm of tort law. The *Fowl Pest* case could be viewed as the *Greenman v. Yuba Power Products, Inc.* of German law. In *Greenman*, Justice Traynor of the California Supreme Court squarely moved strict liability for defective products from contract law to tort law. The *Fowl Pest* case did not adopt strict liability—it couldn't because the court was construing fault-based section 823(1)—but the holding can have the practical effect of imposing strict liability. The court held that when a product causes injury because of a manufacturing defect (*Fabrikationsfehler*), the burden shifts to the manufacturer to prove it was not at fault.

The plaintiff, a chicken farmer, paid a veterinarian to inoculate his chickens from fowl pest, a deadly chicken virus. Despite the vaccination, the disease broke out and spread among plaintiff's chickens, killing more than 4,000 of them. The plaintiff sued the vaccine manufacturer under both contract and tort theories. The high court rejected the contract claim due to a lack of privity of contract between the plaintiff and the manufacturer, but upheld the tort claim under section 823(1).

While affirming that fault is an essential element of a products liability claim under section 823(1), the court reasoned, much like U.S. courts and scholars did in introducing strict liability for manufacturing defects in the 1960s, that proving fault in manufacturing defect cases is extremely difficult and sometimes impossible when the actions creating the defect were likely to have occurred at some distant factory. Accordingly, the court held:

> If someone is injured in his rights protected by section 823 (1) [i.e., the enumerated interests of "life, body, health, liberty, property or any other right"] while using an industrial product in accordance with its intended purpose because the product was defectively manufactured, it is the responsibility of the manufacturer to clarify the events which have caused the defect and thereby to explain that it was not at fault for such event.

The court added that in cases of injury arising within the sphere of the manufacturer's production facility, the manufacturer cannot overcome its burden of showing lack of fault simply "by pointing out possible explanations according to which the defect in the product could have occurred without having been caused within the manufacturer's organization." The holding was grounded in the court's recognition that consumers have no way to gain access or insight into the manufacturer's organizational sphere. This is particularly true given that there is no pretrial discovery in Germany. Essentially, it was a decision rooted in basic notions of fairness. The consumer can't find out what happened. If anyone knows, it's the manufacturer. Therefore, it is the manufacturer's responsibility to come forward with an explanation. The practical result of the holding, as Markesinis and Unberath observed, is that while section 823(1) claims technically remain fault-based, in cases where the burden shifting called for by the *Fowl Pest* case applies, the liability approximates strict liability. *See* MARKESINIS & UNBERATH, at 99.

The *Befundsicherungspflicht* and *Second Mineral Water Bottle* case. Silvia's still not home free, however, because the reversal of the burden of proof under the *Fowl Pest* case applies only to the issue of the *fault* of the defendant. As a prerequisite for shifting the burden to the defendant, the court said the plaintiff must first prove that the defect originated within "the sphere of organization and risk controlled by the manufacturer." Thus, Silvia would still have to show a preexisting product defect and the causality between the defect and her injuries. In other words, we're back to that same problem discussed in the U.S. section of establishing when and where the defect in the jar arose. Fortunately for Silvia, yet *another* judge-made doctrine applicable to particular types of products liability cases may come into play to help her on this point.

In a series of cases involving exploding bottles, the Federal Supreme Court developed a doctrine known as the *Befundsicherungspflicht*, which is a duty imposed on manufacturers to control and preserve records of the quality and status of its products before placing them on the market. *See* BGHZ 104, 323 (the *Lemonade Bottle* case), BGH, NJW 1993, 528 (the *First Mineral Water Bottle* case); BGHZ 129, 353 (the *Second Mineral Water Bottle* case). The *Befundsicherungspflicht* functions sort of like a super form of res ipsa loquitur. It gives rise to a presumption that the defect was created while the product was in the manufacturer's control unless the manufacturer can prove it took all requisite quality control measures to ensure that the product was free from such defects.

Thus, in 1995, in the well-known *Second Mineral Water Bottle* case (BGHZ 129, 353), the defendant sold carbonated mineral water, a popular beverage in Germany, in reusable glass bottles. The plaintiff, a nine-year-old child, was injured when one of the bottles exploded. Pieces of glass caused serious injury to her left eye. Plaintiff relied on an expert report showing a 4 mm external chip at the site of the fracture, but the lower courts rejected her claim because the defendant manufacturer proved it maintained rigid quality control procedures. The Federal Supreme Court reversed and held for the plaintiff, stating that:

> on the issue of whether a particular defect of the product … had already occurred in the manufacturer's area of responsibility or in any case had not been detected, a shifting of the burden of proof may be considered, if the manufacturer was in breach of its *Befundsicherungspflicht*, its obligation to check the product as to its sound composition and to secure such findings.

The defendant had presented detailed evidence of its quality control procedures, which is the principal means by which a defendant can show it has not breached its *Befundsicherungspflicht*. Expert testimony showed the defendant's quality control procedures were state of the art, and that no system of quality control could be foolproof when dealing with this type of product. The bottle, the defendant argued, was simply one that got away, a stray defective product called an *Ausreißer* or "outlier" in German.

While the court agreed that a defendant could avoid liability by demonstrating it was not in breach of its *Befundsicherungspflicht*, it imposed a strict standard for showing compliance with the duty. The court said a mineral water company's *Befundsicherungspflicht* imposes an obligation "to implement a control procedure to assure that the condition of each bottle is ascertained in a reliable fashion using the best available, feasible technology and that all bottles which may pose a danger be eliminated from recycling." It is not sufficient to overcome the presumption that the defect arose while the product was in the manufacturer's organizational sphere for the defendant to use the best possible equipment in its quality control. Rather, "if defects in bottles cannot be detected by means of mechanical inspection but could be seen by visual inspection, the manufacturer has the obligation to have each and every bottle inspected by these means."

The *Befundsicherungspflicht* applies to products that present risks warranting heightened scrutiny and monitoring by the manufacturer. Recyclable lemonade or carbonated mineral water bottles are perfect examples. The Federal Supreme Court has reasoned that the manufacturer must observe the *Befundsicherungspflicht* with regard to such products not only because of the risk of material deterioration inherent in repeat use, but also the foreseeable technical stress to which they will be exposed as they make their way through the distribution chain. The manufacturer is required to keep records of the quality and status of these special products before they leave its sphere in order to establish a means for subsequently evaluating their condition at that time.

As Markesinis and Unberath have noted, *Befundsicherungspflicht* is a somewhat confusing label for the nature of the duty being imposed. A literal translation of the term is the requirement to keep a record of the results of an investigation, but the *Befundsicherungspflicht* duty is broader than that. As applied to glass bottles, it means not simply maintaining a list of the result of checking each bottle, but of establishing and operating a quality control system that permits ascertaining the physical condition of each bottle. *See* MARKESINIS & UNBERATH, at 594.

Whether the *Befundsicherungspflicht* doctrine would be available to Silvia to shift the burden to the producing defendants to prove the peanuts jar did not contain a defect when it was put into circulation is open to question. Jars of peanuts are neither recyclable, nor under internal pressure from carbonation. They are, however, made of glass and travel through a long distribution chain in which they foreseeably will be subjected to rough handling. Case law on whether the *Befundsicherungspflicht* applies to "one-way bottles" is mixed, with two courts applying the *Befundsicherungspflicht* to such bottles, and one court declining to do so. Even the former cases, however, involved carbonated beverages under pressure. It most likely will become necessary for the Federal Supreme Court to step in and resolve the issue of whether the *Befundsicherungspflicht* applies to all glass food and beverage containers.

Strict Liability

The Product Liability Act. In 1989, Germany adopted the Product Liability Act (*Produkthaftungsgesetz*) (PLA) to implement the EU Product Liability

Directive. In theory, the PLA makes life easier for persons injured by defective products by officially adopting strict liability, or liability without fault. In practice, the act has not yet been widely used. Products liability plaintiffs in Germany continue to rely heavily on GCC §823 negligence claims.

One key reason is that the PLA included limitations not applicable to general tort claims under section 823, most importantly, that until 2002 claimants under the PLA could not recover noneconomic losses such as pain and suffering. Additionally, the impact of the most concrete advantage of the PLA to plaintiffs—the imposition of strict liability—is reduced by the judge-made burden-shifting mechanisms discussed above, applicable to some section 823 claims. As observed, applying those mechanisms can result in a kind of de facto strict liability under section 823. With the 2002 amendments to the PLA allowing recovery for noneconomic injuries, it is likely that the PLA will gain more traction with plaintiffs' lawyers.

The PLA is quite short. The entire act consists of nineteen tersely worded sections that fill only a couple of pages. It was intentionally written in a minimalist fashion with the goal of avoiding major changes in prior law. *See* WALTER VAN GERVEN ET AL., at 650.

Test for defect. Section 1 is the operative strict liability provision. It states in pertinent part: "If a person is killed, his body or health injured, or property damaged due to a defective product, the manufacturer of such product is obligated to compensate the injured person for the damages caused by such defective product." Note the absence of any requirement to prove fault. The section goes on to exclude liability for harm to the defective product itself, which parallels the so-called "economic loss doctrine" followed by a majority of U.S. states, holding that harm to the product itself is considered an economic loss not recoverable under tort law, but only under a breach of warranty contract claim.

The test for defect under the PLA, taken directly from article 6(2) of the EU Product Liability Directive, is set forth in section 3 as follows:

(1) A product is defective if, considering all the circumstances, it fails to offer the safety which could reasonably be expected, particularly in light of:
(a) its presentation;
(b) its use which could have been reasonably expected;
(c) the time when it was brought into circulation.

Note that this test for defect is quite similar to the U.S. "consumer expectation test" for determining the existence of a product defect. Under the U.S. consumer expectation test a product is considered defective when it is "dangerous to an extent beyond that which would be contemplated by the ordinary consumer who purchases it, with the knowledge common to the community as to its characteristics." RESTATEMENT (SECOND) OF TORTS § 402A cmt. i (1965). Interestingly, the consumer expectation test, which now reigns supreme in Europe under the EU Product Liability Directive as implemented by the member states, has been abandoned as an independent test for defect by many U.S. states and by the *Products Liability Restatement. See* RESTATEMENT (THIRD) OF TORTS: PRODUCTS LIABILITY § 2 cmt. g (1998). Departure from the consumer expectation test in the U.S. has implications mostly with regard to design defects, which are not at issue in Silvia's case.

Burdens of proof under the PLA. Plaintiffs pursuing claims under the PLA bear the burden of showing a defect, damage, and causality between the defect and the damage. PLA § 1(4). In one sense, it would be easy for a court to conclude that Silvia's jar of peanuts failed the PLA test for defect. A jar that shatters during normal use "fails to offer the safety which could reasonably be expected." For many products, the scope of strict liability under the expectation test depends on the type of product and the manner in which the producer marketed the product. However, for simple everyday products such as Silvia's peanuts jar, reasonable consumer expectations regarding safety can be formed based simply on the product's appearance.

But, quoting former U.S. baseball star and team manager Yogi Berra, "it's *déjà vu* all over again" with regard to that fundamental problem of proving when and where the defect arose. Section 1(2)2 of the PLA provides that the manufacturer is relieved of the duty to pay damages if "according to all the circumstances, it must be concluded that the product did not have a defect at the time the manufacturer put it into circulation." However, section 1(4) provides that product producers bear the burden of proof on this issue when it is in dispute.

In the *Second Mineral Water Bottle* case, the plaintiff raised a strict liability claim under the PLA in addition to her general tort claim under section 823 of the GCC. Invoking section 1(4) of the PLA, the court held that the producer of the exploding bottle of mineral water could avoid liability under the PLA only if it could prove that the bottle did not have a defect at the time it was put into circulation. Thus, assuming the court were willing to infer the existence of a defect in Silvia's peanuts jar, if Levington or Penelope argued that the defect did not exist when the jar was placed into circulation, they would bear the burden of proving that issue under the PLA. It appears that under the PLA they would bear that burden without regard to whether the *Befundsicherungspflicht* was invoked, although the interplay between the judge-made *Befundsicherungspflicht* and the PLA still has not been fully resolved.

"Producer" liability. Section 4 of the PLA defines "producer"; that is, the potential defendants subject to strict liability under the act. It limits claims to those: who manufactured the final product (Penelope); manufactured "a basic substance or a component part of the product" (Levington); represented himself as a producer of the product by attaching his name or trademark to the product (Penelope again); or who imported the product into the European Economic Area (not applicable). Section 5 of the PLA imposes joint and several liability when multiple producers are held liable.

Limited liability for non-manufacturer sellers. Notably, non-manufacturer sellers such as retailers (Value-Store) and wholesalers (Charter) are treated as producers under the act only if the manufacturer cannot be identified. Since Levington and Penelope have been identified in our problem, Silvia would not be able to maintain claims under the PLA against Value-Store or Charter. Thus, a critical difference from U.S. law is seen in that retailers and other intermediaries in the distribution chain generally are not subject to strict liability under German law with regard to defective products they sell or distribute. The liability of non-producer suppliers of products has been a somewhat controversial issue in the European Union. In implementing the EU Product Liability Directive, some countries, including France and Denmark, have passed laws imposing strict liability on suppliers. The Danish government proposed an amendment to the directive that would allow member states to hold suppliers strictly liable, but it was not adopted. Thus, this issue awaits further development.

Contract Liability

Contract claims arising from a product defect are a good example of how courts in civil law systems often are required to deduce principles from a series of code provisions, none of which clearly state the precise principles recognized. All of the following sections of the GCC have been held to be relevant to contract-based products liability claims: §280 (Compensation for breach of contract), §433 (Basic duties of seller and the buyer), §434 (Defective goods), §437 (Rights of purchase in the event of defects), and §633 (Defects as to quality and as to title).

No useful purpose would be served by attempting to explain in detail the complex interrelationship among the various provisions of the GCC that have been held to give rise to contract claims arising from defective products, particularly since a contract claim will be Silvia's least useful claim. For all practical purposes, the adoption of strict liability by the PLA and the expansion of general tort liability under section 823 engineered by the *Fowl Pest* case, the

Second Mineral Water Bottle case, and their successors, have rendered contract-based products liability claims in Germany largely a matter of historical interest. *See* MARKESINIS & UNBERATH, at 94–99 (tracing evolution and demise of contract claims in products liability cases).

Contract-based products liability claims for mass-produced consumer goods are much more limited in Germany than in the U.S. because the applicable law has retained more of its true contractual character than in the U.S. As previously discussed, liability for breach of implied warranty in the U.S. essentially equates with strict liability in tort because courts stripped away most of the limitations that general contract law principles would otherwise impose on such claims, including the requirement that the plaintiff be in privity of contract with the defendant. German law is to the contrary.

As in the U.S., manufacturers have a duty to deliver products that are suitable for the purposes for which they are intended. Selling products unfit for normal use constitutes a breach of contract. German law, however, retains privity of contract as a requirement for contract claims. Third-party contractual claims, including breach of warranty claims, exist only if such claims are expressly agreed to by the parties to the contract. Thus, in the *Fowl Pest* case, the Federal Supreme Court rejected the plaintiff's contract claim against the manufacturer of the defective vaccine because the plaintiff was not in privity of contract with the manufacturer, but only with the veterinarian who supplied the vaccine.

For mass produced products sold through a distribution chain, German manufacturers typically do provide a type of express warranty called a *Herstellergarantie*, which translates to "producer's guarantee," but this guarantee is usually limited to liability for repair and/or replacement of the defective product. It does not in most cases extend to personal injuries. Again, a variance is seen between U.S. and German contract law. U.S. courts have held that limitations of remedies and disclaimers of warranties in cases involving personal injury to consumers from defects in new products will not be honored.

The privity requirement would thus limit Silvia's contract remedy to a claim against Value-Store, where she would confront yet another obstacle. German product sellers are liable under contract law only if they were at fault in breaching the contract. The fault requirement comes from judicial interpretation of section 280(1) of the GCC, which states that the duty to pay compensation for breach of contract "does not apply if the debtor is not responsible for the breach of duty." While the requirement to prove fault is mitigated in products liability cases by a reversal of the burden of proof on the issue to the seller, German courts take the position that retail sellers do not have a duty to investigate products for defects unless facts exist putting the retailer on notice of a defect. No facts in our case problem indicate that Value-Store was on notice that the jar of Penelope Peanuts was defective. Accordingly, even though Value-Store would bear the burden of proving it was without fault in a breach of contract claim, that should be an easy burden to carry.

As a result, it is unlikely Silvia would have a viable contract-based claim under the facts presented. The good news is that she does not need one. Her general tort claim (GCC §823) and claim under the PLA would be easier to establish and, if successful, provide an opportunity to obtain full compensation for her injuries.

Conclusion

In Germany, Silvia's best hope for recovery lies in claims based on general tort liability (negligence) under section 823(1) of the GCC and strict liability under the PLA. Given the limitations on non-producer liability under German law, Levington and Penelope are the most promising defendants. Contract liability does not present much hope for Silvia due to the privity of contract limitation combined with the fault requirement for contract claims.

With regard to her section 823(1) general tort claim, Silvia would have to prove fault in creating a defect, that the defect existed at the time the peanuts jar was in control of one of the producing defendants, and that the defect caused her injury. The *Fowl Pest* case probably would relieve her of the burden of showing fault. Thus, her real problem, just as in the U.S., would be in proving the existence of a product defect and the point in the distribution chain at which the defect arose. The *Anscheinsbeweis* inference-drawing principle could help her on that issue, but German courts have not stretched the *Anscheinsbeweis* as far as American courts have stretched res ipsa loquitur in this type of case. With other plausible explanations for why the jar shattered, a German court would be less likely to draw an inference that the jar had a preexisting defect.

Silvia's best chance for prevailing on her section 823(1) general tort claim would be if the court applied the *Befundsicherungspflicht* doctrine, which would create a presumption that the defect existed while in the control of the producing defendants and force the defendants to prove otherwise to escape liability. There is a chance that Silvia would get the benefit of the *Befundsicherungspflicht* doctrine, but it is not a sure thing since the doctrine was developed in cases involving reusable carbonated-beverage containers, which present greater and more frequent risks of explosion and injury than other glass food or beverage containers.

Silvia might be able to avoid this problem under her PLA strict liability claim. Under the PLA, once the plaintiff proves the existence of a defect that caused harm, the defendants bear the burden of showing that the defect did not exist when the product was placed in circulation. The Federal Supreme Court so held in the *Second Mineral Water Bottle* case. However, because the PLA has not been extensively relied on by plaintiffs and, hence, has not been thoroughly fleshed out by the courts, the full ramifications of the act on this point are unknown. Even under the PLA, Silvia would have to prove the existence of a defect, which the plaintiff in the *Second Mineral Water Bottle* case did with expert evidence. Although a court might be willing to infer that the peanuts jar was defective, the issues of the existence of a defect and when the defect arose are so closely intertwined in a case like Silvia's that it is impossible to predict how the court would rule.

In short, subject to the defenses discussed in chapter nine, just as in the U.S., Silvia's case is not a long-shot, but neither is it an odds-on winner.

Argentina

In Argentina, Silvia would be likely to name as defendants all those who have had any relevant contact with the peanuts jar (Levington, Penelope, Charter, and Value-Store). Under the doctrine of *iura novit curia* (the court knows the law), Silvia would not have to opt for a particular legal theory in her complaint. The judge can decide the appropriate legal theory on his or her own. On the other hand, as emphasized in chapter five, it is very important that Silvia allege all relevant *facts* in the complaint.

Typically, there are four prerequisites to a successful tort claim in Argentina, which apply regardless of the specific legal theory on which the plaintiff is relying. They are: (1) unlawful conduct; (2) damage; (3) causation; and (4) a legal standard to attribute a damaging consequence to a given person. *See* BUSTAMANTE ALSINA, TEORIA GENERAL DE LA RESPONSABILIDAD CIVIL 108 (9th ed. 1997). According to article 1066 of the Argentine Civil Code (ACC), unlawful conduct is that which is in direct breach of a code or statutory provision, but Argentine courts have construed this requirement much more broadly. Basically, under modern law, any act that breaches a legal obligation or duty and results in harm to a third person is considered an unlawful act for purposes of civil liability. In products liability law, this includes both breaches of contracts (for contractual liability) and violation of the general principle of *alterum non laedere* that one shall not harm another (for extracontractual liability). Cognizable damages, which are discussed thoroughly in chapter ten, generally include all damages that are monetarily appraisable. ACC Art. 1068. The standard for causation is one of "adequate causation" which, oversimplified, means responsibility for "[t]hose consequences which tend to naturally and ordinarily result from actions." ACC Art. 901. As in other countries, the issue of causation is one of the most confusing and controversial in Argentine legal doctrine. Regarding the fourth element, in a products liability case, the legal standard upon which to attribute liability can be negligence or strict liability, either of which can be grounded in tort or contract theory.

The specific legal theories available to Silvia are quite similar to those already outlined for the U.S. and Germany: negligence, strict liability in tort, and a contract theory. As is true in all three of our countries of study, the lines between fault-based liability (called "subjective liability" in Argentina) and strict liability ("objective liability") have become increasingly blurred in products liability cases. The lines demarcating extracontractual liability (tort liability) and contractual liability are similarly fuzzy.

Negligence

Article 512 of the Argentine Civil Code (ACC) establishes the general definition of fault, which includes negligence. In fact, "fault" is one of the few terms actually defined in the civil code. Article 512 states that "[a] person is at fault when he fails to perform those duties which the nature of his obligations demand," specifying further that a person's "obligations correspond to the circumstances of the parties, the time, and the place." This translates in practice to the same basic standard of "reasonable care under the circumstances" that applies under the U.S. common law. Article 1109 ties in with article 512, laying down the general principle that "[a]ny person that either through fault or negligence causes harm to another is obligated to repair the injury."

As in the U.S. and Germany, the plaintiff bears the burden of proving negligence. The res ipsa loquitur doctrine, however, also applies. It does not deviate substantially from its U.S. counterpart. As strict liability has now emerged as the dominant standard in products liability cases, negligence and the res ipsa loquitur doctrine have seldom been invoked as core grounds of liability in the last decade. Most products liability cases in Argentina are going to be decided by strict liability standards. Nevertheless, negligence terminology still appears in many judicial decisions. It is not uncommon to read opinions that elaborate on some sort of negligence by the defendant, but end up finding the defendant strictly liable. See, e.g., Cámara Nacional de Apelaciones en lo Civil, Sala D [CNCiv.], 3/11/03, "Herrero Morales, Daniela et al v. Arcos Dorados S.A. McDonald's/daños y perjuicios," La Ley [L.L.] (2003-F-617) (suggesting McDonald's restaurant was negligent in not adopting measures to prevent spill of hot coffee on child, but imposing strict liability under a contractual breach of implied warranty of safety theory; reversed on extraordinary appeal to the Federal Supreme Court). Just as in the U.S., Argentine plaintiffs usually make a point of arguing that the defendants "did something wrong." Judges, in turn, seem to feel a need to justify their decisions by pointing to wrongdoing by one or more defendants. Perhaps it's partly a case of old habits die hard. Whatever the reasons, negligence wording stills pops up with frequency in Argentine products liability decisions. Plaintiffs will typically allege and argue negligence, but not expend great effort trying to prove it.

Strict Liability

Two different strict liability avenues are available in Argentine products liability: a specific statutory products liability claim and a claim arising under an article of the civil code.

Article 40 of the Consumer Protection Law. In 1993, Argentina adopted the Consumer Protection Law (CPL), which, as amended in 1998, greatly expanded the rights of consumers in products liability cases. Law No. 24.240, Sept. 22, 1993, as amended by Law No. 24.999, July 30, 1998. This statute is the most important basis of liability in products liability cases. Article 40 is the key provision. It has been unanimously construed as a strict liability provision intended to ease the ability of consumers to recover. Article 40 reads as follows:

> Liability. If the injury to the consumer is a result of the defect or risk characterizing the product or service, the producer shall be liable, along with the manufacturer, the importer, the distributor, the supplier, the salesperson, and whoever has placed his markings on the product or service. The carrier is liable if the product was damaged while he performed or attempted to perform his service. The liability is joint and several, and is not impaired if two or more parties similarly acted. One may liberate himself from liability, either wholly or in part, if he can demonstrate that the cause of the injury was foreign to him.

Article 40 is an expansive provision that imposes joint and several liability on each and every player in the commercial chain. These players can then file claims against each other in a separate lawsuit, but the injured consumer is not required to prove the degree of fault or contribution to her injuries by each of these parties. Thus, unlike in Germany, strict liability applies to nonproducing suppliers such as wholesalers and retailers, in Silvia's case, Charter and Value-Store, respectively. Note also that article 40 includes strict liability for consumer services, which has been rejected in the U.S.

The CPL applies only to those who can be labeled as "consumers." As one who purchased a food product for final consumption, Silvia is a paradigmatic consumer. Her burden would be to prove: (1) the existence of a product defect; (2) damages arising from that defect (both the existence and extent of the damages); (3) and the causal link between the product defect and the injuries she suffered. In Silvia's case, as has been observed repeatedly, proving a product defect caused by one of the defendants would be difficult. Typically, in every Argentine products liability case, the report from a court-appointed expert is the most persuasive item of evidence to the judge. Because of the impossibility of having an expert inspect the pieces of the broken jar, Silvia's case loses considerable strength. Arguably, a glass jar can break for many reasons other than a preexisting defect. But the res ipsa loquitur-type inference-drawing process or the dynamic burden of proof (see chapter seven) might be enough to get her past this proof problem.

Article 1113 of the Civil Code. In addition to the CPL, Silvia would invoke a strict liability provision from the ACC: article 1113. This article played a key role in the early development of Argentine products liability law, and it still receives prominent attention in modern cases. Much ink has been spilled by Argentine scholars and judges in attempting to ascertain the meaning of article 1113. It is difficult to try to summarize it in a few paragraphs, but, of course, we won't let that stop us from trying. Article 1113 imposes a rule that the owner, guardian or whoever else controls or makes use of a "thing" or object is responsible for damage caused by the thing.

Article 1113 applies to harm caused "with things" and harm caused "by things." In the first scenario, a human tortfeasor uses a thing to cause injury. In these cases the law presumes that the owner or guardian is liable. The plaintiff does not need to prove fault to recover. The owner or guardian may be freed from liability only by proving that he or she was not at fault. Products liability cases involve harm caused "by things." The thing is the cause of harm without direct human intervention. If the thing is deemed either defective or simply "risky," the owner or guardian is liable. The only defense is to prove the victim or a third party was at fault. It is not sufficient to escape liability for a defendant to show he was free from fault.

Article 1113 has been construed by Argentine courts and scholars to subject sellers to liability even when no specific defect can be shown, if the nature of the product renders it "risky." Risky products can include those that are risky per se, as well as products that, while not inherently risky, nevertheless present foreseeable risks to consumers, users or bystanders under particular circumstances. For instance, a firearm is a product that is risky per se. A glass food or beverage container is not risky per se but can become risky under certain foreseeable circumstances (e.g., exposure to heat, twists, shakes, etc).

As one court explained: "[A]ll things when put to practical and concrete use may attain the status of risky or dangerous things. The concept must be judged according to the concrete circumstances of each case, since many things are not intrinsically dangerous or injurious, but they attain this characteristic through their utilization or operation and end up playing an active causal role." Cámara de Trabajo en lo Civil y Comercial de Venado Tuerto [C. Civ. y Com. y Trab. Venado Tuerto], 3/13/1997, "Herrera, Francisco J. v. Ciba Geigy Argentina S.A.C.I. y F.," Jurisprudencia Argentina [J.A.] (2001-III-Síntesis). Under this broad interpretation, even a sack of cotton could be found risky under the particular circumstances of the case, subjecting the seller to liability unless the seller could prove fault by the victim or a third party. Echoing the "enterprise theory" of strict liability in the U.S., Argentine judges have concluded that since manufacturers benefit from the commercialization of products that present inevitable risks of injury, it is fair that they should be required to respond for damages when their products cause injury. Thus, in one sense, Argentine products liability is broader than U.S. law, which has rejected liability for products that are merely risky, but lack a specific defect.

An obstacle to injured consumers inherent in article 1113 that has troubled scholars and judges is that, by its terms, article 1113 applies only to those who are the "owner or guardian" of a thing. Technically, a manufacturer or other seller is not the owner or guardian of a product once the product has left the seller's control and entered the distribution chain or exited the distribution chain into the hands of the consumer.

Some courts have held and some scholars have argued (remember that because case law is not binding in civil law countries, scholarly opinions carry great weight) that manufacturers are not subject to products liability under the plain language of article 1113. The clear modern trend, however, is for courts to broadly interpret article 1113 to include manufacturers on the theory that they are the "guardian of the structure" with regard to the overall process of manufacturing and distributing their products. Another method by which some courts and scholars have reasoned their way around the explicit language of article 1113 is by looking at who was the owner or guardian of the product at the time the risk was created, rather than at the time the injury occurred. For example, in a case involving a beer bottle that exploded in the plaintiff's home, a court of appeals in Buenos Aires concluded that article 1113 would be the appropriate basis for liability against the manufacturer because "when the defect was created, the manufacturer was indeed the 'owner or guardian of the thing.'" Liability was rejected, however, on other grounds. Cámara Nacional de Apelaciones en lo Civil, Sala K [CNCiv.], 5/28/04, "Baños, Alicia v. Cervecería y Maltería Quilmes S.A.I.C.A. y G.," Jurisprudencia Argentina [J.A.] (2004-III-206).

As discussed in chapter nine, a sound defense for the defendants under both article 40 of the CPL and article 1113 of the ACC would be to prove fault by the victim (e.g., Silvia's using the Exacto knife to cut out the label) or by a third party (e.g., Norah or Marco dropping the jar or otherwise handling it improperly). Nevertheless, if the dynamic burden of proof is applied, Argentine judges would expect Penelope and the other defendants to prove that the jar was free from any defect at the time it left their respective control, which would be difficult to do. Proof of diligent quality control procedures or other diligent conduct would not, by itself, exempt the defendants from liability under the strict liability standard.

Contract Liability

In Argentina, contractual liability was developed through judicial decisions, which, as is often the case, were influenced by a wealth of doctrine (i.e., scholarly opinions). Thus, reading the sterile words of the ACC leads one nowhere in trying to understand Argentine contract law. Interpreting contract law in Argentina is a good example demonstrating why many comparative law studies fall short in trying to explain a given civil law system: they look for answers in the code that simply cannot be found. Pursuant to article 1198 of the ACC, contracts must be executed, construed, and fulfilled in "good faith." From this broad, vague provision, interpreted in conjunction with other articles of the ACC (e.g., articles 512 and 902), courts and scholars developed three theories of contractual liability that are now widely applied. These theories are: (1) the obligation to deliver a sound result (*obligación de resultado*); (2) a duty of guarantee (*obligación de garantía*); and (3) an implied warranty of safety (*obligación de seguridad*).

"Result" and "means" obligations. As to the obligation to deliver a result, civil law doctrine distinguishes between "result obligations" (*obligaciones de resultado*) and "best efforts obligations" (*obligaciones de medios*). Argentine law adopted these theories from French and Italian scholars. French law professor Rene Demogue may have been the first to clearly draw the distinction in his famous treatise on the law of obligations. Under some contractual schemes the debtor (breaching party) accepts the obligation to deliver a certain "result," meaning to achieve an objective that is duly specified or at least naturally expected by the creditor for a given sort of obligation. For instance, a consumer buying a bottle of shampoo expects that the product will have some washing effect on the consumer's hair. When these sorts of results obligations are not fulfilled, strict liability-like consequences apply. Liability arises simply from not achieving the result. There is no need for the creditor to prove the debtor's fault, and the debtor does not free himself from liability by proving that he acted diligently. Many contractual relationships involving consumer products fall under this strict liability category of result obligations.

For other types of contracts, such as service contracts, "best efforts" or "best means" obligations (*obligaciones de medios*) apply. The debtor is not obliged to deliver a certain result, but only to use all reasonable means to obtain a result. The best example of an *obligación de medios* is the relationship between physician and patient. Doctors promise to use their best efforts and state of the art scientific means to treat the patient. However, doctors neither assure patients they will be cured nor are they obliged to actually cure them. When a creditor pursues redress under a "means" obligation scheme, the plaintiff must prove the debtor was at fault. The debtor, in turn, frees himself from liability by proving diligence. Few consumer products relationships fall into the *obligaciones de medios* category.

Duty of guarantee. As refers to products liability, the duty of guarantee (*obligación de garantía*) imposes on the professional seller the obligation of delivering a product suitable for the purpose for which it was originally designed, manufactured, and sold. Generally, a kind of strict liability arises from not honoring the duty of guarantee. When a product fails to fit to its natural purpose under normal or foreseeable circumstances, seller liability follows regardless of whether the seller acted diligently. Diligence and fault are irrelevant. The resemblance between the duty of guarantee and the U.S. implied warranty of merchantability under the UCC is apparent.

Implied warranty of safety. Somewhat similar to the duty of guarantee is the implied warranty of safety (*obligación de seguridad*). The implied warranty of safety arising from this obligation means that every party to a contract is held to a duty to other contracting parties that no damage will ensue from the fulfillment of the contractual obligation. As with the obligation to deliver a result and the duty of guarantee, the obligation of safety is a strict liability obligation.

It is perhaps not surprising in light of the above descriptions that overlap exists among the obligation to deliver a sound result, the duty of guarantee, and the implied warranty of safety. In Silvia's case, a court might find any of the three applicable and, since each can result in strict liability, she would benefit no matter which one was applied.

However, in Argentina, as in Germany, contract liability runs only to parties in direct contractual privity with one another. Accordingly, Silvia's only viable contract claim would be against Value-Store, from which she purchased the peanuts. It would be a good claim *if* Silvia could show that the defect in the jar existed when she purchased the jar. Even assuming diligent conduct on the part of Value-Store, the sole fact that Silvia sustained injuries could lead to this defendant having to respond in damages.

In addition to this strict contract liability, Value-Store would fall under the blanket strict liability provision of article 40 of the CPL. Value-Store would be jointly and severally liable with Penelope and the other players in the commercial distribution chain, assuming they were found liable on Silvia's extra-contractual claims.

Conclusion

Silvia would sue all the parties in the distribution chain and pursue extra-contractual (tort) strict liability claims against them under both article 40 of the CPL and article 1113 of the ACC. She also would pursue a strict liability breach of contract claim against Value-Store. While Silvia would also allege negligence as a matter of course, she would not waste much time or effort investigating or trying to prove negligence because of the availability of strict liability.

Her main focus would be attempting to prove the existence of a preexisting defect in the jar and the injuries she sustained. Because of her inability to show evidence of a specific defect existing in the jar at the time she purchased it, application of a res ipsa loquitur-type inference-drawing process or the dynamic burden of proof likely would be critical to Silvia's ability to prevail on the merits. Just as in the U.S. and Germany, Argentine courts have gone both ways in cases like Silvia's.

In a recent case, a fifteen-year-old boy suffered an eye injury when a plastic cork popped off a bottle of cider while the safety strip restraining the cork was still partially in place. The National Civil Court of First Instance No. 47, a trial court sitting in Buenos Aires, imposed extracontractual liability on the defendant bottler under both ACC article 1113 and article 40 of the CPL. Liability was appropriate, the court said, "because there was causation proven between the injury and the inherent characteristics of the bottle." Although there was testimony by an expert that plastic corks are less able to withstand the pressure of a cider bottle than traditional corks, the court implied that it made no difference whether the injury was caused by a defect in the bottle or resulted simply because the bottle was inherently risky. Juzgado Nacional de Primera Instancia en lo Civil No. 47 [Juz. Nac. de 1ra Inst. Civ. No. 47],

8/18/04, "L. D. L. c/ Sáenz Briones y Cía S.A.I.C./daños y perjuicios," *available at* http://www.diariojudicial.com/nota.asp?IDNoticia=23097#. The court did reduce the damages by 35% because of the boy's negligence in opening the bottle with the cork pointed at his face and because his parents failed to warn him to point it away (thus, imputing the parents' fault to the boy). Because *Sáenz Briones* was a trial court decision, it generally would not be cited as authority, yet the case has been described as a "valuable precedent" by one Argentine legal scholar, whose description of the case has subsequently been cited by other scholars. *See* LILIANA SCHVARTZ, DEFENSA DE LOS DERECHOS DE LOS CONSUMIDORES Y USUARIOS 147 (García Alonso 2005). Surprised by this assertion, Sprovieri sent a paralegal to the court that decided *Sáenz Briones* to see what happened to the case on appeal. The paralegal reported back that the case settled during the appellate process. Thus, the trial court's decision in *Sáenz Briones* can, in fact, be considered "firm" or final.

However, in two other somewhat similar cases, two divisions of the National Civil Court of Appeals in Buenos Aires ruled in favor of the defendants. In *Baños v. Quilmes*, a beer bottle exploded in a home, causing eye injuries to the plaintiff, a child who was helping her mother and a domestic worker clean the house. The child was placing a basket of potatoes beneath the sink when a bottle of beer stored there exploded. The court held that the proper basis for recovery was ACC article 1113, but ruled for the defendant because the plaintiff presented insufficient evidence explaining what happened. The shards of glass were not saved and the primary witness was the domestic worker, who did not actually see the accident. Cámara Nacional de Apelaciones en lo Civil, Sala K [CNCiv.], 5/28/04, "Baños, Alicia v. Cervecería y Maltería Quilmes S.A.I.C.A. y G.," Jurisprudencia Argentina [J.A.] (2004-III-206).

Similarly, in *Roncelli v. Aguas Dadone de Argentina*, a plastic bottle of carbonated mineral water exploded in the plaintiff's home, breaking his glasses and causing lacerations to his face. The bottle was equipped with a plastic lever attached to a valve. The National Civil Court of Appeals in Buenos Aires rejected liability. Experts testified extensively that it would be difficult for such a bottle to contain a defect given the meticulous safety standards to which such bottles are submitted. The plaintiff retorted that "the safety procedures at Chernobyl were no less meticulous," but that they didn't prevent the 1986 nuclear accident at that site in the former Soviet Union from occurring. Relying primarily on the expert testimony, the court concluded there was no evidence of a defect and held in favor of the defendants. Cámara Nacional de Apelaciones en lo Civil, Sala C [CNCiv.], 6/1/04, "Roncelli, Eduardo c. Aguas Dadone de Argentina S.A.," Jurisprudencia Argentina [J.A.] (2004-IV-401). All three of the above cases are discussed in SCHVARTZ, at 146–47.

Thus, as unsatisfying as the answer may be to readers, in Argentina, just as in the U.S. and Germany, success in a case such as Silvia's depends to a large extent on how liberally or stringently the particular court is willing to construe the inferences of defect and attribution of the defect in the absence of specific proof on the issue. Application of the dynamic burden of proof, which places the burden on the party with the most information, could certainly benefit Silvia, but as explained in chapter seven, there is no way to know whether this doctrine would be applied until the trial judge rendered a final decision.

Summary Chart—Theories of Recovery

	United States	Germany	Argentina
Products liability claims are recognized in negligence, contract, and strict liability.	Yes	Yes	Yes
Through judicial interpretation, negligence, contract, and strict liability claims overlap.	Yes	Yes	Yes
Negligence claims require proof of an objective failure to exercise reasonable care under the circumstances.	Yes	Yes	Yes
In negligence claims, courts have recognized procedural devices to aid plaintiffs in proving fault and attributing fault to the defendant.	Yes	Yes	Yes

In strict liability claims, courts have recognized procedural devices to aid plaintiffs in proving a product defect and attributing the defect to the defendant.	Yes	Yes	Yes
Non-manufacturer sellers (e.g., wholesalers and retailers) are subject to liability in negligence if it can be proved.	Yes	Yes	Yes
Non-manufacturer sellers are subject to strict liability in tort.	Yes, except in states with statutes limiting liability of non-manufacturer sellers to negligence.	Not in most cases.	Yes
Contract-based liability in defective products cases is essentially strict liability.	Yes	Fault is required, but the burden of proof is shifted to the defendant.	Yes
Parties not in privity of contract with plaintiff are subject to contractual liability for breach of warranty in defective product cases	Yes	No	No
Scholarly opinions carry great weight in fashioning the law, including theories of recovery.	No	Yes	Yes

CHAPTER 9

DEFENSES

We've seen that Silvia has three closely parallel theories of recovery available to her in each country: negligence, strict liability, and breach of contract. Application of these theories also functions similarly for the most part, with each country recognizing either formal or informal mechanisms that work to ease or shift the burden of proof for plaintiffs like Silvia in cases where, if the normal burden of proof applied, the plaintiff usually would lose. Now the subject turns to defenses, where we again find substantial convergence in approach among the U.S., Germany, and Argentina.

United States

In discussing defenses to Silvia's claims under U.S. law, one must distinguish between true "affirmative defenses" and defense strategies for attacking the plaintiff's case that do not constitute affirmative defenses. The difference is more than semantic. Defendants bear the same burden of proof with regard to affirmative defenses as plaintiffs bear with regard to claims. They must prove the facts supporting each element of the defense by a preponderance of the evidence (more likely than not) standard. To the contrary, when a defendant simply attacks the plaintiff's case, the defendant bears no burden of proof. Rather, the defense strategy is aimed at persuading a fact-finder that the plaintiff has not met *the plaintiff's* burden of proof as to one or more elements of her claims.

The line between what constitutes a true affirmative defense and other defense strategies is sometimes blurry. Because the failure to plead an affirmative defense constitutes a waiver of the defense, even veteran trial lawyers err on the side of pleading many defense strategies as affirmative defenses even when they do not technically qualify as such. Rule 8(c) of the Federal Rules of Civil Procedure identifies the following affirmative defenses: accord and satisfaction, arbitration and award, assumption of risk, contributory negligence, discharge in bankruptcy, duress, estoppel, failure of consideration, fraud, il-

141

legality, injury by fellow servant, laches, license, payment, release, res judi-cata, statute of frauds, statute of limitations, and waiver.

In Silvia's case, the only viable affirmative defense is that of contributory negligence. Today, the defense often travels under the name "comparative neg-ligence" or "comparative fault," but as seen from Rule 8(c), the defense is still technically called "contributory negligence."

Contributory Negligence/Product Misuse

The defendants would raise as an affirmative defense that Silvia was con-tributorily negligent in handling the jar; specifically, in using the Exacto razor to remove the rebate coupon from the jar. They might also raise "product mis-use" as a separate defense, but, properly viewed, product misuse is simply one type of contributory negligence. U.S. courts have been all over the map in how they treat product misuse as a defense in products liability cases. Some courts have treated product misuse as a type of contributory negligence to be ap-portioned under modern comparative fault principles, some have treated it as no defense at all if the misuse was foreseeable, and some have treated it as a complete bar to recovery.

The clear modern trend is to treat all varieties of product misuse as a type of plaintiff fault to be considered and apportioned by the jury on a percent-age basis in comparison to the defendant's fault or product defect, unless the misuse is so unforeseeable or egregious as to negate causation or a finding of product defect. The *Products Liability Restatement* adopted the majority ap-proach in section 17, which provides that a plaintiff's recovery can be reduced if the conduct of the plaintiff combines with a product defect to cause harm. RESTATEMENT (THIRD) OF TORTS: PRODUCTS LIABILITY § 17 (1998). A com-ment adds "that some courts accord different treatment to different types of plaintiff conduct, but that the majority position is that all forms of a plain-tiff's failure to exercise reasonable care are to be considered in apportioning responsibility under comparative fault principles." *Id.* § 17 cmt. d.

Contributory negligence is a failure by the plaintiff to exercise reasonable care under the circumstances. Just as defendants have a legal duty to exercise reasonable care to protect others from risks, plaintiffs have a duty to exercise reasonable care to protect themselves from risks. Until several decades ago, contributory negligence was a complete defense to a negligence claim. If the defendant proved the plaintiff's negligence contributed to the injury, even if only to a small degree, the plaintiff was completely barred from recovery. The case credited with, or blamed for, the "no recovery" rule of contributory neg-ligence is *Butterfield v. Forester*, 103 Eng. Rep. 926 (King's Bench 1809), in which the plaintiff rode his horse into a pole that the defendant had extended across a portion of the road while making repairs to his house. Although the defendant was negligent in extending the pole into the road, the court barred the plaintiff from recovery because the plaintiff was also negligent in riding too fast and failing to see the pole. This harsh rule was carried over to the U.S. and at one time was recognized by all U.S. states.

Today, all but four U.S. states (Alabama, Maryland, North Carolina, Virginia) have altered this "all or nothing" result by adopting, either judicially or by legislation, comparative fault principles that call on the fact-finder to apportion fault between the plaintiff and defendant on a percentage basis. If the plaintiff is found to be at fault, she can still recover, although her damages will be reduced by her percentage of fault (subject to the 50% cut-off rule discussed below). Although courts have struggled with the semantic and conceptual difficulties of applying comparative fault to strict liability claims (how does one compare the plaintiff's "fault" to the defendant's "product defect"?), the issue is now well settled. Comparative fault is a defense in products liability actions, even as to claims grounded in strict liability.

Two basic systems of comparative fault exist: pure and modified. Under a pure system, followed in about a dozen U.S. states, including Florida, the plaintiff is entitled to recover her damages reduced by her percentage of fault, regardless of the percentage. A plaintiff found to be 90% at fault, for example, can still recover 10% of her damages. In a modified system, the plaintiff is entitled to recover her damages reduced by her percentage of fault, unless her fault equals or exceeds 50%, in which case the claim is barred. About twenty states bar recovery if the plaintiff's fault is *greater than* the defendant's fault, while about a dozen states bar recovery if the plaintiff's fault is *equal to or greater than* the defendant's fault. In other words, the only difference in states following modified comparative negligence is in the 50–50 situation where the plaintiff's fault is found to be equal to the defendant's fault. *See generally* Owen § 201, at 505 (describing the different systems of comparative fault and giving the above estimates as to the number of U.S. states adhering to each system). Thus, if a jury found Silvia was 50% at fault, she would recover: (1) 50% of her damages in a pure comparative fault state like Florida; (2) 50% of her damages in a *greater than* comparative fault state; and (3) nothing in an *equal to or greater than* comparative fault state.

Because contributory negligence is an affirmative defense, the defendants would have to raise the defense in their answers and prove the facts supporting the defense by a preponderance of the evidence at trial. Whether Silvia's conduct in using the Exacto knife constituted a failure to exercise reasonable care, whether it caused the jar to shatter, and, if so, whether a non-defective jar would have shattered as a result of such conduct normally would be questions for the jury. Silvia would argue that using a razor knife to remove rebate labels is foreseeable consumer conduct and rely on her materials expert to attempt to persuade the jury that a non-defective jar would not have shattered because of the Exacto knife. Indeed, Silvia's lawyer might argue Penelope, the manufacturer, was negligent to use a rebate label on a jar that required a razor knife to remove it. If the jury decided Silvia was negligent, her recovery would be reduced by her percentage of fault.

In the *Welge* case, the trial court granted summary judgment to defendants because the plaintiff did not exclude possible causes for the jar's breaking other than a defect. In particular, defendants pointed to the fact that the plaintiff's roommate had used an Exacto knife to remove a portion of the label necessary to obtain a rebate. The U.S. Court of Appeals for the Seventh Circuit reversed. Regarding the use of the Exacto knife, the court stated that "nothing is more common or, we should have thought, more harmless than to use a knife or a razor blade to remove a label from a jar or bottle," analogizing the activity to the common practice of using a knife or razor to remove a price label from a wine bottle. 17 F.3d at 210–11. Additionally, to the extent using the knife could be considered product misuse, the court said that the defendant retailer, by participating in the rebate promotion, invited the misuse. "Invited misuse," Judge Posner wrote, "is no defense to a products liability claim. Invited misuse is not misuse." *Id.* at 211. Similar reasoning could be applied to Silvia's case, although another court might view the case differently. Such fact-specific reasoning would not constitute binding precedent on any court.

"No Defect" Finger-Pointing Strategy

Apart from asserting the affirmative defense of contributory negligence, the defendants would attempt to show more generally that the defect in the jar causing it to shatter did not exist at the time the product was in their respective control. This strategy would not constitute an affirmative defense, but rather an attack on the plaintiff's ability to prove the necessary elements of her claims, which includes proving that the product had a defect at the time it left the hands of the entity upon which Silvia attempts to pin liability. Pursuant to this downstream "finger-pointing defense," Levington, for example, would point down the chain and assert the defect was created after the jar left its control. The other defendants would do likewise. Because the defendants might benefit from a joint defense strategy, this finger pointing could take the form of each defendant generally pointing away from itself rather than specifically at another defendant. The defendants would be united, however, in pointing their blame fingers at Silvia, Norah, and Marco.

The advantage of such a defense strategy is that it does not require the defendants to prove anything. Silvia carries the burden of proving the defect existed when the jar left the control of the respective defendants. The defendants would only have to raise sufficient questions to persuade the judge or jury that Silvia failed to meet her burden of proof. Remember, however, that the negligence doctrine of res ipsa loquitur and a similar inference-drawing process for strict liability claims could work to relax Silvia's traditional burden of proof.

Germany

Under German law, defenses available against Silvia depend to some extent on the basis of the particular claim. Most defenses apply to all claims, but some apply only to specific claims. Let's first address the general defenses applicable to all claims.

General Attack on the Plaintiff's Case

The most basic and widespread defense strategy is simply to contest the plaintiff's factual allegations and, thus, deny liability. Generally, the plaintiff bears the burden of proof for most of the necessary facts supporting her claims. Thus, defendants would seek to avoid liability by arguing that Silvia failed to prove the facts supporting one or more essential elements of her claims. This attack could cover the gamut of factual issues present in most products liability cases. Thus, defendants would contest that the product was defective or, if defective, that the defect was the cause of Silvia's injury. Also, although there are no facts suggesting that Silvia's injuries were aggravated by a preexisting condition, that is an issue that the defendants' lawyers typically would investigate.

Attacking the plaintiff's case is a comfortable strategy in most cases. Here, however, because of the burden-shifting devices previously described (see chapter eight), Levington and Penelope in particular would need to do quite a bit more in fashioning and pursuing their defense strategy. As previously explained, Charter (the wholesale distributor) and Value-Store (the retailer) do not have much liability exposure under German law.

Contributory Negligence

Just as in the U.S., the defendants would be likely to raise the defense that Silvia acted negligently and contributed mainly or at least partly to her dam-

age. Contributory negligence is an oft-used defense in Germany. It is estimated, for example, that the defense comes into play in 80% of all motor vehicle accident cases. *See* Jörg Fedtke & Ulrich Magnus, *Contributory Negligence
Under German Law, in* UNIFICATION OF TORT LAW: CONTRIBUTORY NEGLI-
GENCE 76 (Ulrich Magnus & Miguel Martín-Casals eds., 2004).

The fundamental provision for contributory negligence under German law
is section 254(1) of the German Civil Code (GCC), which states: "If the negligence of the injured party contributed to causing the damage, the obligation
to compensate and the extent of the compensation due shall depend on the
circumstances, in particular on how predominantly the damage was caused
by the one or the other party." Section 254 would apply to Silvia's general tort
claim under section 823 of the GCC.

It also would apply to her claim under the Product Liability Act (PLA). Section 6(1) of PLA provides for reduction of the amount of damages in the event
of the plaintiff's contributory fault with regard to strict liability claims brought
under the act, but it specifically incorporates section 254 of the GCC as the
operative provision, stating: "If the injured party by his own fault contributed
to the origin of the damage, section 254 [GCC] applies...." Here, we see a
good example of the point made earlier. Germany's implementation of the EU
Product Liability Directive, pursuant to which the PLA was adopted, was
specifically made with the goal of not wanting to dramatically change prior
law. Also observe that, as in the U.S., the German legal system applies the defense of contributory negligence to strict liability claims, setting aside the in-
commensurability problem of comparing the plaintiff's fault against the defect in the defendant's product.

There is an almost identical parallel in the development of the contributory fault defense in Germany as compared with the U.S. Just as in the U.S.,
early in German law, before the GCC was established in 1900, contributory
fault on the part of the plaintiff to any degree was a complete bar to recovery.
This all-or-nothing rule was known as the *Culpakompensation*, or culpa-compensation, doctrine. The adoption of the GCC, in particular section 254, put
an end to the culpa-compensation doctrine.

In modern times, application of section 254 usually results in an apportionment of damages on a percentage basis if it is found that the plaintiff's
fault contributed to the injury. As is true in most civil law countries, in Germany the defense of contributory negligence resembles the "pure" approach
to comparative negligence in the U.S., rather than the "modified" approach.
No automatic percentage cut-off point exists at which the plaintiff is barred
from recovery. Nevertheless, a plaintiff who was disproportionately at fault
can be denied all recovery. This is apparent from the code itself. Section 254(1)

expressly speaks both to the issue of *whether* the defendant should be obligated to compensate the plaintiff at all and to the *extent* of such compensation. *See* Fedtke & Magnus, at 75. Conversely, if the plaintiff's fault contribution is small, the defendant might bear full liability. In cases of co-equal fault, damages will be apportioned on a 50–50 basis. Thus, depending on the amount of Silvia's fault, if any, contributory negligence under German law could operate as a complete defense, a partial defense, or no defense at all. As in the U.S., the defendants bear the burden of both pleading and proving the defense of contributory negligence.

In Silvia's case, the defendants would assert that she negligently misused the jar when cutting the rebate label from it with the Exacto knife, arguing that the knife caused a micro-crack that weakened the jar. Alternatively, it could be argued that the knife contributed to the injury by worsening a pre-existing defect, so as to make the knife a superseding proximate cause of the glass breaking. The court probably would appoint an expert witness to report on whether the use of the Exacto knife under the circumstances of Silvia's case would cause a non-defective jar to shatter. However, remember what was said back in chapter five. Given the absence of discovery mechanisms in Germany, it is quite possible that Silvia's use of the Exacto knife would never become known to the defendants.

Assuming the defendants became aware of the use of the Exacto knife, two other aspects of the case weaken a contributory negligence defense. First, Penelope conducted the rebate promotion and, as noted by the U.S. court that decided the *Welge* case, effectively "invited" customers to cut the labels from the jars using a knife. Relatedly, Silvia could argue that many other consumers no doubt used a knife to cut rebate labels from Penelope jars without incident. How else could they be removed? The fact that these other jars did not shatter, while Silvia's did, would strengthen her claim that the cause of the shattering was not the knife, but more likely a manufacturing defect in the jar.

Finger-Pointing Strategy

The strategy of pointing fingers at others described for the U.S. would also apply under German law. Any party might assert that the product was not defective at the time it was within its control and that someone else damaged it after the jar left the particular defendant's organizational sphere. Thus, Levington might point down the distribution chain to Penelope, Charter, Value-Store, Silvia, Norah, and Marco as possible suspects. Penelope might do the same thing.

In part to limit the misuse of this strategy, however, the Federal Supreme Court developed the *Befundsicherungspflicht*—the producer's duty to control product quality and to keep records of the status of its products. If the *Befundsicherungspflicht* were applied, the finger-pointing strategy for Levington and Penelope would be severely limited. As discussed in the previous chapter, breach of the duty of the *Befundsicherungspflicht* to keep records of quality control and other records relating to the condition of the producer's products while they are in the producer's control creates a presumption that the product was defective at the time it left the producer's sphere. A similar presumption can arise in practical effect under the provisions of the Product Liability Act, elaborated on below.

Product Liability Act Defenses to Strict Liability Claim

In addition to the defenses discussed above, which apply regardless of the theory of the claim, the PLA codifies several defenses to strict liability claims brought under the act. Pursuant to section 1(2), the manufacturer is not liable if:

1. The manufacturer did not place the product into circulation;
2. It can be assumed under all the circumstances that the defect did not exist when the product was placed in circulation;
3. The manufacturer did not produce the product for sale or any other form of distribution involving economic gain;
4. The defect resulted from the product being in compliance with compulsory design regulations in place at the time of marketing; or
5. It was not possible to detect the product defect under the state of science and technology existing at the time the product was placed on the market.

The defenses in subsections 1, 3, and 4 are not applicable to Silvia's case. The defense provided for in subsection 2, however, will be vigorously asserted by Levington and Penelope, both of which would argue that the defect arose after they released the product into the chain of distribution. Unfortunately for Levington and Penelope, as discussed in chapter eight, the PLA places the burden of proof on the defendants with regard to this defense.

The PLA places the general burden of proof on the injured party to prove the existence of a product defect and that the defect caused injury, but makes an explicit exception with regard to disputes arising under paragraph 2 above. If a producer contends that the defect did not exist when the product was placed into circulation, it bears the burden of proof as to that issue. Section 1(4) explicitly provides: "The person who has suffered the damage has the burden of proving the defect and its causal connection with the damage. If it is in dispute whether the obligation to pay compensation is excluded according to [paragraph 2 above], the burden of proof lies with the producer."

While it is not technically impossible for the defendants to carry this burden, the Federal Supreme Court has made it very difficult to do so, as shown in the *Second Mineral Water Bottle* case, where, despite evidence that the defendant followed state of the art quality control procedures, the court held that the defendant failed to carry the burden of proving the exploding mineral water bottle was not defective when it left the defendant's sphere.

Paragraph 5 above refers to what is known in Germany and the rest of the European Union as the "developmental risk defense." PLA § 1(2)5. The same defense travels in the U.S. under the label "state of the art defense." The defense recognizes that while product makers are expected to observe up-to-date technology and science in designing, manufacturing, and marketing their products, they are not responsible for risks that could not be detected or eliminated under the state of technology and scientific knowledge available at the time of manufacture or marketing. Thus, if a defendant proves that at the time the product was placed on the market it was not possible to detect or eliminate the defect under the existing state of science and technology, the defendant is not liable.

Theoretically, the developmental risk defense could be applied to a case such as Silvia's. Although the risk of a glass container breaking is well-known, it probably is not scientifically feasible to develop a quality control system that is one hundred percent effective in eliminating the risk. Regardless of the degree of care exercised, in mass-producing and distributing glass containers, a defective unit is going to slip through from time to time. In an important portion of the *Second Mineral Water Bottle* case, however, the Federal Supreme Court held that the developmental risk defense does not apply to manufacturing defects. Rather, the court held that only design defects fall within the scope of the defense.

This portion of the decision has been questioned as being in conflict with article 7(e) of the EU Product Liability Directive, the article mandating the adoption of the developmental risk defense. The court in the *Second Mineral Water Bottle* case declined to refer the issue to the Court of Justice of the European Communities, which is the procedure when an interpretation of a concept of European Community law is in dispute. While the decision is not binding on other courts, it has been a very influential opinion.

It should be noted that the court's decision holding that the developmental risk defense does not apply to manufacturing defects is consistent with U.S. law. The state of the art defense in the U.S. has generally been limited to cases involving design defects (where the defendant asserts that the method of eliminating the risk was unknown or scientifically unknowable under the state of science and technology existing at the time of manufacture) and informational defect cases involving failure to warn (where the defendant asserts the risk was unknown or scientifically unknowable under the state of science and technology existing at the time of manufacture).

In short, Levington and Penelope could face difficulty in asserting viable specific defenses to Silvia's claim under German law apart from the general contesting of her factual assertions.

Argentina

Within the broad concept of "defenses," the Argentine system—as may be the case in most Latin American jurisdictions—distinguishes between "defenses" and "exceptions." "Defenses" is the generic label for all possible responses from the defendant while "exceptions" are specific, named defenses.

There really is no essential difference between a defense and an exception other than the desire of legislators to have exceptions addressed and decided at the introductory stage of the lawsuit. Exceptions are listed in article 347 of the National Code of Civil Procedure (NCCP). One of the most commonly argued exceptions is the "legal defect in stating a complaint," which is similar to a motion to dismiss the complaint for failure to state a claim in the U.S. If the exception is recognized as valid, the court usually will give the plaintiff a chance to attempt to repair the defect. To avoid succumbing to this exception, a complaint must: (1) identify the plaintiff and defendants by name and address; (2) explicitly state the relief sought; (3) state the facts upon which the claim depends, "explaining them clearly"; (4) give a succinct statement of the party's claims; and (5) contain a clear demand for the amount claimed, unless it is impossible to do so (as is usually the case in personal injury cases). *See* NCCP Art. 330.

Another substantial exception is the "lack of legitimation" (*falta de legitimación*), an argument equivalent to lack of standing, by which the defendant asserts that the plaintiff is not the person legally entitled to claim (without reference to the merits of the claim) or that the defendant is not a proper defendant (e.g., the defendant has been named by mistake and has no relationship to the matter in dispute). Other exceptions include lack of jurisdiction in the intervening court, res judicata, pending action, and settlement.

Apart from the "exceptions," the defendant can advance "defenses." Defenses essentially are all the allegations and arguments that the defendant makes in opposition to the plaintiff's claim. There is no way to concretely label these defenses, but in products liability cases they can include issues such as assumption of risk, victim fault, and product misuse. *See, e.g.,* Cámara Nacional de Apelaciones en lo Civil, Sala H [CNCiv.], 2/26/01, "Lodoli, Roberto v. Massalín Particulares S.A.," LexisNexis Argentina, Lexis No. 30010404 (stating that smokers assume the risk of consuming a potentially harmful product); Cámara Nacional de Apelaciones en lo Civil, Sala H [CNCiv.], 8/31/01, "Koch, Eva. v. Medtronic S.A.," Revista de Responsabilidad Civil y Seguros [RCyS], LexisNexis Argentina, Lexis No. 10/8916 (finding plaintiff at fault for failing to monitor a medical device after the product's projected life expectancy had passed); Cámara de San Martín en lo Civil y lo Comercial, Sala II [C. Civ. y Com. San Martín], 12/5/98, "Zarate, Antonio v. Cerámica Tropezón S.A./daños y perjuicios," LexisNexis Argentina, Lexis No. 14/11810 (discussing product misuse as a way to exempt manufacturer from liability).

In theory, a defendant can limit his answer to denying the plaintiff's factual allegations and all liability. However, this might prove to be a bad strategy. Although it is true that a defendant can sometimes succeed by simply denying liability, experience shows that defendants in Argentine products liability cases do better when they pursue a comprehensive defense strategy that includes offering a sound alternative factual scenario and addressing the core allegations of the plaintiff's complaint.

We previously listed the four essential elements of an Argentine tort claim: (1) unlawful conduct; (2) damages; (3) causation; and (4) a legal standard to attribute a damaging consequence to a given person. Most of what would be considered defenses under Argentine law amount to raising questions about whether one or more of these elements are unsatisfied. In Silvia's case, these arguments might unfold as follows:

Unlawful conduct. As the law has developed, a manufacturer behaves "unlawfully" within the meaning of this civil law concept when it puts into the stream of commerce a defective or risky product that injures a person. At the core of this element is the existence of a product defect.

In Silvia's case, the defendants would argue and attempt to prove that the peanuts jar was not defective. Ideally, this defense would focus on the particular jar that injured Silvia. Given that the jar is not available for examination, however, the defendants would have to resort to alleging and attempting to prove that a defect in this *type* of jar would be impossible or at least highly improbable. The court would appoint an expert on this issue. Levington and Penelope would enlist consulting experts to supplement the report of the court-appointed expert. These experts might provide information about matters such as the defendants' quality control procedures and scientific information concerning the structure and materials of the jar. For instance, Sprovieri was part of a defense team that vigorously produced scientific evidence to successfully rebut allegations that silicone breast implants were defective or inherently dangerous. *See* Cámara Nacional de Apelaciones en lo Civil, Sala A [CNCiv.], 3/8/06, "Juarez de Mas, María Esther v. Dow Corning de Argentina S.A.I.C. et al./daños y perjuicios," La Ley [L.L.] (2006-C-Supplement 6/7/06-9).

As useful as this approach would be for the defendants, establishing the existence of a particular defect is not essential in all cases. As covered in chapter eight, per article 1113 of the Argentine Civil Code (ACC) and article 40 of the Consumer Protection Law (CPL), strict liability applies both to defective products and "risky" products, which could include Silvia's jar. In one sense, this means that distributors of products deemed to be risky serve as a kind of insurer for injured consumers. As those businesses benefit from the lucrative activity of putting the risky products into the stream of commerce, it is thought to be fair as a matter of policy to hold them accountable for injuries caused by the products, even when a specific defect cannot be shown. As Argentine legal doctrine does not distinguish between avoidable or unavoidable product risks, often the best defense strategy is to argue and prove that the product poses no substantial risk to consumers. This may be a sound defense in Silvia's case. A glass jar is not a risky product per se, although it obviously can pose some risk in given circumstances.

If an absence of defect and/or risk would be sound defenses for Levington and Penelope, the distributor and retailer (Charter and Value-Store) would be well-advised to adapt their positions to accord with those defenses, emphasizing their limited roles. Both Charter and Value-Store should allege that their participation was limited to simply passing the product down the commercial chain. Further, Charter and Value-Store would allege that they handled the jar with all due care. Nevertheless, they could still face strict liability under the theories previously discussed in chapter eight.

Damages. More detailed commentary about damages is still to come in chapter ten. Here, it can simply be noted that defendants would be likely to contest nearly every aspect of the plaintiff's claimed damages. Normally the defendants would devote a significant portion of the briefs filed in support of their answers to the issue of damages.

Causation. Causation is the third prerequisite for a successful claim. Although we, in effect, "wrote causation out of the case" as an issue back in chapter seven, it is necessary to reintroduce the issue here because in Argentina, causation is the issue under which Silvia's alleged contributory negligence would arise. Per article 1111 of the ACC, damage caused by the victim's own fault should not be borne by third parties. This rule, coupled with other relevant civil code provisions (*see* ACC Arts. 1109, 1113, 1198), allows judges to reduce compensation in a percentage equal to that of the victim's fault.

Technically, rather than comparing "fault," Argentine practice focuses on comparing the causal contribution of each party. For clarity, we could call it "comparative causation" rather than "comparative fault," although the principle exists in Argentina under the official name of "concurrent liability." It is similar to the approach taken in some U.S. strict liability products cases in which courts have opted for a comparative causation analysis in place of a comparative fault analysis to get around the conceptual and semantic difficulties of comparing the plaintiff's fault to the defect in the defendant's product. *See, e.g.,* Murray v. Fairbanks Morse, 610 F.2d 149, 158–61 (3d Cir. 1979) (after addressing the conceptual and semantic problem in a strict liability products case that "[t]here is no proven faulty conduct of the defendant to compare with the faulty conduct of the plaintiff," the court agreed that a comparative causation approach is a more precise conceptual analysis).

In practice, however, a comparative causation analysis leads to the same results that would be reached by applying a comparative fault analysis. Judges will reduce the plaintiff's damages on a percentage basis according to the judge's determination of the degree to which the plaintiff's fault contributed to or caused her injuries. In a case such as Silvia's, for example, the court might conclude that Silvia contributed to causing 10–20% of her damages. Her use of the Exacto knife could serve as a basis for such a conclusion. For example, in *L. D. L. c/ Sáenz Briones*, a minor was injured by a popping cork while opening a bottle of cider. The court reduced his damages by 35% due to his own fault (opening the bottle while it was pointed at his face) and that of his parents (not properly supervising or instructing him). Juzgado Nacional de Primera Instancia en lo Civil No. 47 [Juz. Nac. de 1ra Inst. Civ. No. 47], 8/18/04, "L. D. L. c/ Sáenz Briones y Cía S.A.I.C./daños y perjuicios," *available at* http://www.diariojudicial.com/nota.asp?IDNoticia=23097#. Should the court determine that liability apportionment is the most just result, such apportionment would apply to all of Silvia's theories, including strict liability. Defendants would carry the burden of proving their allegation of Silvia's concurring liability.

As alleging and proving an interruption in the causal link between product and damage would be so important, the defendants would be likely to investigate the factual scenario and even the plaintiff's background to form a basis for attacking Silvia's allegations, although the absence of discovery would hinder this effort. The defendants would at least try to form a basis for arguing that either Silvia or her friends mistreated the jar in a way that caused it to shatter. Silvia's cutting the jar with an Exacto knife would be a good basis for alleging victim fault, but as in Germany, it is possible the defendants would never learn about the knife issue.

Legal standard to attribute a damaging consequence to a given person. Finally, with regard to the fourth essential element, the defendants would essentially try to show "we weren't at fault and we didn't do it," just as in the U.S. and Germany. As analyzed in chapter eight, defendants in a case like Silvia's could be placed in a position where they would more or less have to prove someone else was at fault to avoid liability. This would be true if the court deemed Silvia's peanuts jar to be a "risky" product. Under the "strict liability for risky products" judicial interpretation of ACC Art. 1113, defendants are freed from strict liability only by proving the harm resulted from the conduct of a third party or from the victim's fault. Likewise, pursuant to article 40 of the CPL, strict liability does not apply if the defendants can prove they were "alien" to the damage. The same standard applies to contractual strict liability. Pointing fingers at other defendants is also sometimes invoked as a strategy. Experience, however, shows that a lack of coordination among defendants in this regard may end up hurting all of them.

Summary Chart—Defenses

	United States	Germany	Argentina
Defendants bear the burden of proving defenses they raise.	Yes	Yes	Yes
A prominent defense strategy in manufacturing defect cases is for defendants to point fingers at others as the most likely defect-creating suspects.	Yes	Yes	Yes
Comparative fault by the plaintiff may reduce or entirely bar recovery in a products liability case.	Yes	Yes	Yes, but uses "comparative causation" analysis.

CHAPTER 10

DAMAGES, ATTORNEYS' FEES AND COSTS

How much is it worth in money damages to suffer a cut wound such as Silvia's? How much is it worth, both tangibly and intangibly, to experience not only the pain, trauma, and expense of the incident itself, but to go through life with a 20–25% disability in one's dominant hand and wrist and an overall 5% body disability? How much is it worth in lost earning capacity or the ability to perform household services? How much is it worth to be unable to play the piano, or at least not play it as well, an endeavor Silvia has pursued for most of her life?

We devote substantial attention to the damages issue because, when all is said and done, the most important "question of comparative law" for Silvia and all real tort plaintiffs and defendants is the ultimate amount of the monetary recovery. This may sound insensitive or even crass. A student reader noted indignantly on a pre-publication draft: "The most important question for the plaintiff will be the quality of her life!" That's true, of course. But the tort systems in all three nations rely on monetary awards as the imperfect means to attempt to restore plaintiffs to the quality of life they enjoyed before the injury. Putting a definite price tag on Silvia's case is impossible, although this chapter does offer projected "ballpark" recovery amounts for each country to give readers an approximate frame of reference. One conclusion appears quite certain. Were Silvia to prevail on the merits, she would reap her largest award in the U.S.

Before proceeding to the country summaries, an introduction to the issue of damages provides context within which to process the specific country rules. Also included in this chapter is a discussion of attorneys' fees and costs, which are inextricably intertwined with the question of damages. The manner in which responsibility for attorneys' fees and costs is assigned has a direct effect on plaintiffs' recoveries, the ability to obtain counsel, and the level of litigation.

Many areas of convergence have been observed in the products liability law of the U.S., Germany, and Argentina, including similarities in burdens of proof, theories of recovery, and defenses. To these we can add similarity in the types of tort damages available in the three countries, with one major exception: punitive damages. U.S. law allows punitive damages to punish particularly wrongdoing defendants and deter future wrongful conduct. Punitive damages are not available in civil law countries. Punitive damages are not an issue in Silvia's case, but, given that they represent the largest difference in the law of damages among the three countries, a brief discussion of them is warranted.

Punitive damages. The issue of punitive damages is a controversial one in the U.S., in part because large punitive damages awards generate widespread media attention. A majority of U.S. states have passed legislation imposing restrictions on punitive damages, and the U.S. Supreme Court has weighed in on the issue several times in the past twenty years. In 1996, the Court squarely held that excessive punitive damages awards violate the due process clause of the federal constitution. BMW of North America, Inc. v. Gore, 517 U.S. 559 (1996).

Punitive damages are awarded in only a small percentage of cases. U.S. Justice Department statistics show that juries awarded punitive damages in 5% of all tort cases decided in state courts in 2001 in which the plaintiff was the prevailing party, a figure that has remained relatively stable over the years. Some punitive damages awards are shockingly large, but most laypersons probably are unaware that large punitive damages awards often get reduced or eliminated when challenged in post-verdict motions or on appeal. As just one example, in *Boeken v. Philip Morris, Inc.*, a California jury awarded the plaintiff a whopping $3 billion in punitive damages in a tobacco lawsuit in 2001. The trial judge reduced the punitive damages to $100 million. An appellate court reduced the amount further to $50 million, which was roughly nine times the compensatory award of $5.5 million. Boeken v. Philip Morris, Inc., 26 Cal. Rptr. 3d 638 (Cal. Ct. App. 2005). The U.S. Supreme Court let the reduced award stand by refusing to review it. Thus, the final punitive award was only 1/60th of the amount that most people read or heard about. On the other hand, $50 million is still a lot of money. Most punitive damages awards are much smaller. In 2001, the median punitive award in state court tort trials was $25,000.

Plaintiffs must prove some type of particularly reprehensible conduct by the defendant to recover punitive damages. The precise language of this aggravated fault standard varies from state to state, but it generally requires proof of some type of willful or malicious conduct. The U.S. Supreme Court set forth the following factors to consider in assessing the reprehensibility of a defendant's conduct for purposes of awarding and calculating punitive damages: (1) whether the harm suffered was physical as opposed to merely economic; (2) whether the conduct evinced an indifference to or a reckless disregard of the health or safety of others; (3) whether the target of the conduct was financially vulnerable; (4) whether the conduct involved repeated actions or was an isolated incident; and (5) whether the harm was the result of intentional malice, trickery or deceit, or mere accident. State Farm Mutual Automobile Ins. Co. v. Campbell, 538 U.S. 408, 419 (2003).

The facts of Silvia's case, as we know them, do not show any reprehensible conduct by the defendants. We could easily hypothesize additional facts that would support a punitive damages award, such as, for example, facts showing that Levington, the jar maker, knew of a defect in its jars and actively concealed such information. But we will proceed on the assumption that punitive damages would not be available to Silvia.

Compensatory damages. With regard to *compensatory* damages, all three countries recognize the same basic components of compensable harm. The big difference is in the size of the awards. U.S. damages awards in products liability cases are substantially higher than in other countries. According to data compiled by Jury Verdict Research (JVR), a company that collects and analyzes verdict and settlement data, the median compensatory recovery in U.S. products liability cases in 2003 was $2 million. Based on more limited data, and taking into account only jury verdicts (i.e., omitting settlements), U.S. Department of Justice figures show lower median jury awards for products liability cases than the JVR figures. Specifically, Justice Department numbers show a median jury verdict of $450,000 in products liability trials in state courts in the nation's seventy-five largest counties in 2001, and a $350,000 median jury verdict in products liability trials in the U.S. District Courts in 2002–03. Even these amounts, however, are larger than what could be expected in other countries.

Comparatist Mathias Reimann has observed that products liability awards in countries throughout the world are vastly lower than in the U.S. Although some economically advanced systems provide fairly substantial awards, "others are incredibly cheap." Reimann, at 808. He notes that in no jurisdiction outside the U.S. can a plaintiff recover more than $300,000 for noneconomic damages, and that while awards for pain and suffering are growing outside the U.S., "they started from such a low point that they have a long way to go before they can come even close to United States levels." Id. at 809.

Explanations for discrepancies in damages. Many reasons, too numerous and complex to be analyzed in detail here, help explain the damages disparities. Volumes could be written simply about the cultural differences among persons of different nations that influence their views about personal injury damages. Moreover, it must be appreciated that the law of damages is tied to substantive law and cannot be understood in isolation from it. *See* MARKESI-

NIS ET AL., at 200 (asserting that the law of damages cannot be separated from substantive law giving rise to rights of recovery and suggesting "that the substantive law of a particular system may be explicable by the fact that its law of damages is less generous than others").

Juries. Some concrete observations can be made. It is widely believed that having juries rather than judges decide cases leads to higher damages awards in the U.S. common law system. "A common perception," wrote John Fleming, "prevalent especially among critics of the jury, is a bias against corporate and other defendants credited with deep pockets." FLEMING, at 111. Fleming observed that to the extent such bias is reflected in larger awards, it may be attributable to a "popular, latent hostility against powerful interests widely viewed as oppressors and exploiters of the common man." *Id.* On the civil law side, Markesinis and colleagues assert that leaving damages determinations to civil servant judges possessed of middle class values and economic perceptions, rather than to populist juries, helps explain lower damages awards in European civil law nations. MARKESINIS ET AL., at 17. As seen in this chapter, civil law judges, at least in Germany and Argentina, do indeed value tort damages more consistently, objectively, and in lower amounts than do juries in the U.S.

Even within the U.S., data bear out the assumption that juries award higher damages than judges, although the discrepancy is perhaps smaller than one would think. Justice Department figures show that the median award for state court tort jury trials in 2001 was $28,000, while the median award in bench trials (trial by judge only) was $23,000. Tort plaintiffs actually won a higher percentage of bench trials than jury trials, prevailing in 65% of state court bench trials compared to 51% of jury trials. Juries awarded punitive damages in 5% of 2001 state court tort cases in which the plaintiff won, while judges awarded punitive damages in 11% of cases. These comparisons suggest that damages awards in the U.S. are the product of institutional and cultural factors more complex than only the procedural feature of having juries decide cases. Nevertheless, the data should not obscure the fact that virtually all of the notoriously large U.S. tort awards, the ones that generate public attention, are returned by juries.

Contingency fees vs. loser pays rule. In comparing damages awards between the U.S. and civil law countries, appearances can be quite deceiving. Larger absolute damages awards in the U.S. do not come close to telling the whole story because they fail to account for critical legal and social structural distinctions between the U.S. and other countries. One legal difference that packs a potent punch involves how responsibility for attorneys' fees is assigned. Most nations, including most civil law systems and the English common law system, follow a fee-shifting "loser pays" rule under which the losing party pays the winning party's fees and costs. The U.S. is the exception to the rule. Under the "American rule" parties are responsible for their own attorneys' fees and most costs, win or lose.

Virtually all U.S. personal injury lawyers represent plaintiffs pursuant to contingency fee agreements. Under a contingency fee agreement, the plaintiffs' lawyers receive a substantial percentage of the award (usually 30–40%) if they win, but nothing if they lose. Contingency fee arrangements are prohibited in most civil law countries, including Germany, although they are permitted in Argentina. Taking account of the disparate approaches to attorneys' fees casts damages awards in a very different light. A $100,000 award in the U.S. in a case with a 40% contingency fee is really a $60,000 damages award for the plaintiff.

Costs must be figured in as well. In nations following loser pay rules, the losing litigant is responsible for the winner's costs in addition to attorneys' fees. In the U.S., losing litigants are required to pay only very basic costs, such as filing fees and service of process fees. They are not required to reimburse the winner for the costs of big-ticket items such as expert witness fees. Under standard contingency fee agreements, the client is responsible for the costs of investigation, depositions, expert witness fees, travel, etc. Depending on the wording of the agreement, such costs can be deducted from the client's award *after* the attorneys have deducted their contingency fee percentage from the gross recovery. Costs in complex products liability cases often exceed six figures.

Medical expenses. A critical social distinction that goes a long way toward explaining disparate tort damages awards between the U.S. and other nations is the relative lack of publicly funded medical care in the U.S. In most developed countries, publicly funded health care covers most of the population. The U.S. is the major exception. In the U.S., most medical care is privatized, although some residual coverage is provided by the Medicaid and Medicare programs. In countries where injured tort plaintiffs do not pay for their medical expenses, they do not and cannot sue to recover them.

To a considerable extent, the national social security systems of many countries serve as a substitute for tort liability with respect to accident compensation. FLEMING, at 26. In most developed countries, Silvia could go to the emergency room, undergo surgery multiple times if necessary, see specialists, undergo therapy, all with minimal out-of-pocket expense. Likewise, she could apply for a permanent state-funded disability supplement to her wages. This social support net may discourage her from filing a lawsuit, where she would have to incur personal expense and wait perhaps several years to receive—if she were victorious—a relatively low monetary amount.

To the contrary, U.S. plaintiffs, lacking similar social support, might feel compelled to consider litigation as a way to pay their medical expenses. Critics of large tort awards in the U.S. often overlook the fact that past and future medical expenses comprise one of the largest (often *the* largest) portion of a plaintiff's damages award. In cases involving catastrophic injuries, U.S. compensatory awards for medical expenses can reach extraordinary levels. A 2006 Florida automobile accident case provides an eye-opening example. A jury returned a verdict of $23.5 million to a severely brain-damaged plaintiff and his wife, of which $21 million—roughly 90 percent of the judgment—was for the present value of future medical expenses. Mejia v. Manheim Auctions Gov't Serv., 930 So. 2d 657 (Fla. Dist. Ct. App. 2006) (upholding medical expense award as well as trial court's additur of $9.3 million in additional noneconomic damages). Here are a few other examples: Meader v. United States, 881 F.2d 1056, 1057 (11th Cir. 1989) (awarding plaintiff $6.6 million in total damages, of which $4.7 million was for future medical expenses); Richardson v. Chapman, 676 N.E.2d 621, 627 (Ill. 1997) (quadriplegic plaintiff received jury verdict for $22 million, of which $11 million was for future medical expenses); Hardy v. State, 412 So.2d 208, 213–15 (La. Ct. App. 1982) (awarding plaintiff $4.6 million in total damages, of which $2.6 million was for future medical expenses).

Were one to deduct medical expenses from U.S. compensatory damages awards, the disparity in damages awards between the U.S. and other countries would be smaller, in many cases substantially so. In reality, medical expenses incurred *prior* to judgment often do end up being deducted from a U.S. plaintiff's recovery. U.S. health insurers who have paid medical expenses on behalf of a tort plaintiff are entitled to reimbursement out of the plaintiff's judgment through what is known as the right of subrogation. Thus, if Silvia had private health insurance that paid a portion of her estimated $26,000 in U.S. medical expenses, the insurer would be entitled to reimbursement from Silvia's tort recovery for amounts it paid.

Economic disparity. Finally, differences in per capita income and living costs among different nations cannot be overlooked. If one were creating Rawlsian-style first principles, perhaps it would be fairer to value similar injuries similarly, wherever they occur. That, of course, does not accord with the reality of a world in which wealth is unequally distributed. Economic disparities among nations naturally contribute to disparate results in calculating tort damages. The Gross Domestic Product per capita in 2005 was $42,000 for the U.S., $29,800 in Germany, and $13,700 in Argentina. Thus, a $100,000 damages award would have a very different impact on Silvia's life in each country. In the U.S., such an award would be 2.4 times the per capita GDP, in Germany it would be 3.4 times the per capita GDP, and in Argentina, it would be 7.3 times the per capita GDP.

Keep these important distinctions in mind when reading the country summaries below. First, attorneys' fees and costs are addressed, followed by a discussion of damages.

Attorneys' Fees and Costs

United States

The contingency fee system. U.S. tort litigation is funded on the plaintiff's side by the contingency fee system under which plaintiffs' lawyers receive, pursuant to written agreements with their clients, a percentage of any recovery if the plaintiff wins, but nothing if the plaintiff loses. The particular percentages vary by agreement and state regulation.

In Florida, home to Silvia's U.S. case, the *Rules Regulating the Florida Bar*, which are typical of the rules in many states, contain express provisions governing contingency fees. *See* FLA. BAR REG. R. 4-1.5(f) (2005). Contingency fee agreements must be in writing, inform the client that the agreement can be cancelled within three business days from the date it is signed, state the method by which the fee will be determined, and specify whether costs are to be deducted before or after the contingent fee is calculated. The rule also establishes upper limits on contingent fees. Any fee exceeding the specified limits is presumptively excessive. The maximum limits are:

• Fees in cases that settle before the filing of an answer:
33 1/3% of any recovery up to $1 million; plus
30% of any portion of a recovery between $1 million and $2 million; plus
20% of any portion of a recovery exceeding $2 million.
• Fees in cases that are not resolved until after the filing of an answer:
40% of any recovery up to $1 million; plus
30% of any portion of a recovery between $1 million and $2 million; plus
20% of any portion of a recovery exceeding $2 million.
• An additional fee of 5% of the total recovery is authorized for any case reaching the appellate stage.

The U.S. contingency fee system is a source of intense debate. Depending on which side is speaking, the contingency fee system is either an essential portal to justice that allows tort victims without financial means to obtain high-quality representation or a tool for making "greedy trial lawyers" rich while depriving clients of a large portion of their needed compensatory damages. As with most disputes, there is truth on both sides. Because contingency fee agreements are tied to results, rather than work expended, situations can arise where an attorney reaps a windfall in cases that settle early. Even in cases that require substantial expenditures of time and money by the plaintiff's attorney, large judgments or settlements can result in compensation that, in hindsight, looks unreasonably high. Such cases are not, however, the norm. Empirical research suggests that in most cases contingency fee agreements generate hourly rates that are not dramatically out of kilter with the rates of lawyers who charge by the hour. *See* Herbert M. Kritzer, *Advocacy and Rhetoric vs. Scholarship and Evidence in the Debate Over Contingency Fees: A Reply to Professor Brickman*, 82 WASH. U. L.Q. 477 (2004) (commenting on empirical evidence); *but see* Lester Brickman, *Effective Hourly Rates of Contingency-Fee Lawyers: Competing Data and Non-Competitive Fees*, 81 WASH. U. L.Q. 653 (2003) (disputing and critiquing such evidence).

Additionally, borrowing a classic line from ABC's Wide World of Sports, one cannot fairly consider the "thrill of victory" without also looking at the "agony of defeat." In contingency fee cases where plaintiffs lose, the plaintiff's lawyer receives nothing. Tort plaintiffs in the U.S. lose about as often as they win. When personal injury plaintiffs lose, their lawyers not only receive no compensation for the labor they expended, they usually never recover the costs of litigation they advanced on behalf of the client. While contingency fee agreements often make the client responsible for costs, win or lose, most injury victims do not have the resources to reimburse their lawyers for the costs of litigation.

One advantage of the U.S. contingency fee system is that it allows even the most disadvantaged members of society—assuming they have suffered serious injuries and possess a reasonably strong claim on the merits—to obtain representation from the best personal injury law firms, firms with the talent and resources necessary to engage in complex, extended litigation.

The contingency fee system might, as critics argue, encourage more litigation than in countries following the loser pays rule. Under the loser pays rule, the prospect of losing and being obligated to pay not only one's own attorney's fees and costs, but those of the other side, surely deters some injured persons from pursuing litigation. Does the contingency fee system encourage *frivolous* litigation? Rational economic judgment would seem to discourage attorneys operating on a contingency fee basis from taking on frivolous cases. If cases are truly frivolous, the plaintiffs' lawyers should lose every one, wasting much time and money. On the other hand, precisely because each side does bear its own fees and costs in the U.S., there is economic pressure for defendants to settle even some weak cases.

In small cases, the contingency fee system discourages litigation. Due to the expenses of litigation, many lawyers will not accept expensive cases, such as products liability and medical malpractice cases, involving insubstantial amounts of damages even when liability is fairly clear. In this regard, it has been argued that the loser pays rule actually encourages litigation because people with strong claims on the merits but trivial damages have a stronger incentive to sue, secure in the knowledge that their costs and fees will be paid by the other side. With regard to the perception that Americans are hyper-litigious in general, it should be noted that empirical studies have shown that the vast majority of injured persons never bring lawsuits or even consult lawyers. *See* WILLIAM HALTOM & MICHAEL MCCANN, DISTORTING THE LAW: POLITICS, MEDIA, AND THE LITIGATION CRISIS 77–90 (2004) (discussing several empirical studies related to these issues).

Obscured in the U.S. contingency fee debate is the fact that some states, including Florida, have passed fee-shifting "offer of settlement" statutes designed to encourage (plaintiffs' lawyers might say *coerce*) settlements. These statutes can have the same effect as the loser pays rule. A Florida statute, for example, provides that if a defendant makes a settlement offer that is rejected and the plaintiff fails to recover at least 75% of the settlement offer, the plaintiff must pay the offering party's attorneys' fees and costs that accrue after the date of the offer. FLA. STAT. §768.79 (2005).

Finding a lawyer for Silvia. In our case facts, Silvia's professor referred her to a lawyer, but even without that reference, finding a lawyer would be easy in the U.S., where personal injury lawyers are plentiful. They advertise heavily on the Internet, in phone directories, on television, billboards, and bus benches. State and local bar associations also operate referral services for people seeking legal representation. Numerous online directories of plaintiffs' personal injury lawyers exist, allowing people to locate lawyers in their area by typing in a zip code. Many of the top-rated Google ad words relate to personal injury lawyers and lawsuits. Silvia's case is attractive enough in terms of both the prospect of success and the severity of her injuries that she should have no problem finding a competent lawyer willing to accept her case under a contingency fee arrangement.

Germany

If the manner in which attorneys' fees are handled in the U.S. can be said to encourage personal injury litigation, some might argue that the way fees are handled in Germany has the opposite effect. In addition to any deterrent effect of the loser pays rule, contingency fees are prohibited in Germany. The prohibition comes from the Federal Lawyers' Act (*Bundesrechtsanwaltsord-nung*), which lays out a basic code of professional conduct for attorneys. Section 49B(2) prohibits "[a]greements in which the compensation or the amount of compensation is contingent on the final disposition or the success of the attorney's work or any agreement where the fee for the attorney is paid in the form of a portion of the amount recovered."

The ban on contingency fees has been the subject of increasing and increasingly heated public debate as more and more German lawyers have called for relaxation of the prohibition. In 2004, a German lawyer filed a complaint with the German Constitutional Court asserting that the prohibition on contingency fees violates her right of occupational liberty, protected by article 12 of the German Constitution. The right guarantees the freedom to choose and practice a profession. The whole German Bar is awaiting the decision, which is expected in 2007, with much curiosity.

Fee amounts are regulated by a different act, the Statute for the Compensation of Attorneys (*Rechtsanwaltsvergütungsgesetz*), which sets forth detailed fee schedules based on the specific tasks performed—not the time it takes to complete the tasks—and amount in controversy. Enumerated tasks include items such as case preparation, filing a complaint, and attending court hearings. An additional fee is added if the lawyer is successful in settling the case, a feature that encourages settlement. Because lawyers do not get paid for their time under the act, an incentive is built into the system for lawyers to limit the time they expend pursuing each compensable task. One consequence of this payment structure is that lawyers rely on the court to do much of the "heavy lifting" in civil litigation. MURRAY AND STÜRNER, at 115.

Fees under the attorneys' fees act are substantially lower than a lawyer could expect to receive in the U.S. for a similar case. For example, if we assume for purposes of illustration that Silvia's case resulted in an award after a trial of $50,000 (41,667 euros), her attorney's fee in Germany, as calculated under the act, would be $4,700 (3,917 euros). In the U.S., a 40% contingency fee from a $50,000 judgment would be $20,000 (16,667 euros), more than four times as much. On the other hand, German lawyers get their fees even if they lose.

Persons with assets can hire an attorney of their choosing and agree to pay them higher amounts than specified by statute. Corporate defendants in products liability cases who retain large law firms usually do agree to pay fees higher than the statutory schedules. Personal injury claimants without substantial assets, like Silvia, do not enjoy that luxury.

With contingency fee agreements prohibited, how would a plaintiff such as Silvia, laden with debt and unemployed, obtain legal representation? Three alternatives are available: government-paid legal aid, legal services insurance through a private company, and an emerging arrangement in which finance companies agree to underwrite the costs of strong personal injury cases in return for a percentage of the recovery.

Legal aid. As a student with no assets and no income, Silvia could apply for legal aid to finance her litigation. Section 114 of the German Code of Civil Procedure (GCCP) provides that one who lacks the ability to pay legal costs can receive funding from the government to pay her attorneys' fees and costs, provided that the case presents a reasonable likelihood of success on the merits and is not for the purpose of vexation. Whether a reasonable likelihood of success exists is determined by the court, based on the complaint. Remember that, unlike in the U.S., complaints in Germany are fairly extensive presentations of the case. One test for making the requisite "likelihood of success" determination is for the court to consider whether parties who could afford to hire a lawyer would spend their own money to pursue the case. In cases such as Silvia's, the mere fact that further evidence is needed to confirm or reject the validity of her claim might be deemed a sufficient basis for granting legal aid. Legal aid is refused mainly when the claim clearly lacks merit on the facts presented.

Thus, Silvia probably would qualify for legal aid, but the aid would not come free. Under the legal aid system, the state will pay a lawyer's fees and court costs, but the court will, based on the party's income and assets, set up an installment plan requiring the party to make monthly payments to repay the state, limited to a maximum of forty-eight payments. The amount of the repayment is based on a statutory formula, taking into account the party's income, living expenses, and property. Silvia would have to make the decision whether to bring a lawsuit and risk losing, with the consequence that she would be in debt not only to the other side under the loser pays rule, but also to the government for her legal aid. A couple of bright spots exist for losing plaintiffs. For someone in Silvia's poor financial position, the statutory installment repayments of her legal aid would be small and far less than the actual costs of the lawsuit. Also, fees paid pursuant to the loser pays rule are limited to the fee rates set by statute, even if the defendant paid higher amounts to its lawyers pursuant to a fee agreement, which is usually the case for corporate products liability defendants.

If Silvia applied for and received legal aid, she would be permitted to find and retain her own lawyer, as the GCCP provides that a person who is granted legal aid may hire "a lawyer of the party's choice who is willing to accept such representation." GCCP § 121(1). Unfortunately for Silvia, while she would have no problem finding a willing lawyer, she might have great difficulty finding a products liability specialist. Highly trained specialists can command and naturally prefer higher hourly rate contracts to the more limited fees payable under the statutory fee schedules. The problem is aggravated by the fact that statutory fees for legal aid are substantially lower than statutory fees in other cases. Realistically, this means that, contrary to the U.S., usually only defendants can retain highly specialized products liability lawyers in Germany.

Legal services insurance. Offsetting the impact of the prohibition on contingency fees and the loser pays rule is the fact that, unlike in the U.S., a large percentage of the German population carries insurance for legal expenses. The insurance typically covers both the person's own attorneys' fees and costs, as well as any fees and costs ordered to be paid by a losing litigant under the loser pays rule. Legal insurance, however, carries the same basic drawback as legal aid in that the fee schedules are too low to allow the insured to obtain highly trained specialists. Nevertheless, legal services insurance goes a long way toward enhancing access to the courts for ordinary citizens in a system without contingency fees, in no small part by relieving them of the fear and burden of having to pay the other side's fees and costs if they lose. Some have argued that by shifting the risk of loss to third-party payers, the widespread use of legal services insurance has increased litigation in Germany.

Underwriting personal injury cases. A recent development in German litigation practice is an arrangement whereby finance companies agree to underwrite the fees and costs of a personal injury plaintiff's case, including the opponent's fees and costs if the plaintiff loses, in return for a substantial percentage of any recovery. This arrangement is basically a contingency fee arrangement in disguise. Technically, however, it does not violate the prohibition on contingency fees because that prohibition applies only to lawyers. While such an arrangement may make it easier for some personal injury victims with good claims to obtain counsel, it does not facilitate obtaining the best counsel because the lawyers themselves are still limited to recovering the fees set by statute. The practice is still quite new and it is unlikely a plaintiff with an ordinary case like Silvia's would pursue financing of her case through this means. The companies engaged in this practice only accept cases with a strong likelihood of success and tend toward cases with high potential damages. Some of them only finance cases with damage values of more than 100,000 euros.

Finding a lawyer for Silvia. Silvia would have no problem finding a lawyer in Germany. As in the U.S., complaints are frequently heard in Germany that there are "too many lawyers," although the number of lawyers per capita is substantially lower than in either the U.S. or Argentina. But as noted above, she would have a problem finding a products liability specialist.

Lawyer advertising is permitted in Germany. It is strictly regulated by statute and professional conduct rules, although there has been a profound trend toward liberalizing the restrictions, particularly in light of the new means and opportunities for advertising provided by the Internet. So far, Germany has not permitted advertising on television.

Argentina

A dual fee system. Contrary to the practice in Germany and most other civil law nations, contingency fee agreements are permitted and routinely used in Argentine personal injury cases. Lawyers are allowed to agree with their clients on a fee to be calculated as a percentage of the recovery. This percentage ranges from 10–40%, with the most common agreements providing for a 20–25% contingency fee.

Argentina also follows the loser pays rule. The loser is obligated to pay the winner's fees and costs. However, fees resulting from contingency fee agreements are independent from the fees that will be assessed by the court in implementing the loser pays rule at the time of final judgment. In other words, a prevailing plaintiff's attorney can "double-dip" and cash both fees. Assume Silvia entered into a contingency fee agreement with her lawyer, which would probably be the case, and won her suit. Silvia's lawyer would receive both the full contingent fee percentage from the recovery as well as the court-imposed fees and costs taxed against the defendants under the loser pays rule.

In theory, if Silvia lost, her lawyer would still be entitled to payment from Silvia, not under the contingency fee agreement, but from the general rule that losers are obligated to pay both their own attorneys and their opponents' attorneys. In practice, however, plaintiffs' personal injury lawyers usually agree to take nothing if they lose. In other words, the plaintiffs' personal injury bar in Argentina operates similarly to the U.S. system in that plaintiffs can obtain lawyers without having to pay them.

The benefit to litigate without expenses. Additionally, pursuant to the national procedure code, citizens lacking adequate financial resources are entitled to request the "benefit to litigate without expenses" (*beneficio de litigar sin gastos*). NCCP Art. 78. Although the benefit to litigate without expenses is a type of "legal aid," it must be distinguished from U.S.-style legal aid services, which also exist in Argentina, where government-funded lawyers or private lawyers working pro bono provide legal assistance to indigents. It is very common for injury-case plaintiffs such as Silvia to request the benefit to litigate without expenses at the time of filing the complaint. The basis for such a petition is the plaintiff's lack of funds to finance the litigation and the unlikelihood of obtaining such funds in the foreseeable future. Once the benefit has been granted, the beneficiary is freed from paying court-appointed expert and other costs, as well as the Argentine court tax, which is assessed at 3% of the amount claimed and must be paid at the time of filing the complaint.

The benefit to litigate without expenses, although provided for in the procedure code, is a matter of constitutional right. Pursuant to due process, lack of funds cannot be a reason to deprive people of the opportunity to enforce their rights before a court of law. As noble as this principle sounds, it is often subject to abuse, especially in personal injury cases. This abuse often takes the form of outrageously inflated claims. Plaintiffs' lawyers sometimes move their clients to artificially inflate their claims so as to assure that the benefit is granted. For example, a school teacher might be able to pay the 3% court tax on a claim of $10,000 (which would be $300), but not on a claim of $100,000 (which would be $3,000). Increasing the amount of the claim increases the likelihood that the court will sympathize with the plaintiff and grant the benefit. By this means, middle-class plaintiffs who otherwise might be capable of paying their own expenses are able to obtain a government grant that was initially created to serve only the truly needy. Moreover, since the standard for qualifying for the benefit to litigate without expenses is not indigence, but only an inability to cope with the expenses of the case at hand, even commercial entities have been able to receive the benefit, although this has been a matter of controversy.

Unlike in Germany, the benefit to litigate without expenses does not include government payment of the plaintiff's attorney, but that does not present a problem because of the availability of contingency fee agreements. Also unlike Germany, personal injury plaintiffs in Argentina without financial resources usually escape having to pay anything to the other side under the loser pays rule. This result derives from article 84 of the NCCP, which as interpreted by courts, basically lets recipients of the benefit to litigate without expenses off the hook for the other side's fees and costs when there is no prospect that the plaintiff's economic situation is going to improve. As a result, plaintiffs without financial resources can end up with a completely free ride even with respect to frivolous claims.

With regard to legal services insurance, although a few companies offer such insurance in the federal capital of Buenos Aires, legal insurance has not caught on in Argentina.

Finding a lawyer for Silvia. It would not be difficult for Silvia to find a lawyer in Argentina, which has a per capita ratio of lawyers to population similar to that in the U.S. A caveat, however, is that, as discussed in the final chapter, it might be difficult to find a lawyer willing to fight the case all the way through trial, as opposed to one simply seeking a quick mediation or other settlement. As noted, Silvia normally would pay nothing for her lawyer's services. As for selecting among lawyers, Silvia normally would have to seek references, as she did in our case where she found her lawyer through a reference by one of her professors. Unlike the U.S., where lawyer advertising is common, Argentine lawyers are prohibited from engaging in almost any type of advertising. Infringing this rule has resulted in severe sanctions from the bar association.

Summary Chart—Attorneys' Fees and Costs

	United States	Germany	Argentina
The loser must pay the winner's attorneys' fees and costs.	No	Yes	Yes
Plaintiffs may obtain legal representation on a contingency fee basis.	Yes	No	Yes
Government assistance is available to tort plaintiffs who cannot afford to hire a lawyer or pay litigation costs.	No	Yes	Yes
Losing parties without financial assets are relieved from the burden of the loser pays rule.	Not applicable.	Generally not.	Yes

Damages

United States

While there are competing theories as to the purposes of the U.S. tort system, it's fair to say that the most widely accepted goal of awarding compensatory damages is to make the plaintiff whole again; that is, to restore the person, as nearly as possible, to the position she would have been in but for the tortious conduct.

Categories of compensatory damages. The damages designed to fulfill this goal are called "compensatory damages." Compensatory damages can be broken down into the following categories: (1) past and future medical expenses; (2) past lost wages and future lost earning capacity; (3) past and future mental and physical pain and suffering; (4) disfigurement and disability; and (5) the plaintiff's lost ability to enjoy some aspect of life (in Silvia's case, her piano playing).

Compensatory damages come in two varieties that usually travel under the labels "economic" and "noneconomic" damages. Economic damages are the plaintiff's past and future tangible out-of-pocket losses (items 1 and 2 above). Noneconomic damages are for intangible harms (items 3, 4, and 5 above).

With regard to the classes of noneconomic damages, arguably, disfigurement and disability and loss of the ability to enjoy life should be grouped with and treated as part of mental and physical pain and suffering since that is the nature of the noneconomic harm suffered from such injuries. Most states have rejected that argument with regard to disability and disfigurement, allowing separate damages for them in addition to pain and suffering damages. On the other hand, a majority of states do not allow separate damages for loss of the ability to enjoy life. Rather, such injuries, while compensable, are included as part of pain and suffering. These distinctions are not simply matters of form. Typically, a jury will receive a "special verdict form" on which each component of potential compensable damages will be listed as a separate line item. The more blanks on the page, the more likely the jury will fill them in, resulting in a higher damages total.

Intangible injuries. A formidable challenge for any jury is placing a monetary value on intangible injuries such as pain and suffering. Pain and suffering, while real, are difficult to quantify and incommensurate with money. Subject to limitations imposed by a mounting inventory of tort reform statutes, American juries have broad discretion in calculating damages, subject to judicial review for excessiveness, with the result that damages awards can be unpredictable and can lack uniformity from case to case. In his book, *Adversarial Legalism*, Robert Kagan offers several reasons for the lack of uniformity among tort verdicts, including that juries receive no objective guidelines for measuring damages, are not informed about decisions in comparable cases, and are not compelled to explain their decisions. ROBERT A. KAGAN, ADVERSARIAL LEGALISM: THE AMERICAN WAY OF LAW 138 (2001). He cites a study that showed experienced medical malpractice insurers were "seriously off the mark" in estimating jury awards and were unsuccessful in attempting to arrive at anything resembling a "going rate" for specific types of injuries. *Id.* at 139.

Under Florida law, which is typical of other states, the only guidance juries receive in calculating damages for intangible harm comes in the form of a jury instruction that, after listing the various types of noneconomic injuries, states: "There is no exact standard for measuring such damage. The amount should be fair and just in light of the evidence." Fla. Std. Jury Instr. (Civ.) 6.2(a) (2004).

Future damages. Note that tort plaintiffs are entitled to recover both past damages (damages accruing prior to trial) and future damages (damages that will accrue after the trial). Proving the past component is much easier than proving the future component. It would be easy for Silvia to prove her lost wages from her part-time job at the health club and her pretrial medical expenses. But without a crystal ball, how does one predict future damages? Will Silvia require future medical care? If so, what care and how much will it cost? If Silvia cannot work as a physical therapist, or is limited in the jobs she can perform, how much has she lost in future earning capacity, measured in today's dollars, projected over her working life?

Adding to the complexity of calculating future damages, the jury would be called on to reduce Silvia's future damages for medical expenses and lost earning capacity to "present value." By definition, future damages are an advance payment for damages that have not actually been sustained yet. In recognition that a dollar received today, if invested, is worth more than a dollar received in the future, juries are supposed to take into consideration the ability of money to earn interest in calculating future economic damages. Simply put, the present value of a future sum is the amount an unsophisticated investor would require today to achieve, through investment, the future amount at the future date when the money would actually be due.

Sound complicated? It gets even worse. Juries also are expected to consider the offsetting effect of inflation on the theory that a dollar received today, if not invested, will be worth *less* in future. The whole undertaking is marvelously complex and it is folly to believe ordinary jurors are capable of performing these complicated accounting tasks. In large cases, it is common for the parties to hire economists to testify as expert witnesses about present value and inflation adjustments to future damages. In most cases, the lawyers rely on the jurors to just "wing it." Because of the uncertain nature of pain and suffering and other intangible injuries, courts do not require that future awards for noneconomic damages be reduced to present value.

Tort reform. No aspect of the American tort system is more hotly contested than the issue of damages, as evidenced by the fact that most legislative tort reform efforts are aimed at limiting damages. Approximately one-half of U.S. states have passed statutes placing maximum caps on noneconomic damages, although about half of the caps apply only in medical malpractice cases. *See, e.g.,* ALASKA STAT. §09.17.010 (2006) (imposing cap on noneconomic damages in personal injury cases of $400,000 or an amount equal to the plaintiff's life expectancy in years multiplied by $8,000, whichever is greater; exception for cases involving severe permanent physical impairment or disfigurement, where the cap increases to $1 million or $25,000 multiplied by expectant years of life, whichever is greater); IDAHO CODE §6-1603 (2006) (noneconomic damages in personal injury cases capped at $250,000, except where defendant acted willfully or recklessly; such amount to be adjusted annually in accordance with average annual wages as computed by the Idaho Industrial Commission); KAN. STAT. ANN. §60-19a01 (2005) ($250,000 cap on pain and suffering damages in personal injury cases).

Several cap statutes have been declared unconstitutional on a variety of grounds by state high courts. *See, e.g.,* Smith v. Schulte, 671 So. 2d 1334 (Ala. 1995) (declaring unconstitutional $1 million cap on noneconomic damages in wrongful death actions brought against health care providers); Best v. Taylor Mach. Works, 689 N.E.2d 1057 (Ill. 1997) (declaring unconstitutional statute capping noneconomic damages at $500,000 in personal injury cases). Several other cap statutes, however, have been upheld. *See, e.g.,* Fein v. Permanente Medical Group, 695 P.2d 665 (Cal. 1985) (rejecting constitutional challenge to $250,000 cap on noneconomic damages in actions against health care providers); Kirkland v. Blaine County Medical Center, 4 P.3d 1115 (Idaho 2000) (rejecting constitutional challenge to statute capping noneconomic damages at $400,000 in personal injury negligence cases).

In addition to damages caps, a majority of states have legislatively abrogated or substantially modified the common law doctrine of joint and several liability, which allows a plaintiff with a judgment against multiple tortfeasors to collect the full amount of the judgment from any one of them, regardless of their percentage of culpability. In 2006, the Florida legislature abolished joint and several liability. FLA. STAT. §768.81 (2006). Absent joint and several liability, each defendant is liable according to its percentage of fault as determined by the fact-finder. About half of U.S. states have abolished or modified the collateral source rule, which prohibits defendants from receiving credit for compensation plaintiffs receive for their injuries from outside sources such as health insurance, disability insurance or sick leave. While not at issue in Silvia's case, most states also have imposed restrictions on the recovery of punitive damages.

Silvia's goal. Silvia would seek to recover all five categories of compensatory damages discussed above. While most U.S. law school courses in torts and products liability focus on rules of liability, a substantial portion of any personal injury trial is devoted to proving damages. As with her liability issues, Silvia would bear the burden of proving all damages, including future damages, by a preponderance of the evidence. Proving damages often entails extensive expert testimony: physicians testify about future medical care; physicians and psychologists testify about pain and suffering and other noneconomic injuries; economists testify about lost earning capacity and the cost of future medical care. In Silvia's case, a physical therapy or vocational rehabilitation expert might be needed to testify about Silvia's reduced job prospects, if any, due to her injury. As a prelude to any recovery for lost future earning capacity as a physical therapist, Silvia would have to prove that she would have successfully become a physical therapist but for the injury (i.e., that she did or would have completed her degree program and licensing requirements, etc.).

Estimating Silvia's damages. So what's the bottom line? What amount would Silvia be likely to recover in her U.S. suit should she prevail on the merits? For reasons already articulated, there obviously is no reliable answer. However, to give readers a comparative reference point and to contextualize the discussion of damages, we decided to offer some very rough estimates of Silvia's recovery in each country in the event she prevailed on the merits.

For the U.S., the estimate comes from Jury Verdict Research (JVR), a company that has been valuing personal injury cases since 1961. JVR donated its fee-based case evaluation services to this academic project. JVR doesn't claim infallibility, but only that its database of more than 245,000 verdicts and settlements allows it to provide "descriptive statistics" regarding personal injury case evaluation by type and region. JVR analyses begin with a base verdict value which is then augmented or reduced in percentage terms by various factors. For example, amounts are added for circumstances such as non-surgical scarring (plus 17%) and location (plus 7% for an action in Miami-Dade County, Florida), and subtracted where medical impairment is contested (minus 6%) or both sides present expert medical witnesses (minus 4%).

JVR used our hypothetical facts (supplemented with some reasonable assumptions) to do an analysis of Silvia's case. For comparative purposes, we requested two analyses, one based on the assumption that Silvia suffered no future lost earning capacity and one based on the wholly arbitrary assumption that she suffered and would be able to prove $250,000 in lost lifetime future earnings. JVR's analyses showed Silvia's case carried the following probable gross verdict amounts in 2006:

Silvia's projected gross recovery:

$345,000 (assuming no future lost earnings)
$609,000 (assuming lost lifetime future earnings of $250,000)

While these amounts might sound large, remember that Silvia wouldn't get to keep all of her damages. Her lawyer would receive a large portion of the judgment pursuant to their contingency fee agreement. The Florida Bar's contingency fee schedule would permit Silvia's lawyer to charge a 40% contingent fee on the above amounts, which, rounded to the nearest thousand, would be $138,000 and $244,000, respectively. In addition to the lawyer's fee, prior to cutting a check to Silvia, the lawyer would deduct, pursuant to the fee agreement, all litigation costs advanced on Silvia's behalf for expert witnesses, travel, investigation, depositions, exhibits, photocopying, etc. Costs vary by case. Previously, we consulted a Florida personal injury lawyer who said that in a case like Silvia's, he would try to keep the out-of-pocket costs below $50,000. They could be higher or lower, but we'll use that amount as an estimate. Finally, Silvia would be obligated to pay her medical expenses from the award. She doesn't have health insurance, so the bills remain unpaid and owed in full. Even if she had health insurance, the insurer would be entitled under its right of subrogation to recoup amounts it paid on Silvia's behalf.

Taking into account attorneys' fees, costs, and medical expenses, Silvia's projected net recovery would be reduced as follows:

Silvia's projected net recovery:

$131,000 (assuming no future lost earnings)
$289,000 (assuming $250,000 lifetime lost earning capacity)

The differences in gross and net recovery are obviously quite large. One unofficial justification advanced in favor of noneconomic damages awards in the U.S. is that they help plaintiffs pay their attorneys and litigation costs, allowing them to retain a larger portion of their economic losses for lost wages and medical expenses. Congress has provided one silver lining to victorious personal injury plaintiffs. Section 102(a)(2) of the Internal Revenue Code exempts recoveries for personal injuries from federal income taxes. But don't start giving Silvia investment tips yet. We've been talking only about her projected recovery amounts *if* she won. She could lose.

Germany

The basic rules for damages under German law are codified in sections 249–54 of the German Civil Code (GCC). Because they are part of the broad law of obligations, most of the damages rules apply equally to tort and contract claims. MARKESINIS ET AL., at 22. The overriding principle is that of *Naturalrestitution*, which combines the goals of restitution and compensation. Codified in section 249 of the GCC, it is essentially the same "make whole" principle applicable to tort damages in both the U.S. and Argentina. Section 249(1) provides: "A person obligated to make compensation shall restore the condition which would have existed if the instance giving rise to the duty to make compensation had not occurred." Restitution in kind is called for where possible. Where restitution in kind cannot be achieved, the civil code allows the injured party to recover compensation in money damages. *See* GCC § 251(1) ("If reparation in kind is impossible or not sufficient to compensate the creditor, the person liable for compensation shall compensate the creditor with money.").

Apart from the prohibition on punitive damages, the categories of tort damages in Germany are nearly identical to those in the U.S. Compensatory damages in Germany could be differentiated using the same five categories outlined for the U.S. (past and future medical expenses, past and future lost wages, past and future pain and suffering, disfigurement and disability, and loss of enjoyment of life). Also as in the U.S., Germany distinguishes between economic and noneconomic damages, except that it uses the labels "material" and "nonmaterial" damages, respectively.

Material (economic) damages. Material, or economic, damages are provided for in the general damages sections of the GCC (§§ 249–53), as supplemented by section 842, which applies specifically to tort claims. Together, the sections have been construed to allow recovery of all expenses reasonably necessary to restore the health or property of the tort victim. This includes past and future medical expenses, both of the typical variety (physicians, hospitals, pharmaceuticals) and atypical variety (home nurse, value of health care services provided by relatives). In Germany, medical expenses are regularly paid by state-run social security systems called health insurance funds, to which about 90% of the population belongs. The remaining 10% or so carry private insurance. As an unemployed student without significant assets, Silvia most likely would be a member of a state health insurance fund. Thus, if her medical expenses were paid by the health insurance fund, she could not claim them in her lawsuit. As explained in the introduction to this chapter, the lack of out-of-pocket medical expenses for most tort plaintiffs in Germany helps account for lower tort awards.

The health insurance fund would be entitled under law to reimbursement from the tortfeasors for any medical expenses paid out on Silvia's behalf, somewhat similar to the way the right of subrogation functions in the U.S. If the tortfeasor refuses to pay the reimbursement, which happens only rarely, the health insurance fund can file its own action to collect the amount. In the unlikely event that Silvia was not a member of a health insurance fund and was forced to bear the costs of her treatment, she would be entitled to claim those costs as material damages.

Material damages also include lost past and future wages and other income, as provided by both section 252 (a general damages provision) and section 842 (specifically allowing recovery of lost earnings in tort actions) of the GCC. For persons at the beginning of their careers, like Silvia, courts estimate the future development of the person's career and the income such a career would be likely to generate. In unclear cases, courts rely on average career development and income for the particular profession as setting the basis. However, if the plaintiff is able to work in a different profession, those expected earnings would offset any recovery for lost future earning capacity. The basic principle, consistent with the "make whole" theory of restitution, is to calculate the differential between what the plaintiff would have earned without the injury and what the plaintiff would be able to earn in light of the injury. In Silvia's case, the court would rely on experts to determine whether and to what extent Silvia's ability to work in her field of physical therapy would be affected by her injury.

The Product Liability Act (PLA) contains a separate damages provision relating to material damages that is largely duplicative of the preexisting GCC sections. Section 8 of the PLA states: "In case of injury to body or health, compensation must be given for the medical expenses as well as for pecuniary losses the injured person suffers because of a temporary or permanent disability or temporary or permanent reduction in earning capacity or due to his increased needs."

The PLA also imposes an aggregate damages ceiling of 85 million euros (roughly $102 million) for damages that can be awarded in any case or series of cases arising from a product defect of the same type (PLA § 10), but the cap applies only to strict liability claims under the act. It does not apply to general tort or contract claims brought pursuant to the GCC. This cap is designed to max out the total damages arising from a given product defect regardless of the number of injuries caused. The cap would not come into play in Silvia's case because her individual damages certainly would not reach the cap level and because it has been assumed Silvia's injury was caused by a manufacturing defect in the individual peanuts jar rather than a generic design defect affecting all jars. As such, there would be no danger of multiple claims aggregating toward the cap level.

Nonmaterial (noneconomic) damages. German law also allows recovery for noneconomic intangible losses, which are referred to as "nonmaterial damages" or *Schmerzensgeld*, which translates to "money for pain." Nonmaterial damages encompass what typically are referred to in the U.S. as damages for pain and suffering. Traditionally, German law has not favored nonmaterial damages. The authors of the GCC expressed repugnance for money awards for intangible injuries and the broad discretion inherent in calculating such damages. Ulrich Magnus, *Damages Under German Law, in* UNIFICATION OF TORT LAW: DAMAGES 94 (U. Magnus ed., 2001). This is another explanation for the disparity between U.S. and German tort awards. Even when granted, nonmaterial damages for physical injuries are much smaller than in the U.S.

Until 2002, the right to claim nonmaterial damages for pain and suffering existed only for fault-based general tort claims under section 823 of the GCC. This restriction greatly reduced the usefulness to injured persons of strict products liability law in Germany, and helps explain why the PLA has not yet been extensively relied on in German products liability actions. A critical 2002 amendment to the GCC extended the availability of pain and suffering damages to all cases involving personal injuries, regardless of the basis of the claim. This amendment took the form of an added paragraph to GCC § 253, which now reads:

§ 253 Nonmaterial Damages
(1) For a damage which is not a financial loss, monetary compensation can only be demanded in cases where specifically provided by law.
(2) For an injury to the body, the health, the liberty or the right to sexual self-determination, one can demand monetary compensation for a damage that is not a financial loss.

Prior to 2002, only the first paragraph existed, which had the effect of limiting nonmaterial damages to the few instances where they were expressly provided for by law. Adding paragraph 2 had the effect of making nonmaterial damages (i.e., "damage that is not a financial loss") available in all cases involving injury to the person. This change is one of the most important changes in German tort law since the GCC was adopted in 1900. Correspondingly, section 8 of the PLA was amended to allow recovery for nonmaterial damages with the addition of the sentence, "For damages that are not of a pecuniary nature, fair compensation in money can be claimed."

Nonmaterial damages include compensation not only for pain and suffering, but for disfigurement and disability and loss of the ability to enjoy life. Again, a close parallel can be seen between the categories of noneconomic damages recoverable in the U.S. and those recoverable in Germany.

Finding the "correct" amount of damages. As in all legal systems, calculating the correct amount of compensatory tort damages is a formidable challenge in Germany. Obviously, there are fewer problems determining past material damages (e.g., medical expenses, property damage, and lost wages) than future material damages or nonmaterial damages of any type.

Section 287 of the German Code of Civil Procedure (GCCP) grants judges broad discretion to estimate damages. It provides that where damages are in dispute, the court "in its free evaluation" shall decide the appropriate amount of damages. The provision grants the court the authority to decide whether or not to take evidence on the issue or to appoint experts to assist the court. Judges regularly exercise their authority to appoint experts to evaluate injuries. In Silvia's case, the court probably would appoint a hand surgeon and perhaps an expert witness on economics to estimate Silvia's lost future income. Alternatively, the court might estimate Silvia's lost income based on publicly available economic statistics or ask the German Federal Institute for Statistics to provide relevant employment and income data.

Regarding nonmaterial damages, amounts are estimated by the court on the basis of judgments in similar cases. Several books exist that provide tables of pain and suffering judgments in German low and high courts, and include descriptions of the basic case facts. The most famous of these sources is SUSANNE HACKS, AMELI RING & PETER BÖHM, SCHMERZENSGELDBETRÄGE (23rd ed. 2005), containing summaries of more than three thousand German court decisions. Judges consult these works in search of similar cases with the goal of awarding similar amounts of nonmaterial damages for similar injuries. It is an accepted principle that comparable injuries should be treated comparably to promote consistency and equal treatment. MARKESINIS ET AL., at 67. The Federal Supreme Court has held that trial judges whose awards for nonmaterial damages deviate from those in prior similar cases must explain the reasons for the deviation in writing.

Thus, take note of an interesting comparative point. In the hugely important area of assessing tort damages, Germany, a civil law nation, relies heavily on case precedent for assistance whereas the U.S., a common law nation, does not. U.S. juries are not told about prior judgments in similar cases in calculating damages. Such evidence would be considered irrelevant and inadmissible. Even in appeals challenging damages awards as excessive or inadequate, U.S. courts do not usually consult or refer to awards in other cases in evaluating damages awards.

Of course, German judges don't just follow the tables by rote. Similar cases simply provide guidance in assessing damages. Each case is adjudged on its facts and merits, and the result must be justified in writing. All damages must be supported by facts and logical analysis, although as discussed in chapter seven, the burden of proof in Germany with respect to damages is lower than the burden with respect to proving liability.

Concerning future damages, an important difference from U.S. practice is that German plaintiffs can incorporate within their lawsuit filings a declaratory action (*Feststellungsklage*) seeking to establish a "legal relation" with the defendant (such as the defendant's liability to the plaintiff) pursuant to which the defendant can be ordered to pay all future damages of the plaintiff as they occur. *See* GCCP § 256. Such a judgment amounts to a continuing obligation on the part of the defendant to pay both material and nonmaterial damages whenever they might arise.

Relatedly, German courts have the power under section 843 of the GCC to award periodic payments for damages to be paid out over time, rather than in a lump sum, and, in fact, periodic payments are the norm, at least in large cases. Section 323 of the GCCP allows either party to an action to seek a variation in these payments (called an *Abänderungsklage*) due to a substantial change in circumstances.

The combination of the availability of the *Feststellungsklage* and the power to revise periodic payments via an *Abänderungsklage* builds flexibility into the German system of damages awards with regard to future events. This is all much different from U.S. practice where the jury returns a verdict in a single lump sum, with no ability of the court to raise or lower that sum based on future developments. More than half of U.S. states have passed "periodic payment" statutes, which authorize and sometimes require the trial judge in certain cases where the damages meet a specified threshold (usually ranging from $100,000 to $250,000) to order that the damages be paid out in future installments over a period of years. But these statutes simply effect a divvying up of the jury's verdict amount into future payments. They do not authorize revisions in the payments of future damages based on future events. The only exception is that some U.S. periodic payment statutes cut off payments for future medical expenses in the event the plaintiff dies. They do not, however, authorize termination of future lost earnings or future pain and suffering upon death. Although a logical argument could be made for doing so (since a dead person cannot earn money or experience pain and suffering), such a result was simply thought to be too harsh to write into the statutes, especially given the reality that noneconomic damages help fund the plaintiff's attorneys' fees.

The availability of the declaratory judgment action and revisable periodic payments under German law make it less critical that the court "get it right" in the first instance in terms of estimating damages. For example, suppose that two years into the future Silvia suffered unforeseen complications in her right hand and wrist that caused additional medical expenses and increased her disability to the point where she was unable to perform any job requiring use of both hands. Under the U.S. system, she would be out of luck. She could not return to court and ask for more money to compensate her for this new development. In Germany, however, she could request additional funds from the defendant based on this substantial change in circumstances. If the defendants refused to pay, Silvia could return to court and ask the court to order payment of the additional funds. The only issue in the subsequent litigation would be whether the additional expenses were related to the initial injuries.

Note, however, that the flexibility of the German system also can work to the disadvantage of a tort plaintiff. Suppose it turned out that in two years Silvia's hand and wrist healed completely, allowing her to successfully pursue all jobs in her chosen field of physical therapy. If the German court had awarded her periodic payments for lost income, the defendants would be permitted to seek a downward adjustment based on this new development. In the U.S., Silvia would not be required to return any funds to the defendants based on her improved physical condition and job prospects.

To avoid the uncertain financial future of new or revised payments, German defendants often settle cases for a flat amount with a provision in the settlement agreement that there is no right to seek additional damages in the future. The settlement payment releases all past and future damages claims so that the case is completely terminated. To achieve a settlement that disposes of a case once and for all, German defendants often are willing to pay an additional flat sum as compensation for any potential future expenses. Such settlements also benefit plaintiffs, who do not have to wait to receive their compensation for future damages and are relieved of the burden of making future recovery requests.

Estimating Silvia's damages. For comparison purposes, the following analysis estimates Silvia's recovery in her German action. Although the estimates are rudimentary, making damages predictions in Germany is not as speculative as in the U.S. because of the more limited ranges for noneconomic damages and the fact that German judges consult compilations of prior cases in valuing damages.

Assuming she prevailed on the merits without any reduction for contributory negligence, Silvia would receive complete recovery for her material damages, including lost income from her part-time job at the health club, future lost income if the need for it is established, and an amount for her "increased needs" due to her medical condition. "Increased needs," as provided for in GCC §843, are additional living expenses arising from the plaintiff's injury and disability. In Silvia's case, they could include items such as temporary home help, laundry services, travel expenses to visit doctors and physical therapists, other travel expenses due to the disability, and expenses for typing or writing services due to her hand and wrist injury.

If a government insurance fund paid her medical expenses, which would likely be the case, Silvia would not be able to recover those expenses in her lawsuit, although the fund would recover them from the defendants either by agreement or separate litigation. If Silvia paid her own medical expenses, she would recover the full amount. The case facts use an estimate for medical expenses based on U.S. costs ($26,000), but in Germany, Silvia's medical treatment would cost substantially less, probably in the range of 6,000 euros or $7,200. U.S. citizens are accustomed to hearing about the high costs of medical care in the U.S., and this contrast perhaps adds some support to that perception, at least in comparison to Germany. German doctors consulted for this book attributed part of the disparity to the low level of earnings for doctors in Germany.

For Silvia's lost income from her part-time job at the health club, we'll estimate 2,250 euros ($2,700). This is based on the assumption that Silvia worked twenty hours a week at an hourly rate of 8 euros ($9.60), which would be a typical salary rate in Germany for an unskilled part-time student worker. Additionally, an amount would be added for her "increased needs" as described above. Although pursuant to GCC §843, the recovery for increased needs is to be paid monthly, it is common in small cases to award a lump sum. Given that Silvia has not been able to use her right hand and that the hand and wrist remain disabled, 2,500 euros ($3,000) is a reasonable "guesstimate" for her increased needs.

Silvia's nonmaterial (pain and suffering) damages would be likely to range from 5,000–15,000 euros ($6,000–18,000). This estimate is based on German court decisions summarized in *SchmerzensgeldBeträge*, as well as Koyuncu's experience litigating personal injury cases. In a similar case decided by a State Appeals Court in 2001, a nine-year-old boy who suffered a cut injury to his right hand due to an exploding Coca-Cola bottle was awarded 5,000 euros ($6,000) for his nonmaterial damages, including pain and suffering, disability, and lost ability to enjoy life. *See* Regional High Ct., Koblenz, File No. 11, 10 U 838/100, May 2001, *available in* NJW-RR 2001, 1315.

Like Silvia, the boy suffered severed nerves, tendons, and blood vessels. He spent one week in the hospital and received physical therapy for two months. Following the therapy, his hand still suffered paresthesia (a burning or prickling sensation), lowered sensitivity, scarring, reduced strength, and functional disability. Also like Silvia, the boy suffered an overall body disability of 5%. The boy played keyboard (as did Silvia) and also participated in judo. Because of the injury he gave up the keyboard and reduced his judo participation markedly.

In estimating nonmaterial damages in Germany, one must take account of a general upward trend in such damages in recent years, as well as the fact that some regions of the country are known to award higher nonmaterial damages than others. There is no particular geographic pattern to this phenomenon.

Rather, it depends on the tone set by the State Appeals Court for the particular region, which, in turn, usually depends on the particular judges assigned to the appellate panel responsible for hearing appeals in tort cases on that court. Cologne is in a region in which the State Appeals Court (*Oberlandesgericht Köln*) is known to favor higher nonmaterial damages than courts in some other regions. Judge Lothar Jaeger, a former chief judge at the *Oberlandesgericht Köln* who served on several liability panels hearing tort cases, is a well-known German scholar who stated in the 1990s that nonmaterial damages were too low. He recently went even further in a preface to his co-authored compilation of nonmaterial damages tables, stating it was the authors' intention "to build a platform for higher nonmaterial damages." LOTHAR JAEGER & JAN LUCKEY, SCHMERZENSGELD TABELLE: SYSTEMATISCHE ERLÄUTERUNGEN, MUSTER, URTEILSTEXTE v (2d ed. 2005). This is actually quite an extraordinary statement inasmuch as German judges are normally very reserved about making public statements that could be regarded as criticism of the German legal system.

But remember that we're talking about relative differences within Germany. Compared to the U.S., nonmaterial damages remain low in Germany. A reasonable upward figure to place on Silvia's pain and suffering damages for her action filed in Cologne would be 15,000 euros ($18,000).

Thus, not taking into account potential lost future earning capacity, Silvia's "best case" award would be:

Silvia's projected damages:

Lost past income: 2,250 euros ($2,700)
Increased needs: 2,500 euros ($3,000)
Nonmaterial damages: 15,000 euros ($18,000)

Total damages: 19,750 euros ($23,700)

In the unlikely event she paid her own medical expenses (6,000 euros or $7,200), her total damages would rise to 25,750 euros, or roughly $30,900.

If Silvia suffered lost future earning capacity, her damages would increase further. However, even assuming that Silvia would be unable to function as a physical therapist, she would be expected to seek retraining and find a different job. Her claim for lost future earnings would be the difference between what she earned in the new profession compared to what she could have been expected to earn as a physical therapist. In such cases, German plaintiffs typically receive only very small monthly differential amounts as recovery for lost earning capacity. Remember that unlike in the U.S. where these critical decisions regarding future damages must be made once and for all at the time of judgment, the availability of the declaratory judgment action establishing a continuing obligation by the defendants to pay future damages as they arise (*Feststellungsklage*), as well as the ability to seek revisions in periodic payments due to changed circumstances (*Abänderungsklage*), mean that Silvia would have the potential to seek additional damages in the future if her injury caused greater lost earning capacity than expected.

Argentina

The governing principles of damages calculation in Argentina do not depart significantly from those in the U.S. and Germany. Argentina also follows the "make whole" approach to tort remedies. Argentine courts and commentators call this the principle of *reparación integral* (whole restitution), meaning that every item of damages sustained by the injured person should be compensated to try to restore the person to the status he or she enjoyed before the injury. If actual restitution is impossible, which is usually the case in personal injury actions, the indemnification takes the form of a monetary award. This principle is embodied in article 1083 of the Argentine Civil Code (ACC), which states: "Compensation for damages shall consist in returning things to their original state except if this is impossible, in which case the indemnity will be set in money."

The ACC traditionally recognized two general types of damages: resulting damage (*daño emergente*) and lost profits (*lucro cesante*). *See* ACC Art. 1069. Resulting damage includes just about every type of injury affecting the value of something that can be subject to monetary redress. A 1968 amendment to the ACC introduced a third type of damages, *daño moral* (moral damage). *See* ACC Art. 1078. Moral damages can be conceptualized as the rough equivalent to pain and suffering damages in the U.S. They encompass damages for all types of intangible injuries. In recent years, Argentine courts and scholars, and especially practitioners, have developed a myriad of "new damages" categories, including incapacity, psychological damage, emotional distress, aesthetic damage, damage to life prospects, loss of chance, lost capacity for procreation, lost consortium, etc. The list sounds impressive, but in actuality it represents nothing more than a broadening of the already existing concepts of resulting damage, lost profits, and moral damages. In other words, only the labels are truly new.

As in the U.S. and Germany, it is also possible to recover both past and future damages. The difficulty of concretely determining future loss of income is frequently solved by resorting to a concept known as "loss of chance," which allows recovery for the plaintiff's lost possibility of future earnings when those future earnings are difficult or impossible to assess at the time of judgment. In recognition of the inability to calculate lost earning capacity with any degree of certainty, Argentine judges, if persuaded that a plaintiff's injuries will interfere with his or her ability to pursue a chosen avocation, often estimate a small amount to compensate the victim's loss of some future, hypothetical lost earnings. The amount is not based on a factual determination of the specific lost earnings of the injured person, as occurs in the U.S. Rather, it's labeled as a "lost possibility" and is treated more as a legal conclusion than a factual conclusion.

In determining the amount of the award for this lost possibility, Argentine judges follow article 165 of the National Code of Civil Procedure (NCCP), which provides that in cases where a loss has been proved but the amount of compensation for the loss has not been established in the record, judges still have to estimate an award. This estimation usually is arrived at simply from judges applying their common sense and experience, often with reference to what they or sister courts have granted in similar cases.

To facilitate damages calculations, the National Civil Court of Appeals in Buenos Aires created a database of awards in prior cases accessible through the Internet (www.iijusticia.edu.ar). This database is just a reference and has no binding effect, but courts have increasingly relied on the database in setting damages in recent years. Thus, as in Germany, Argentine courts often refer to prior cases as establishing a baseline for damages awards in tort cases, adding a degree of predictability to calculating damages.

As in both the U.S. and Germany, a substantial portion of an Argentine tort case is devoted to determining the nature and extent of the injuries that the plaintiff sustained. Like the U.S. and unlike Germany, damages are determined once and for all in one final judgment. Parties cannot go back to court in the future and seek adjustments based on changed circumstances.

Estimating Silvia's damages. How much money could Silvia expect to receive in her lawsuit filed in Buenos Aires, the capital and largest city in Argentina? The most relevant case facts that would go into calculating the award would be that she is thirty years old; is a recent university graduate not yet practicing as a physical therapist; suffered a 20–25% permanent disability in her right hand and wrist with a resulting overall body impairment of 5%; underwent three months of physical therapy; had to quit her part-time job at a health club; plays piano as a hobby with the likelihood that her playing ability is substantially impaired; and could find it difficult to practice in at least some capacities as a physical therapist.

Based on these facts, Silvia would claim to have suffered the following damages: physical damage (the cut wound, scar, and permanent disability), emotional distress and other psychological damage, lost past wages, and loss of future earnings or at least a "lost chance" of receiving such earnings. Because she is unemployed and has no assets, Silvia probably would not have paid her own medical expenses. In Argentina, even persons without private medical insurance usually get their medical expenses paid for by labor union health care organizations or, if unemployed and lacking other assets, state-sponsored social security. We'll reasonably assume Silvia did not pay and is not responsible for her medical expenses. Thus, she could not recover them in her lawsuit. Nevertheless, for comparative purposes, we consulted a Buenos Aires physician who, after cautioning that almost no one would pay this amount in real life, roughly estimated the cost of Silvia's medical treatment in Argentina (including emergency room treatment, surgery, anesthesia and other medications, one night hospital stay, follow-up visits with Dr. Schmitt, and three months of physical therapy) at $8,100 or 24,300 Argentine pesos.

In determining awards for physical disability, Argentine courts rely on neutral court-appointed medical experts who, in turn, use one of the *baremos* that are generally accepted as reliable sources for establishing percentages of disability. A *baremo* is a complex reference chart that physicians use to calculate disability. Reliance on a *baremo* is not mandatory. It is simply a tool for harmonizing disability assessments. For instance, Silvia's disability of 20–25% in her right hand and wrist function would be translated into a general laboring permanent disability of 14% for her wrist and 5% for her hand for a total general average permanent disability in hand and wrist of around 20%. For purposes of this calculation, we consulted the *Rules for the Evaluation, Qualification and Quantification of the Disability Degree for the Workers Affiliated to the Integrated System of Pensions and Retirement Benefits*. These rules were promulgated by a presidential decree and are maintained by a federal agency that administers and oversees pension and retirement funds in Argentina.

To approximate a likely award for Silvia in Argentina, we looked for representative cases in *IIJusticia*, the publicly funded database mentioned above, and found the following three similar cases, all decided by the National Civil Court of Appeals in Buenos Aires:

• In *Escobar v. Estigarribia*, a thirty-year-old police officer sustained a wrist rupture. He suffered a permanent disability of 18% (physical) and 5% (psychological). The court of appeals awarded him 28,000 Argentine pesos ($9,330). This award was comprised of the following damages: physical disability, 20,000 pesos; psychological disability, 3,000 pesos; and emotional distress, 5,000 pesos. Cámara Nacional de Apelaciones en lo Civil, Sala M [CNCiv.], 2002, "Escobar, Oscar Juan c/ Estigarribia Julio y otros/daños y perjuicios" (unpublished).

• In *D.C.A. v. Los Constituyentes*, the court of appeals awarded 19,500 pesos ($6,500) to a twenty-eight-year-old male who suffered a wrist fracture and permanent disability of 20%. The award included 15,000 pesos for permanent physical disability and 4,500 pesos for emotional distress. Cámara Nacional de Apelaciones en lo Civil, Sala H [CNCiv.], 2003, "D.C.A. v. Los Constituyentes" (unpublished).

• In *Chavez v. D.O.T.A. S.A.*, the court of appeals awarded 17,000 pesos ($5,667) to a twenty-eight-year-old man who fell from an overcrowded bus when it made a sudden stop. He suffered trauma to his wrist with a resulting permanent physical and psychological disability of 10%. The award included 8,000 pesos for disability, 3,000 pesos for future medical expenses, and 6,000 pesos for emotional distress. Cámara Nacional de Apelaciones en lo Civil, Sala K [CNCiv.], 2004, "Chavez, Juan Carlos c/ D.O.T.A. S.A. de Transporte Automotor Linea 28 y otro/daños y perjuicios" (unpublished).

Using the data from these sample cases as a baseline, Silvia's damages award could be approximated in 2006 as follows:

Silvia's projected damages:

Permanent disability: 7,000 pesos ($2,333)
Lost income (three months of lost part-time wages): 1,500 pesos ($500)
Emotional distress: 7,000 pesos ($2,333)
Lost chance of working as a physical therapist: 20,000 pesos ($6,667)

Total damages: 35,500 pesos ($11,833)

These estimated damages are somewhat higher than the sample cases, but we took into consideration the fact that noneconomic damages have risen in recent years, and also included damages for Silvia's "lost chance" to work as a physical therapist. While it is unknown whether a court would award damages for Silvia's lost, or reduced, chance to work to her full potential in her chosen profession, Sprovieri believes it is likely a Buenos Aires court would grant a small lost chance award in Silvia's case—assuming she prevailed on the merits. In calculating Silvia's lost wages for her part-time job we estimated what a part-time unskilled employee earns in Buenos Aires, which is around 6.50 pesos ($2.17) per hour. In advancing a figure to redress emotional distress, we considered the pain, trauma, and nuisances Silvia was forced to undergo as part of her treatment, as well as her inability to enjoy some aspects of her life (playing piano, for example). The estimated award of 35,500 pesos ($11,833) assumes, of course, that Silvia set forth a well-documented case in which she successfully proved all of her alleged damages.

Silvia's Comparative Compensation

Money may or may not be the root of all evil, but, for the lack of any other means for compensating tort victims, it is at the root of all personal injury actions. Assuming Silvia prevailed on the merits in all three countries, we estimated that Silvia would recover the following gross amounts in 2006 U.S. dollars. As repeatedly emphasized, these are very rough estimates. They are descriptive rather than predictive.

U.S.: $345,000 (or $609,000 assuming proved lost lifetime earning capacity of $250,000)

Germany: $23,700 (19,750 euros)

Argentina: $11,833 (35,500 pesos)

As described in the U.S. section, a more relevant U.S. figure to compare would be Silvia's "take-home" amount. After deducting Silvia's attorneys' fees, costs, and medical expenses, her estimated projected net recovery would be $131,000 (or $289,000 assuming proved lost lifetime earning capacity of $250,000). Applying the 2005 per capita GDP figures for the three countries, Silvia's estimated low-end take-home award of $131,000 in the U.S. would be 312% of U.S. per capita GDP, her German award of $23,700 would be 80% of German per capita GDP, and her Argentine award of $11,833 would be 86% of the Argentine GDP (lower if Silvia entered into a contingency fee agreement with her Argentine lawyer).

The specific figures are unimportant and largely irrelevant. They represent only one set of projections that will change over time and which, in any event, are dependent on several assumptions and do not take account of all variables. The figures are included to contextualize the discussion of damages and attorneys' fees and to provide a *broad relative damages comparison* among the three nations. The figures support the perception that the U.S. tort system produces significantly higher overall tort damages awards than in civil law nations from Europe and Latin America, even in cases not involving punitive damages.

The discussion in this chapter has proceeded on the assumption that Silvia would win her case. But would she? In the last chapter, we give our overall assessments of the merits of Silvia's lawsuit.

Summary Chart—Damages

	United States	Germany	Argentina
The primary purpose of recovery under tort law is to make the plaintiff "whole."	Yes	Yes	Yes
Monetary awards are the primary means of compensation in personal injury cases.	Yes	Yes	Yes
A substantial portion of a tort case is devoted to proving and refuting damages.	Yes	Yes	Yes
Economic damages can be recovered for past and future medical expenses and lost wages and earning capacity.	Yes	Yes	Yes
Noneconomic damages can be recovered for mental and physical pain and suffering and disability and disfigurement.	Yes	Yes	Yes
Punitive damages are available in some tort cases.	Yes	No	No
Medical expenses are regularly paid by state-run social security systems for persons lacking financial resources and private insurance.	No	Yes	Yes

Public and private health insurance funds are entitled to reimbursement for any medical expenses paid on the injured party's behalf.	Yes	Yes	Yes
Courts rely on case precedent in calculating damages awards.	No	Yes	Yes
Damages awards are considerably standardized.	No	Yes	Yes
Parties may return to court to seek adjustments in damages based on changed future circumstances.	No	Yes, in many cases.	No

CHAPTER 11

FINAL JUDGMENT

Here we are at the end of the road and what a long, strange trip it's been. As indicated in the preface, not being comparatists, we started this journey without many preconceived notions of what we would find. Much of what we did discover came as a surprise. Due to short space, we don't attempt to recap here all of the similarities and differences among the tort litigation and products liability systems of the U.S., Germany, and Argentina. Rather, some general observations are offered, followed by our individual assessments of Silvia's case.

Four Comparative Lessons

From a wide-angle perspective, four fundamental comparative points stand out. First, we found remarkable convergence in the substantive products liability rules in all three countries as they relate to manufacturing defects. All three countries recognize similar theories of recovery grounded in negligence, strict liability, and contract, as well as similar defenses. All three countries impose similar burdens of proof on the plaintiff, and, of critical importance to plaintiffs like Silvia Winter, also have developed mechanisms to ease the plaintiff's proof burden in certain types of tort and products liability cases. It is perhaps comforting that the products liability systems in three different cultures in three different corners of the planet have, out of fairness concerns, responded in nearly identical ways to the realities of modern commerce by adopting strict liability and modifying traditional burdens of proof to facilitate the ability of injured consumers to recover for manufacturing defects.

Looking back, this convergence probably should not have come as such as a surprise to us. Law is woven into the fabric of the societies it reflects and is bound to respond to the needs of those societies. While cultures and their legal systems are very different from place to place, human beings and the legal dilemmas they regularly confront probably are not so different. We suspect there are many universal fact patterns, like Silvia's, in tort and other cases in which countries have responded in similar ways despite differences in their legal systems. This realization seems to be one of the great benefits of doing comparative law. As we looked at "the other," we found confirmation of the same concerns that our own legal systems have struggled with in consumer product cases and closely parallel solutions for resolving them. These discoveries not only helped us appreciate other legal systems, but also helped us see better what is going on at home with a fresh perspective and deeper understanding.

Secondly, contrary to the convergence in substantive legal principles, dramatic differences were seen in the procedural realm of fact gathering and presentation. In the U.S., the parties retain complete control over fact gathering, and are provided with a long list of discovery tools to facilitate that quest. In civil law countries such as Germany and Argentina, pretrial discovery does not exist, increasing the likelihood that relevant facts will never be uncovered and brought to bear in the lawsuit. While Germany and Argentina both recognize a principle of party control in civil proceedings, the parties are in reality heavily dependent on the judge to carry out fact development.

Similarly, with regard to fact presentation, in the U.S., lawyers manage all aspects of presenting facts, subject to the rules of evidence, including posing all the questions to witnesses. In Germany and Argentina, the court has primary control over eliciting evidence, although somewhat less so in practice in Argentina than in Germany. In Germany, judges decide which witnesses to call and what questions to ask them, although they're limited to calling witnesses named in the parties' pleadings. In Argentina, the parties have more leeway to summon witnesses of their choice, and to prepare lists of the questions they want the witnesses to answer (although remember that evidence-taking usually occurs before the court clerk or a subordinate—not the judge). In both countries, the lawyers get to ask follow-up questions, but such questioning does not resemble U.S.-style cross-examination. Contrary to the U.S., in Germany and Argentina, parties generally cannot testify as witnesses. In the U.S., the trial is a unified and rigidly ordered event. In civil law nations such as Germany and Argentina, trials are composed of a flexible series of episodic hearings which can continue with no definite ending date in sight.

In the U.S., every word of testimony is recorded verbatim, preserved for subsequent review, whereas in both Germany and Argentina witness testimony is merely summarized. Experts, it was seen, are widely used in all three countries, but are handled very differently. In the U.S., partisan experts are hired by the parties, often resulting in a courtroom "battle of the experts." In Germany and Argentina experts are appointed by the court, and courts usually follow their opinions, although the parties can and frequently do hire their own consulting experts. Since most case resolutions turn on facts rather than law, these procedural differences no doubt greatly impact both the conduct and outcome of litigation. The extent of this impact warrants more extensive scrutiny.

A critical third point that became clear when we reached the chapter on damages and attorneys' fees is that social and legal structural differences better explain outcome differences in the tort systems of the three countries than do rules of law. Key among them is the relative absence of government medical and wage assistance for injured persons in the U.S. as compared to many countries, including Germany and Argentina. Government social security systems serve as a substitute for tort liability in many countries around the world, whereas the U.S. relies on the tort system as a kind of ex post safety net for injury victims. The legal regime governing compensation for injuries caused by defective products in the U.S. amounts, in effect, to a publicly imposed, privately funded insurance system on product makers in which all consumers pay the premiums in the form of higher product prices. Other structural features, such as the use of juries, the contingency fee system, and a highly organized and sophisticated plaintiffs' bar, exert strong force in shaping U.S. tort litigation. Conversely, having professional civil servant judges decide cases, requiring losers to pay winners' attorneys' fees and costs, and wider availability of legal aid for tort plaintiffs all play key roles in setting the contours of tort litigation in civil law countries such as Germany and Argentina.

Finally, with regard to sources of law in the three countries, we learned the fallacy or at least the incompleteness of the bromide that law in common law systems "comes from case precedent" and law in civil law systems "comes from codes and statutes." In the realm of tort and products liability law, law in the U.S. common law system is increasingly being dictated by statutes and administrative rules, whereas most of the specific products liability rules in Germany and Argentina have emanated from case law, usually influenced by scholarly writings. While the case law always tracks back to code or other statutory provisions, many of the provisions are so general or vague in their wording that the interpretations amount to wholly judge-made law.

Take as an example article 1113 of the Argentine Civil Code, the provision that makes guardians or owners of objects liable for harm caused with or by the object. This type of provision is not unique to Argentine law. Italy, for example, has a virtually identical provision in article 2051 of the Italian Civil Code. Although article 1113 on its face appears to have little or nothing to do with products liability, Argentine courts and scholars have constructed an entire regime of strict liability for defective products from the provision. In Italy on the other hand, applications of the same basic strict liability rule have been limited to situations involving present control exercised by the guardian over the thing—the very limitation Argentine courts and scholars have worked to circumvent—and therefore finds little application in products liability law.

The observations that U.S. law is becoming increasingly systematized by statutes and administrative regulations and that civil law courts make law every day when interpreting code provisions and other statutes are not new insights, but our contextualized case study exposed these truths in rather stark relief.

Overall Assessments of Silvia's Case

As we approach the end of our global trek, the last task is to deliver our overall assessments of Silvia's case alleging a manufacturing defect in the jar of peanuts that shattered and injured her. We've covered several fundamental aspects of procedural and substantive law as they would be applied to Silvia's case in the U.S., Germany, and Argentina, yet after all that has been said, the question of whether she would win or lose is still up in the air. Below, an effort is made to pin down that all-critical question a bit more definitively, although the final answers will remain elusive. To make it clear that what follows are our informal, personal opinions, we switch to a first person point of view. For each country, we discuss:

> • Our overall assessments of the factual and legal merits of Silvia's case and the extent to which our opinions changed during the course of the project.
> • Whether we would accept Silvia's case if we were practicing plaintiffs' personal injury lawyers.
> • Whether a person in Silvia's position would be likely to seek legal redress.
> • Brief comparative observations, including desirable features of other legal systems worth considering in our own countries.

The last item requires a disclaimer. Legal systems are polycentric in nature. All features are interrelated. It's not possible to just lop off a legal rule from one country and stick it on to another country. That would be like trying to bolt a fender from a Mercedes automobile onto a Ford. Integrating a new feature of any magnitude would require adjustments, in many cases significant ones, to existing features. Here, the discussion is limited to mentioning a few appealing features of our sister nations we came across during our comparative journey.

United States/McClurg

Overall assessment. We intentionally selected a case with no easy or certain resolution. Nevertheless, it is a bit unsettling, and humbling, that after being immersed in Silvia's case for more than a year, I still have no firm idea of her ultimate chance of success in the U.S. At the beginning, I felt fairly confident that she had a good case. From years of teaching products liability law, I was well aware of the fundamental—and apparently universal—problem she would face in carrying her burden of proving when and where the defect in the jar arose. I also knew that without the jar itself, Silvia probably never would be able to produce evidence establishing those critical facts. In the original draft of the case facts, we had Norah insisting that they save the jar fragments, but that seemed a bit too convenient. The real world of finding objective truth in manufacturing defect cases is often quite messy.

Even if the broken jar had been saved, there is no guarantee experts would be able to determine the origin of the defect. In *Welge*, the pieces of the peanuts jar were preserved and examined by experts, but they could not ascertain what caused the jar to break. The study of materials failure has advanced since *Welge* was decided in 1994, but even assuming experts could determine conclusively that, say, an external impact caused the defect in Silvia's jar, such an impact could have been inflicted anywhere in the distribution chain.

Even with the absence of the jar, I felt good about Silvia's chances. My opinion was formed primarily from the study of appellate cases, which is the realm in which a U.S. law professor dwells in a common law education system dependent on the "case method." I shared the opinion of the Iowa Supreme Court, quoted in chapter eight, that cases involving exploding beverage bottles are "generally resolved" in favor of plaintiffs, and saw no legally relevant distinction between exploding bottles of soft drinks or beer and shattering glass jars of peanuts. Carbonated beverage containers are more intrinsically dangerous because they are under pressure, but are made stronger and sturdier for that reason. I believed judges usually bailed out plaintiffs like Silvia by liberally construing the facts necessary to support the inferences that the product had a defect and that the defect existed when the product was in the hands of one or more of the defendants.

This sunny outlook was reinforced by *Welge v. Planters Lifesavers Co.*, the case from which the legally relevant facts of Silvia's case were derived. Judge Richard Posner, who penned the opinion for the U.S. Court of Appeals for the Seventh Circuit, is one of America's most respected legal minds. A prolific law and economics scholar, Judge Posner is not viewed as a liberal or activist judge. In reversing the summary judgment granted by the trial court to the defendants, Judge Posner was dismissive of the defendants' assertion that the jar of peanuts, bought two weeks before the accident, could have been damaged after purchase. Recall his sarcastic comment that "[e]lves may have played ninepins with the jar of peanuts" while the plaintiff slept, but that the plaintiff was not required to exclude "every possibility, however fantastic or remote" that the defect was caused by someone other than one of the defendants. *Welge* bolstered my perception that Silvia was on solid ground.

Deeper into the project, I became somewhat less sanguine about Silvia's chances. A particular eye-opener was when I called a friend and former colleague who has been practicing as a successful plaintiffs' personal injury lawyer in Florida for more than twenty-five years. His lukewarm response to a description of Silvia's case came as a surprise. "Is there any evidence of similar breakage incidents?" he asked. None that we know of, I told him. He said he probably wouldn't take the case unless he could find such evidence. Knowing that his level of success gave him greater luxury to be picky in choosing cases than most lawyers enjoy, I asked him whether Silvia would be able to find another lawyer. He was confident that she could. "What kind of lawyer?" I asked. "A great lawyer, a competent lawyer, or a bottom feeder?" "Probably a competent lawyer," he said. One insight from this discussion is that the contingency fee system may not be arbitrary or irrational as some people believe. His reticence to take the case was grounded in simple economics. Like all products liability cases, Silvia's case would require a significant investment of time and out-of-pocket costs. Since it was far from a slam-dunk, that investment would be at risk in a system where the plaintiff's lawyer gets paid only if victorious.

Then Jury Verdict Research updated its computer generated analysis of Silvia's case for us. JVR first did an analysis in 2005 estimating a 40% probability of a favorable verdict for Silvia for a food or beverage container case filed in Miami-Dade County, Florida, but when it reran Silvia's case in 2006, the probability declined to 26%. We have mentioned the JVR analysis several times in this book. JVR does not purport to be able to make guaranteed predictions. Still, the decline made me wonder whether, as plaintiffs' lawyers fear, negative publicity of the tort system generated by the tort reform movement could be working to poison the well for tort plaintiffs by making jurors more skeptical of tort claims. *See generally* Haltom & McCann (in-depth examination of how distortion and misinformation have shaped inaccurate perceptions of the U.S. tort system).

Finally, when I asked one of my research assistants to search for broken glass container cases in which the plaintiff lost, I was surprised by the length of the list of appellate cases he brought back to me. Many of those cases are cited in chapter eight.

In short, Silvia has a decent case, but her prospects, especially at the trial level, might not be as rosy in the U.S. as I first thought. Of course, the result would depend to a large extent on facts not known because we did not develop them. In a real litigated case, additional facts could be unearthed along the way that would dictate a result one way or the other. For example, as was hypothesized several times, if facts were discovered showing an unusually high rate of breakage in the particular batch of jars to which Silvia's belonged, that would provide a strong basis for circumstantially proving a preexisting defect. On the other hand, if Silvia broke down on the witness stand and admitted that the accident occurred as she attempted to juggle the jar of peanuts with a couple of flower vases, while drunk, she would lose.

While factual breakthroughs like these do occur, we decided to stay with the reasonable assumption that no tribunal would ever be able to figure out exactly what caused Silvia's jar of Penelope Peanuts to shatter. The defect could have arisen a year earlier at Levington's factory while the glass was being cast or an hour before Silvia purchased the jar when a Value-Store employee dropped the jar on the floor while stocking the shelves. Recently, at the grocery store, I saw a store clerk—a full-grown man—using a twelve-pack of glass beer bottles as a stepstool. Could someone have stood on the crate containing Silvia's peanuts jar, cracking the jar?

With the objective truth in doubt, the outcome of the case could turn in large part on Silvia herself. Our self-created perception of Silvia probably influenced my optimistic assessment of her case from the beginning. In the U.S., witness credibility, demeanor, and appearance are critical to the outcome of cases. In the glare of the spotlight of open court and subject to vigorous cross-examination, Silvia's testimony could prove outcome determinative. That parties generally are not permitted to testify as witnesses in either Germany or Argentina was one of the most surprising comparative differences I came across during this project. In the U.S., cases like Silvia's frequently depend on the plaintiff's testimony.

We always pictured Silvia as a sincere, honest, hardworking "victim" of circumstances. If she came across that way to the jury, she would have a much better chance of winning, particularly if she were attractive. Not attractive in a glamorous way, which could work against her, but pleasant-looking. Many empirical studies show we are inclined to associate good qualities with people—both men and women—who are physically attractive. Studies show that less attractive people are less favored in almost every context of life: by their teachers, employers, even parents. Why should jurors be immune?

Imagine a sincere, attractive Silvia on the witness stand tearing up ever so slightly as she testified how after the accident she tried to play Beethoven's *Für*

Elise on the piano, a piece she's been playing in recitals since she was seven years old, but couldn't do it because of the pain, numbness, and limited range of movement in her fingers and hand. With jurors receiving no limits or guidance in calculating noneconomic damages, the defense lawyers might be hoping that the jury wouldn't request a calculator when it retired to deliberate. Since Norah and Marco were the last people to handle the jar before it broke, their credibility and demeanor also would be important.

Because Silvia's injury occurred in a private household with no physical evidence or disinterested witnesses, the believability of Silvia, Norah, and Marco would be especially important because there is always a possibility of fraud in this type of case. Silvia's case obviously couldn't be a complete fraud, because her injuries are real. But if the jury thought that any of them were being untruthful about their handling of the jar, her case could end badly.

Most U.S. jurors probably wouldn't hold the use of the Exacto knife against Silvia, assuming there was no other readily apparent way to remove the rebate coupon. In fact, there could be a backlash against the defendants if they tried to blame Silvia for the accident. In deciding how reasonable persons would have acted under a particular set of circumstances, most jurors probably consider how they themselves would have acted. With regard to the Exacto knife, they might ask, "What would I do if there was a rebate label on a jar and no easy way to remove it?" Using some type of sharp blade would appear to be a logical course of action. On the other hand, if the rebate coupon was designed with a clearly marked and easy-to-use pull-tab for removal, the jury might very well look askance at taking a knife to a glass jar. This is an example of how altering a single fact could affect the outcome of a case.

Assuming the judge let the case go to the jury, the result would depend in part on the individual jury. Two juries could look differently at the same set of facts. The relative skill of the lawyers often plays a large role. Skilled lawyers can win weaker cases, while less-skilled lawyers can botch better ones.

Given that it is unlikely anyone would ever know exactly what caused the jar to break, the most important *legal* question in the case, apparently in all three countries, is who would end up bearing the burden of proof. U.S. courts take burdens of proof seriously. Normally, Silvia would bear that burden and if held to it strictly, as said many times, would lose. But we saw that an escape avenue exists for plaintiffs like Silvia in the form of res ipsa loquitur for negligence claims and a more or less identical inference-drawing process for strict liability claims. If invoked, the judge would instruct the jury at the end of the case that it may—not must—draw an inference of negligence or defect and attribute the negligence or defect to one or more of the defendants.

This would have the practical, although generally not formal, effect of shifting the burden of going forward with the evidence to the defendants, giving Silvia a fighting chance to prevail since the defendants aren't in a much better position to prove what happened or didn't happen than Silvia. On the other hand, if the judge decided the facts did not warrant such an instruction, he or she might very well grant summary judgment or a directed verdict for the defendants and Silvia would lose. Thus, as explained in chapter eight, Silvia's fate in the trial court would rest largely in the hands of the particular judge, specifically with regard to how liberally or stringently the judge was willing to construe the inferences that the jar had a defect and that the defect existed when the jar was in the hands of one or more of the defendants.

Taking on Silvia as a client. Would I take Silvia's case if I were a practicing plaintiffs' personal injury lawyer? Personal injury lawyers generally weigh three interrelated components in deciding whether to accept representation in a particular case: the likelihood of success on the merits, the amount of damages, and what it's going to cost in time and money to get there. Strength in one component can help make up for weaknesses in others. Thus, for example, a lawyer might be willing to take a chance in accepting a weaker case if it carried the potential for a high payoff. Just as we designed Silvia's case to be a decent but not great case on the merits, we designed it to be an in-between case in terms of her injuries. Her injuries are substantial, but not catastrophic. Assuming my firm had the resources to finance the litigation, the answer as to whether I would accept Silvia as a client would be: yes, if Silvia came across as believable and likeable; and no, if she didn't. Trial lawyers we consulted confirmed that "how Silvia would play to a jury" would be the single most important consideration in deciding whether to take the case.

Would Silvia be likely to seek legal redress? Would Silvia be likely to pursue a legal remedy in the U.S.? Many factors obviously go into such a decision, and empirical evidence suggests that most injured persons in the U.S. do not bring lawsuits or even seek legal advice. Nevertheless, there may be a greater tendency, as well as a greater need, for injured persons to seek legal representation in the U.S. Because lawyers advertise widely and because the U.S. tort system receives substantial, albeit mostly negative, media coverage, Americans may be more programmed than citizens of other countries to think about the possibility of a lawsuit when they get injured. Due to the lack of ready access to public health care and the fact that a substantial percentage of the population lacks private health insurance, there may be a greater need for injured persons to think about a lawsuit than in countries where government social security systems fund medical care. I think there's a good chance that an educated person like Silvia with a fairly serious injury caused by a consumer product would consult a lawyer.

Comparative observations, including desirable features of other legal systems. The most striking legal differences among the three countries were the procedural ones, particularly in the realm of fact-finding. The U.S. discovery system, while costly and inefficient, seems significantly more likely to unearth relevant facts than the civil law systems in Germany and Argentina, where there is no discovery. The cost and efficiency savings of a legal system without discovery may or may not be worth it to a society at large, but as an individual party, I'd feel more comfortable in a system where I knew my lawyer had more control over finding that slippery objective truth. References have been made to the possibility that in Germany and Argentina crucial facts such as Silvia's use of the Exacto knife or documents showing higher than normal breakage rates in the defendants' jars could remain hidden due to the absence of discovery. In the U.S., there is little doubt both sides would pursue and uncover such facts through pretrial discovery unless they were intentionally and fraudulently suppressed, which can and does happen.

The starkest practical difference overall among the three tort systems is in the amount of damages. I went into the project with a vague impression, unsupported by specific information, that U.S. tort damages were substantially higher than in other countries. One commonly offered explanation for the disparity is the availability of punitive damages in the U.S., but Silvia's case didn't involve punitive damages and yet we still found, in our inexact way, substantial disparities in damages estimates, even after taking into consideration relative per capita GDP. As discussed, institutional features such as the relative availability of public health care and the manner in which attorneys' fees and costs are handled explain much of the disparity.

Another explanation for higher damages awards in the U.S. that has not been addressed appears to be a much different cultural mindset toward damages for noneconomic injuries. The amounts of Silvia's projected noneconomic damages in both Germany and Argentina for the pain and trauma of the cut injury and a lifetime of suffering a 20–25% disability in one's dominant hand and wrist with a 5% overall bodily impairment struck me as unreasonably low. But then, noneconomic damages in the U.S. strike many people as unreasonably high.

Three features of the German and Argentine legal systems appealed to me. The first is in how experts are handled. While I see danger in over-reliance on court-appointed experts, I see advantages in the basic concept of using neutral court-appointed experts over partisan experts hired by the parties. The "battle of the experts" in the U.S. has always struck me as an inefficient and unreliable means by which to resolve scientific or technical questions. An observation by John Langbein sticks in my mind. In criticizing U.S. expert witness practice, Langbein observed: "If you need an architect, a dermatologist, or a plumber, you do not commission a pair of them to take preordained and opposing positions on your problem.... [Y]ou take care to find an expert who is qualified to advise you in an objective manner." Langbein, at 837. On the other hand, when a lot is at stake, one is well-advised to seek a second opinion. Perhaps a good approach would be to appoint two independent experts on the key issues and consider their reports together.

I found the German procedures that allow the parties to go back to court to seek an adjustment of damages based on changed circumstances to be fascinating. Predicting future damages for medical expenses and lost earning capacity can be speculative to the point of being meaningless. The casebook I use to teach Torts contains a tragic case about an infant who suffered horrible, permanent injuries from a fire caused by a defective space heater. I use the case in part to demonstrate the "reading tea leaves" quality of predicting future damages. How is a jury supposed to calculate the lifetime medical expenses of a severely disabled infant with a seventy-five year life expectancy? How are jurors supposed to assess the future lost earning capacity of an infant? The child may have grown up to be a neurosurgeon or a convenience store clerk. There is no way to know, yet potentially millions of dollars in differential lifetime earnings can depend on the answer to that question.

Silvia's case is not as striking, but predicting her future damages is nevertheless quite speculative. Would Silvia require future medical care? Would she suffer lost earning capacity due to her disability? Would the condition of her hand and wrist improve or degenerate? In the U.S., experts would be likely to express contradictory opinions on these issues and the jury would be left to sort them out and make predictions forever binding even if they turned out to be dead wrong. Leaving the door open for future damages adjustments would impose considerable additional administrative burdens on already overburdened courts and no doubt be a horrifying prospect to defendants who want to close the books on tort claims, but the basic concept seems logically sound. Torts students invariably ask, "Can't the parties go back to court in the future if the circumstances change?" My old answer was a brusque, "No. It doesn't work that way." My new answer is, "Well, in some countries, such as Germany, they can."

Finally, it is noteworthy that tort damages are much more standardized and, hence, predictable in both Germany and Argentina, with judges consulting books or databases of prior cases and setting damages in line with those cases. That's why we were able to offer reasonably reliable estimates of Silvia's damages in Germany and Argentina. This point is intriguing from a common law versus civil law perspective. It seems ironic that two civil law systems, where case law is theoretically irrelevant, rely on prior cases in calculating damages, whereas the U.S. common law system does not. This divergence is also interesting from a social policy standpoint. One of the most frequently uttered critiques of the U.S. tort system is the "lottery" aspect of leaving damages calculations to lay juries, giving them little guidance in calculating economic damages and no guidance in calculating noneconomic damages. It is no wonder that jury awards for similar injuries can vary widely. While it probably wouldn't be desirable to have jurors considering prior cases in setting damages, it might be useful to allow and encourage trial and appellate judges to consult prior awards when reviewing jury verdicts for excessiveness or inadequacy. Building a reliable, publicly accessible database of prior judgments organized by nature and extent of injuries and other relevant factors could help courts fashion a more consistent template for reviewing damages awards. On the other hand, each case is different. Thus, it would be essential that judges retained discretion to consider the special circumstances of each case.

Germany/Koyuncu

Overall assessment. From the time we started this project, I was sympathetic toward Silvia based on her background, job, studious and hard-working nature, the pain and disability she suffered, and the ordinary course of how she was injured, which is something we could all picture happening to ourselves. But would a judge share this view?

Lawyers must differentiate between their personal feelings toward persons and giving them legal advice. As professionals, we need to detach from the sympathy we feel for Silvia as a person in order to provide "client Silvia" with the best and most realistic legal counsel. This necessitates evaluating the case objectively as a judge would see it, and also putting ourselves in the defendants' place. Such a role reversal makes it easier to see the weaknesses in a case by anticipating defense strategies. Lawyers know there are some situations where no legal remedy is available to a plaintiff even though one might feel she deserves it. In these cases, it is part of our responsibility to give candid advice to prevent more injury to the plaintiff in the form of litigation costs and, particularly, the mental strain of carrying on a lawsuit. If there is no reasonable chance of winning, all the sympathy in the world will accomplish nothing but perhaps additional harm. Having said all that, Silvia does have a chance to win.

In assessing Silvia's case, we face both factual and legal questions. Beginning with the factual uncertainties, the crucial question is: Did a preexisting product defect lead to the event? The facts must be sufficient to convince the judge that the harmful event occurred due to a product defect not created by Silvia, Norah or Marco. Moreover, given the much more limited recourse against retailers and wholesalers in Germany as compared to the U.S. and Argentina, the judge would have to be persuaded that the defect most likely existed while the jar was in the sphere of Levington or Penelope.

In Germany, the fact that the jar was disposed of could turn out to be the crucial reason for Silvia losing the case because it prevents technical evaluation of the broken pieces by experts. In exploding bottle cases, German experts have shown considerable expertise in reconstructing the causes of a glass container shattering, particularly as it relates to differentiating external damage to the jar, which could be inflicted by a consumer, from internal defects that are clearly related to the manufacture of the container. Of course, in Silvia's case, as McClurg noted, because the jar traveled through many entities, even testimony of this nature would not prove conclusive as to the origin of the defect. If an expert determined that the jar broke because of an external defect, that would leave open the possibility that Silvia, Norah or Marco damaged it, but it wouldn't rule out the possibility that one of the defendants inflicted external damage on the jar in filling, packaging, transporting or otherwise handling it.

In any event, it doesn't matter because we don't have the broken jar pieces. Therefore, we and the court need to assess the case on the basis of the available limited facts. What evidence does Silvia have to show the defect? Not much, other than the happening of the accident. She has her version of the events, which would not be considered as formal evidence because parties generally cannot testify as witnesses, and the testimony of Norah, Marco, and Dr. Schmitt. Marco and Norah would have only limited knowledge as to what happened to the jar before it shattered. They were not with Silvia when she bought the jar, placed it in her shopping cart, transferred it to her car, and retrieved it from her car before entering the apartment. They weren't with her when she cut out the rebate label or stored the jar in the cabinet or retrieved a handful of peanuts from it the morning before the accident. Although it hasn't been mentioned, Dr. Schmitt might be able to shed some light on the nature of the breakage by testifying about the injury pattern on Silvia's hand and wrist. This pattern and the jar pieces found in the wound could provide relevant information such as the size of the glass shards, which could possibly be used by a technical expert to draw deductions regarding how the jar broke.

Having only the claimant and two close friends as the main witnesses is a weak position for substantiating a products liability case in Germany. The more so inasmuch as the product has been thrown away by the same people. Certainly, as McClurg said, much would depend on the personal appearance of the three at court. But even if they are consistent in their report and come across as trustworthy, the case would remain difficult.

Let us imagine for a moment how the defendant could proceed. Of course, the defense lawyers would ask all three how they handled the jar and whether they were aware of any improper treatment of the jar. If the Exacto knife treatment came out, the case would become much more difficult for Silvia. "Why in the world did you cut off the rebate label with a knife?" defense counsel would ask. "Why didn't you just pull if off or scrape it loose with a fingernail?" Then, assuming it is accurate, the defendants would argue that they have sold millions of these jars and have never heard of a similar shattering incident. They would build a bridge from this to the Exacto knife, arguing they similarly have never heard of any other customer using a razor-knife to cut into the surface of the jar. The goal would be to show that Silvia's contributory negligence caused the jar to shatter.

Continuing this imagined defense strategy, Levington's quality assurance officer at the factory where the jar batch was produced might appear at court. We'll assume he appears to be an honest, hard-working, and diligent person. He testifies that he takes all possible measures to ensure that no defective products leave the plant. Not as constricted by evidentiary rules precluding opinions and speculation as in the U.S., he might even suggest that Silvia made up the story to receive high damages, which she needs because of her financial predicament—that she's lying to try to make the best out of this negligently self-caused accident. This could explain why the jar fragments were thrown away in the trash instead of collected and saved. He would emphasize that the damages Silvia claims are many times higher than what he earns per year to support his family.

In all likelihood, Silvia would need the court to apply the burden-relieving *Anscheinsbeweis* and/or the burden-shifting *Befundsicherungspflicht* doctrines to her case. There is no way to predict whether the court would apply the doctrines. Just as in the U.S., the crucial aspect would be whether the judge sees enough evidence to support an inference based on common understanding that a product defect for which the defendants were responsible led to the jar shattering.

Despite what has been said, I don't think Silvia's case is at all hopeless. She has going for her the common expectation that a normal, non-defective jar would not shatter when putting the lid on top of it. This consumer expectation is arguably valid even for a case where the consumer touched the jar with a razor-knife to cut off a rebate label. First, as the U.S. court said in the *Welge* case, a jar producer should anticipate that consumers would use a razor-knife to detach a rebate label that had to be removed in order for it to be used by the consumer. Additionally, Silvia would argue that glass jars sold to consumers should be strong enough to withstand such a contact. It is predictable that such a jar would encounter many different types of rough treatment. Silvia could assert that the dangers of shattering are just as high or higher when the jar is jostled during transport or bumped against other hard containers in the consumer's shopping bag or during stocking. In assessing the case, it is not a stretch to conclude that the most probable explanation for Silvia's jar shattering is that it was an outlier, a defectively manufactured unit that "got away." Such stray defective units are inevitable in the mass production of any consumer good. This would also explain why no other reported instances of breakage exist, if indeed that turned out to be the case.

To wrap up, it would be crucial for Silvia to convince the court that a product defect caused the shattering of the jar. If the court drew the inference that the product must have been defective, Silvia would likely win the case. The remaining factual and legal questions are far less problematic. Overall, although this is just my rough guess, I would put Silvia's chances of crossing this hurdle in court at less than 50%, maybe even as low as 20–30%. As noted by McClurg, the outlook could change dramatically if additional facts, such as the discovery of similar breakage incidents, were revealed by research or during court hearings. Silvia's chances also would rise if documents or other facts were unearthed indicating quality irregularities at the Levington or Penelope plants. The same development could occur if Levington's above-mentioned quality assurance officer broke down in court during crossfire questioning by the judge and Silvia's lawyer and conceded that there have been quality problems at the factory in the past. Due to the lack of pretrial depositions and other discovery mechanisms in the German system, one often does not know what a witness might say or what further evidence will emerge in court.

To what extent did my opinion of Silvia's case change during the course of this project? At the beginning I was—like McClurg—a bit more optimistic about the outcome of Silvia's case. One reason was that in our initial case facts the broken pieces of the jar were collected and saved by Marco and Norah, so I saw the option of having an expert figure out why the jar shattered. Also, our opinions about Silvia's chances no doubt were influenced by our knowing the facts that Silvia didn't do anything wrong, apart from using the Exacto knife. But this bias lost its effect as we progressed through the case.

At the beginning of the project I expected to find many similar favorable cases in the German judicature, as a large number of court decisions exist involving exploding bottles. I initially assumed the *Befundsicherungspflicht* doctrine would apply easily to Silvia's case and shift the burden to the relevant producing defendant of showing the jar was not defective while it was in the defendant's organizational sphere. More research, however, led me to question whether this doctrine, which was developed in judgments involving exploding fizzy drink bottles (lemonade and mineral water), would be fully applicable to a peanuts jar not intended for repeat use or under internal pressure from carbonation. However, I still believe there is a chance that the *Anscheinsbeweis* and/or *Befundsicherungspflicht* doctrines could apply to Silvia's case. Also, let's not forget that the Product Liability Act contains a provision shifting the burden to the producing defendants to prove the product was not defective when it left their spheres. While the act's provisions have not yet been substantially fleshed out by the courts, it's possible the act could save Silvia's case for her.

Taking on Silvia as a client. If I were a practicing plaintiffs' personal injury lawyer, I probably would accept Silvia's case, but before the decision to file an action was made I would need to assemble more proof, including conducting research of similar breakage incidents. As has been mentioned, Germany has strict reporting and records-keeping requirements for product defects and injuries. Readers may be wondering, "Why would Koyuncu take a case he thinks has less than a 50% chance of success, maybe even as low as 20–30%?" Think back to chapter ten, where the answers lie. Remember that in contrast to the U.S., a German lawyer does not have to finance the litigation or bear the risk of not getting paid under a contingency fee contract if he loses. Silvia most likely has a strong enough claim to receive legal aid, so the costs of litigation, as well as her lawyer's fee, would be advanced by the government. Unlike his or her U.S. counterpart, Silvia's German lawyer would get paid regardless of the outcome. If Silvia lost, her attorney would receive fees based on the legal aid fee schedule, which are lower than the statutory fees the lawyer would be entitled to if Silvia was a regular non-legal aid client. If she won, the losing defendants would have to pay Silvia's attorney the regular, higher statutory attorney fees. Thus, there is an incentive for the lawyer to win in a case involving a legal-aid client even in the absence of contingency fee.

Would Silvia be likely to seek legal redress? Would Silvia be likely to pursue legal redress in Germany? The answer is yes. German Silvia would be very likely to contact a lawyer seeking legal advice. It is not only Americans who contemplate legal action when injured. German citizens are very sensitive with respect to injuries they perceive as having been inflicted by another party, the more so in a case like Silvia's involving a serious injury with a permanent disability that could affect her future occupational life. As in the U.S., products liability cases receive considerable media coverage so that German Silvia, who is even more highly educated than an "average victim," would be well aware of the availability of a possible legal remedy.

Comparative observations, including desirable features of other legal systems. Many interesting comparative similarities, discussed throughout the book, were discovered during this project. Along with my co-authors, I found remarkable the similarities in the substantive products liability law of the three countries, especially as it pertains to theories of recovery, defenses, and burden of proof rules à la res ispa loquitur.

On the other hand, substantial differences exist as well. The right to trial by jury in the U.S. might rank highest on the list of those differences. For us Europeans, jury trials have always been a fascinating phenomenon. Our bench trials are conducted much more matter-of-factly and less emotionally. Of course, jury trials aren't one big drama as portrayed on television. Like all trials, they are dominated by mundane and often monotonous testimony. But they do present dramatic moments in numbers much greater than bench trials. Because the jury is a different kind of audience from a judge, jury trials seem more challenging in that they require skills beyond simply competent legal skills. The best jury trial lawyers must be quick-witted and skilled in rhetoric, humor, and other presentation techniques. Certainly there is an excitement in a jury trial that any lawyer would admire.

But are jury trials a better legal battlefield from the parties' point of view? Our bench trial system has a few considerable advantages for the parties. The trials are led by the professional judges who narrow the focus to the relevant questions, which accelerates the trial and saves costs. Also, the fate of the parties is not so wholly controlled by the lawyers. The judge retains substantial control of the proceedings. One might legitimately argue that most relevant factual and legal questions *are* matter-of-fact in nature and, therefore, it is appropriate that the procedures for handling them be geared in their design toward matter-of-fact evidence presentation and reception. While jury trials remain fascinating to me, I favor our bench trial system.

Another difference worth mentioning, even though it was not an issue in Silvia's case, is punitive damages. In Germany, punitive damages are viewed as a quirky phenomenon of U.S. tort law. We dismiss the idea of mixing a criminal-type punitive element in private law litigation. Such a mix is quite problematic as the litigation procedures in private and criminal proceedings are so different. As there are stricter procedural protections for criminal punishment (as, of course, there are in the U.S.), we can get different results in civil and criminal proceedings. Punishment, it is believed in Germany, as opposed to compensation, is something that should be reserved to criminal proceedings.

Another point that needs mentioning is the loser pays rule. I do not understand why the U.S. does not follow the loser pays rule. In Germany, as well as in Argentina and most other countries, we have a societal agreement that at court the losing party pays the costs of the winning party. If someone is required to retain a lawyer to defend against an action, it is our natural understanding that if the action turns out to have been unjustified, the party who brought the suit and has caused the other to suffer great costs should bear those costs. Therefore, it is striking to me that in the U.S. winning parties have to pay their own costs. The loser pays rule also imposes self-discipline on plaintiffs and their lawyers in that it makes them have to stop and "think twice" before filing an action.

One more striking aspect that came out during this project is that in some situations Germany and Argentina, both civil law systems, are much more case law oriented than even the U.S. As McClurg elucidated, tort damages are much more predictable in both Germany and Argentina than in the U.S. because judges usually aim to set damages consistent with previous cases. Indeed, it is surprising that in the U.S. common law system prior damages awards in similar cases are considered largely irrelevant in calculating tort recoveries.

Finally, I am surprised that the U.S. and Argentina have not established instruments similar to the German declaratory action or revisable periodic payment procedure which provide the parties with more flexibility regarding the compensation of non-predictable future medical expenses and other future damages. There is definitely a practical need for such flexibility, particularly in personal injury cases.

Regarding interesting features of my sister nations which Germany might consider borrowing, here are three:

Should we borrow higher damages awards from the U.S.? As discussed, there are several sound explanations for the disparities in damages amounts between the U.S. and Germany. Nevertheless, from the perspective of an ordinary citizen, I agree with Judge Lothar Jaeger, mentioned in chapter ten, that amounts awarded in Germany for noneconomic damages in personal injury cases are too low. This may be changing, as an upward trend in noneconomic damages has been witnessed in recent years.

Pretrial discovery is another feature of U.S. litigation that is worth investigating for Germany. It is already the subject of sometimes controversial discussion. Some legislators believe there is a clear need to adopt procedures that enable plaintiffs to review the defendant's documentation to find "the truth." Thus, in recent years the German legislature has adopted discovery-like instruments known as "disclosure claims" (*Auskunftsanspruch*) that allow plaintiffs access to documentation in a few areas of tort law such as pharmaceutical industry liability and environmental liability. Even though I see risks for defendants from implementing broader discovery in Germany, I do agree that plaintiffs have both a need and justification to obtain relevant information from within the defendant's sphere. At the same time effective controls should be in place so that discovery devices are not abused to harass defendants and press settlements. Also, discovery should be a two-way street, as in the U.S., so that defendants would be entitled to disclosure of information within the plaintiff's sphere.

Finally, when I review the regulation of the German legal profession in a new comparative perspective, I really see the need for more liberalization in the overall practice of law. It seems that attorneys in the U.S. and also Argentina practice much more freely. Although U.S. lawyers are regulated to a significant extent by bar associations, regulation of the legal profession goes further in Germany, where we have statutes that, among other things, restrictively regulate lawyer advertising, set attorneys' fees, and prohibit contingency fees. Particularly regarding the prohibition of contingency fees, the reasons offered for the existing rules are not convincing. We need more flexibility here, all the more so because the commercial and competitive environment of our profession has changed. The dangers attributed to contingency fees in Germany, usually accompanied by ominous comparisons to "American conditions," seem overstated. The comparison among the three countries in our journey has revealed that contingency fees are not unique to the U.S., as we encounter them in Argentina too. In Germany, we should at least give them a try.

Argentina/Sprovieri

Overall assessment. At the time of shaping the mock case on which this book was based, we decided on an interesting set of facts—simple yet complicated—to enrich the comparative exploration. We wanted to make the facts resemble real life. Straightforward factual and legal cases exist mostly only in theory, not in actual practice. This is true whether one is learning or functioning under the U.S. case method or in a civil law country like Argentina, where legal training does not focus on cases. The reality is that the factual bases of many "ordinary" cases, especially in the sometimes murky world of products liability, do not provide clear-cut solutions. For instance, as was the case with Silvia and her peanuts jar, injured laypersons do not anticipate a claim at the time of being injured and, thus, often do not preserve key pieces of evidence. This common oversight, as has been discussed throughout this book, can be all critical to the parties and outcome of a products liability case. Arguably, corporate defendants in products liability cases—especially manufacturers—are sophisticated businesses and repeat players who should anticipate injuries and lawsuits and prepare for them by tracking their products, keeping detailed records, and gathering and preserving other evidence. The plaintiff's lack of knowledge and evidence-gathering ability could result in a considerable strategic imbalance between Silvia and, say, Penelope, the peanuts manufacturer. This type of imbalance helps explain why judges in all three countries have developed legal mechanisms designed to help consumers like Silvia.

Nevertheless, although Argentine judges, aided by local scholars, have come forward with devices designed to ameliorate the imbalance, plaintiffs in products liability cases still carry the difficult burden of proving a product defect and the casual link between that defect and the alleged damages. Argentine judges have gone far in leveling the battlefield of products liability disputes (e.g., by means of the doctrine of the dynamic burden of proof), but they still may be reluctant to jump to the inferences necessary to support a plaintiff recovery. As shown by recent products liability decisions, Argentine judges are not necessarily consumer sympathetic. *See, e.g.*, Cámara Nacional de Apelaciones en lo Civil, Sala F [CNCiv.], 11/16/05, "Cabrera Cal, Sheila et al. v. Renault Argentina S.A./daños y perjuicios," Jurisprudencia Argentina [J.A.] (2006-I-347) (holding for defendant in an airbag case because the plaintiff was not using a seatbelt when the accident occurred); Cámara Nacional de Apelaciones en lo Civil, Sala C [CNCiv.], 6/1/04, "Roncelli, Eduardo c. Aguas Dadone de Argentina S.A.," Jurisprudencia Argentina [J.A.] (2004-IV-Supplemento 11/17/2004) (holding for defendant in case involving an exploding bottle of carbonated mineral water on the basis that evidence was insufficient to show a defect).

In my view, Marco's and Norah's disposing of the pieces of the shattered jar should be of great concern to Silvia's lawyer. Silvia would have to demonstrate that the particular jar she was handling had a defect, and with the jar pieces no longer in Silvia's possession, any direct evidence on that point is unavailable. The peanuts jar, as we well know, underwent handling by many people who could have mistreated the product. Unfortunately for Silvia, some of the most important individuals were all within Silvia's dwelling, not exactly a neutral venue. One would of course expect that Silvia and her close friends would insist that they acted with complete propriety. Silvia has the ability to prove the nature and extent of the damages caused by the shattering jar, but a judge would examine evidence on damages only after determining that the injuring event was attributable to one or more of the defendants. It is a two-tier logical process in which the event and its etiology come first and damages are examined only after that first exam has been passed satisfactorily.

Glass food jars are not supposed to shatter. In one sense, this bolsters Silvia's claim, but because of the absence of concrete evidence, it could also be a hindrance. As a division of the National Civil Court of Appeals in Buenos

Aires recently held, defects in products are not the rule. They are exceptional. Being that they are the exception, a plaintiff alleging a product defect should deploy a rather cohesive set of evidence able to convince the judge that the case at hand departs from what normally happens. *See* Cámara Nacional de Apelaciones en lo Civil, Sala B [CNCiv.], 4/7/06, "Núñez, Wenceslao v. Cervecería y Maltería Quilmes S.A.I.C.A. y G./daños y perjuicios" (unpublished) (holding that absent a context of evidence suggesting a defect, defect inferences do not apply).

Using the Exacto knife would probably not be a problem in Silvia's case. Since U.S.-like discovery is not part of Argentine procedure, Silvia and her lawyer would never mention the Exacto knife. No party to a lawsuit is obliged to disclose facts that can jeopardize its case. Further, it is likely that Silvia's core witnesses—Marco and Norah—would be well-advised by Silvia's lawyer not to mention the Exacto knife unless directly questioned and required to do so. If the issue did come out, it would be subject to the same type of analysis as has already been posited for the U.S. and Germany. Silvia would argue that it was foreseeable to Penelope that a consumer would use a razor-knife to remove a rebate label and also that a well-constructed jar should have been able to withstand such contact in any event.

Silvia's best strategy in this case would be to try to demonstrate that the supposed exceptional defect is not only possible but also likely. This evidence could take the form of a report of a court-appointed engineer stating that other jars from Levington or Penelope were prone to shatter or records of a public agency overseeing consumer products that showed prior similar incidents. *See* Cámara Nacional de Apelaciones en lo Civil, Sala A [CNCiv.], 5/30/06, "Morelli, Miriam Noemí y otro v. Kalvanco Argentina S.A." (unpublished) (finding in a gas-tank explosion case that records showing the occurrence of other similar incidents and intervention by a public agency on the matter served to prove a manufacturing defect and knowledge of the defect by the manufacturer). Defects can also be shown by citation to other cases involving similar facts and the same product. *See* Cámara Nacional de Apelaciones en lo Civil, Sala B [CNCiv.], 2/24/06, "Pagnotta, Marta M. v. Unilever de Argentina S.A.," Semanarios de Jurisprudencia Argentina [S.J.A.] (5/31/06) (finding that a product defect could be indirectly proved or inferred through reported judicial decisions in similar cases or through complaints filed with the *Dirección General de Defensa y Protección del Consumidor*, the public agency entrusted with consumer protection). Once again, we see that case law plays a powerful role even in a civil law country like Argentina.

Summing up, since the jar is no longer in Silvia's possession and cannot be examined, it is impossible to predict the outcome of Argentine Silvia's case. If the court invoked res ipsa loquitur or the doctrine of the dynamic burden of proof, she might win even without additional evidence. Otherwise, her only hope would be to find some evidence of other similar incidents. Since the judge would never hear the witnesses' testimony or even see a full transcript of it, their credibility and demeanor would not play the critical role they would play in the U.S.

Picture a record ripe for decision that showed, from one side, written summaries of the testimony of three witnesses: Norah, Marco and Dr. Schmitt, two of them being close friends of Silvia's and one testifying principally with regard to injury rather than liability issues. Recall that as a party, Silvia would not be permitted to testify as a witness. Her only opportunity to be personally heard would come in the form of the confessional hearing, where her statements, while they would be considered by the court, would not qualify as evidence. From the other side, the record would be likely to reflect a complete battery of well-researched and professionally organized evidence showing compliance with international manufacturing standards such as those maintained by the ISO (a network of international standards institutes from 156 countries), an absence of similar complaints, registries clean of incidents involving shattering jars manufactured by Levington or sold by Penelope, the testimony of quality control managers, and so on. I believe that any Argentine judge would have a hard time finding solid grounds to decide in favor of Silvia. Moreover, even if the trial judge felt sympathy for Silvia and ruled in her favor, the case would almost definitely be appealed and stand a good chance of being reversed. Thus, although I am sorry to disappoint readers who are in Silvia's corner, my overall assessment based on experience is that, absent the development of other favorable facts, Argentine Silvia probably would have only a 20–30% chance of prevailing.

On the other hand, I am not completely pessimistic about Silvia's case. In Argentina, as in many civil law countries, cases can drag on for years. While a case is pending, the judicial approach and attitude toward a particular product or type of incident can change, other similar cases can be filed or consumer complaints about similar incidents can get the attention of the public agencies overseeing food production. It's even possible and has happened before that an employee of one of the defendants could decide to air production problems at the defendant's plant to get media attention. From a more romanticized, but not implausible perspective, sometimes the law evolves through the voice of persistent claimants unwilling to give up in their pursuit of justice. For Argentine Silvia, carrying forward a claim against Penelope and the other defendants would not be financially expensive to her personally due to the benefit to litigate without expenses. If she were willing to hang in there,

Silvia could give it a costless try and see if something useful for her case developed somewhere down the road.

To what extent did my opinion of Silvia's case change during the course of this project? I concur with some of what has been said by McClurg and Koyuncu. At the beginning I was more optimistic for Silvia about the outcome of the case. The main reason for this optimism was that, as noted, in our first draft of the case facts the broken pieces of glass were preserved. In my Argentine-lawyer mindset my first impression was: "Well, we have the key piece of evidence, capable experts are locally available to find out what happened to this particular jar, and there is a complete set of favorable cases to cite involving shattering bottles. Silvia has already won her case. Good for her." Further, while discussing the case over the telephone and through dozens of email messages we all probably unconsciously depicted Silvia as an honest, hardworking, and unfairly injured student who deserved sympathy and redress.

My opinion changed as the project progressed without my being even completely conscious of the change. It changed more firmly when called on to make this final assessment. Four principal reasons can be identified. First, as just explained, having the jar pieces being disposed of made a big difference. Second, all the Argentine cases I found along the way involved shattering beverage bottles which, unlike Silvia's jar, are subject to internal pressure. Third, I squarely imagined myself on the other side of Silvia's case as the manufacturer's lawyer, which is my current usual role. I pictured the full set of evidence I would be able to develop for a client with resources and could imagine it overwhelming Silvia and her lawyer. Finally, I played the judge role. Before practicing law, I served for many years as an Argentine court officer and drafted many opinions for judges. I can still feel the impotence I felt then when going through a record involving a claim that appeared to deserve redress, yet lacked the evidence necessary to sustain it. Or even worse, a case file showing a severe imbalance in the evidence presented by an impecunious plaintiff and well-funded defendants.

Taking on Silvia as a client. These observations take me to another question each co-author has asked and answered. Would I take Silvia's case if I were a practicing plaintiffs' personal injury lawyer? My answer would be "yes," but with some qualifications.

As briefly mentioned in chapter four, the Argentine legislature has imposed a unique procedure of mandatory mediation *prior* to filing a lawsuit in the national courts of Buenos Aires, the forum for Argentine Silvia. Since coming in force some ten years ago, mediation has been a useful means to free the courts from hearing cases that probably would settle anyway shortly after filing. Some repeat players in tort litigation, such as insurance companies, prefer to settle and avoid the costs of litigating cases that are not worth defending. Silvia's case could fall into that category.

It is much cheaper to bring a case to mediation than to prepare a formal complaint. By some accounts, mandatory pre-filing mediation has facilitated many frivolous claims. Mediation, as it can be used in Buenos Aires, makes claiming a sort of free fishing expedition. Plaintiffs' injury lawyers sometimes expect to attend a couple of meetings, reach a rapid settlement and walk away without ever having to put together a sound complaint. My point is that Silvia would easily find a lawyer to represent her during mediation. Almost no personal injury lawyer would refuse the possibility of reaching settlement before having to actually work on the case. The amount of recovery and contingency fee would be quite modest at this stage, but the investment for the lawyer in terms of time, work, and technical consultants' fees (if needed at all) would be negligible.

Finding a lawyer to represent Silvia before a court of law would be quite a different matter, especially finding someone competent to provide effective legal representation in the complex area of products liability law. The number of products liability cases seems to have risen steadily in the last decade, at least as shown by the private collections that specialize in reporting judicial decisions. This trend of filing more products liability cases has resulted in a well-developed set of new judicial precedent addressing most of the major issues, but we should not ignore that in many of these "new" cases judges continue to adhere to the "old" ways of finding for the defendants due to a shortage of evidence backing the claim. Plaintiffs frequently have come up short in proving a product defect and/or causation. In other words, plaintiffs may be shooting more frequently than ten years ago, but the bullets often are not finding their targets.

After mediation, some entrepreneurial plaintiff lawyers move forward and file a formal complaint with the court. The objective at this point is to reach settlement at the preliminary hearing; i.e., the hearing to which the judge must summon the parties before entering the evidentiary stage. In my experience, if settlement is not reached at or shortly after this hearing, the enthusiasm of most plaintiffs perishes. The evidentiary stage is generally an arena in which well-represented defendants accumulate and present a host of complex technical evidence whilst the plaintiff continues plodding around in the dark or, in some cases, just gives up.

Thus, despite the apparent rise in case filings, Argentine consumers and especially plaintiffs' injury lawyers are far from adopting the aggressive approach that their U.S. counterparts take against manufacturers in product-related injury cases. Personal injury lawyers in Argentina are likely to shy away from products liability cases (as are many U.S. plaintiffs' lawyers for that matter) due to their complexity and expense. In my experience, even in the face of a plausible products liability case like Silvia's, many members of the plaintiffs' bar would prefer to pursue other types of cases, such as automobile cases against properly insured drivers and medical malpractice cases against solvent doctors. For example, in cases involving allegedly defective medical devices such as prostheses, heart valves or arterial stents, plaintiffs' lawyers continue to concentrate on suing the physicians rather than the medical device manufacturers, which is the reverse of the way things usually work in the U.S.

While medical malpractice cases can also be complex and expensive, the law governing medical malpractice is much more clearly developed than products liability law. There are thousands of reported malpractice cases handy for citation. Relatedly, medical malpractice is a more well-known and, hence, comfortable litigation arena. This is true even though medical malpractice cases require proving negligence, whereas we have seen that strict liability is available in defective product cases. In any event, medical malpractice is a popular cause of action in local practice.

The bottom line is that product sellers in Argentina receive a degree of protection simply from the fact that most plaintiffs' lawyers lack the resources, expertise or doggedness to pursue challenging cases. Having said this, there are some good plaintiffs' lawyers in Buenos Aires who would take on Silvia's case. The trick for Silvia would be getting lucky enough to get referred to one, a task made more difficult by the fact that Argentina prohibits lawyer advertising.

Would Silvia be likely to seek legal redress? Would Silvia be likely to pursue legal redress in Argentina? The answer would depend very much on personal factors such as the plaintiff's level of education, affluence, and place of residence (e.g., rural vs. urban). The type of product also plays a role. Argentine consumers are more likely to bring claims with regard to mass-produced products such as automobiles, bottles, and food products, than specialized products such as medical devices. In general, Argentine consumers are not inclined to file lawsuits absent serious injuries or death. While products liability case filings are rising, the vast majority of injured consumers do not file or probably even consider filing lawsuits. This is particularly true with regard to economically disadvantaged consumers who are less aware of their rights, may not have ready access to a lawyer to consult or just feel that misfortune in life is commonplace and inevitable. On the other side of the social landscape, very wealthy people also tend not to sue, probably because it is not worth their while. Hence, my perception based on experience leads me to conclude that products liability cases are, at present, most likely to be brought by middle-class consumers. Silvia comes from a working class family, but lives in the metropolis of Buenos Aires where lawyers are abundant. She also is well-educated, and has been referred to a lawyer by one of her professors, whose opinion she is likely to respect. These facts all increase the likelihood that she would seek legal redress for her injuries.

Comparative observations, including desirable features of other legal systems. The project that resulted in this book was an enlightening experience for me as I hope the book will be for all readers. McClurg and Koyuncu have already said it, but I must add my confirmation of the point about how surprised we were—and readers probably are—at the number of similarities in substantive products liability law among the three countries, as well as the marked dissimilarities in critical procedures. After studying law in the U.S. and working with U.S. clients, I believe that, while common law and civil law look very different in theory, the distances between the two traditions have narrowed in recent decades and probably will continue to do so. Because of the global marketplace in which we live, this is particularly true in the area of products liability law. Strict liability under common law is a matter of case-by-case construction, while in civil law systems it originates in code and other statutory provisions. But we've seen how case law has put meat on the bare-bones codifications of strict liability in both Argentina and Germany in a manner not unlike the way U.S. case law fleshes out rules one case at a time. As mentioned, there seems to be a universal sense of fairness that has moved judges, scholars, and legislators from very different regions and cultures to find similar solutions to the inevitable risks posed by defects in mass-produced products and the difficulties in proving those defects.

Procedural law does not follow that pattern. As I have taught students enrolled in my courses on civil procedure, substantive law can be a marvelous intellectual engagement, but it means nothing if the instruments to put the substantive principles into practice—procedure law—do not work properly. In my view, and that of many local scholars, Argentine civil procedure, although having improved in the last two decades, is ill-designed to accompany the evolution of products liability substantive law principles and is not in tune with the consumerist and globalized world we live in. U.S. scholars, judges, practitioners, and, increasingly, legislators may have a host of complaints against U.S. discovery and class actions, but from a foreign observer's perspective, I believe those devices account for a large part of the protection that consumers enjoy in the U.S. I believe these are devices other countries should borrow, at least in part and always taking into account the local culture and practice of the borrowing country.

Without discovery there is no way for Argentine consumers to unearth the truth about an alleged damaging product. This would seem to hold true in most other civil law countries, which also do not allow discovery. Thus, in one sense, the entire search for objective truth is doomed before it ever starts. As a result, some guilty tortfeasors escape liability and justice is not served. Likewise, without class actions or some similar type of mass aggregation device, wrongdoers that inflict harm on a broad scale are able to minimize their exposure by dealing with each claimant separately, often overwhelming their resources or patience. To be sure, I do not advocate adopting in Argentina discovery or class-action approaches that encourage or permit harassing tactical claims, but tools could be adopted to prevent that from happening, such as close monitoring by judges who are much more active than in current practice.

Another feature of the U.S. litigation system that Argentina, and all countries, should pursue is the practice of conducting empirical studies and other information gathering on the legal system and legal institutions. Certainly, one cannot well manage—much less improve—something that cannot be assessed based on reliable and complete information. Argentina lacks thorough assessments of its legal system. This became apparent at many points during this comparative journey when McClurg would request data on various points. One telling inquiry was an email stating he had come across three different sources giving very different figures as to the number of law schools in Argentina. Even on this basic point, I was unable to give him an exact number. We ended up selecting what we believed to be the most reliable figure of the three, but with no way of knowing for certain whether it was accurate. This lack of reliable data is one reason why my opinions on some aspects of Argentine law and procedure are more a matter of my personal experience and perception than of good science. Due to this shortage of data, changes in Argentine law and procedure often follow a trial and error pattern and sometimes ignore the difference between reality and perception. The recent amendments giving judges broad investigative powers, which they seldom use in fact, may be a good example of this gap between law and reality.

I do not want to finish this book without addressing some words to the U.S. law students who are one of the principal intended audiences. Many U.S. law students still may not be aware of the rapidly changing global situation with regard to the practice of transnational law. You are, whether you know it or not, preparing to practice law around the world. In my practice, I witness daily the cliché that "the world is shrinking." Many of the clients I work with are U.S. companies engaged in worldwide business. I often work closely with their in-house and outside counsel. Coping with the challenges of the borderless marketplace will depend in part on one's ability to understand foreign law, culture, and legal traditions. All U.S. lawyers would benefit simply from having some clue about what their foreign colleagues and adversaries are talking about when, for example, they make references to basic procedures and principles of the civil law tradition. In other words, international training will pay dividends to today's law students.

Conclusion

There is no escaping the fact that lawyers without some grounding in the legal systems of other nations increasingly will be at a competitive and intellectual disadvantage in a rapidly "flattening" world. *See* THOMAS FRIEDMAN, THE WORLD IS FLAT (2005). In his bestselling book, Friedman presented a compelling case that the leveling effects of technology, particularly in computer software and networking, have moved us into a new era of globalization that "is shrinking the world from a size small to a size tiny."

While the Internet and other communications technology have transformed us into a borderless virtual world, a profusion of world trade agreements and regional cooperation pacts, either already in place or in progress, continue to dissolve physical borders. Visit the foreign trade statistics page on the U.S. Census Bureau's website and pick a country, any country. No matter how small or remote the nation, the chances are good that the U.S. is importing and exporting consumable goods and materials to and from it. *See* http://www.census.gov/foreign-trade/statistics/country/index.html. Using our three countries of study as samples, U.S. Census Bureau data show that in 2005 the U.S. imported goods and materials valued at $84 billion from Germany and $4.5 billion from Argentina, while exporting goods worth $34 billion to Germany and $4 billion to Argentina.

Given the vast global market in consumer goods, products liability is an area in urgent need of more comparative study. Silvia Winter's story is just one chapter in this study, but in one sense it is a paradigm of the universal complexities and uncertainties of allocating risk and assigning responsibility for product injuries in a modern commercial life in which a web of actors—raw materials sellers and fabricators, component part and final product manufacturers, packagers, transporters, wholesalers, retailers, and consumers—play intertwined but legally distinct roles. Short of adopting absolute liability for injuries caused by products, "whodunit?" mysteries like Silvia's will remain common and inevitable in manufacturing defect cases. The intricate framework of interwoven substantive and procedural law erected to address these types of conundrums is part of what makes products liability such a fascinating legal playground, not only in the U.S., but, as we have seen, in other countries as well.

In the end, navigating Silvia's products liability case through the legal systems of the U.S., Germany, and Argentina really was like a journey for us. Because we started out knowing little about each other's legal systems, the path of discovery often was confusing and maze-like. Like tourists driving for the first time in Miami, Cologne or Buenos Aires, we proceeded tentatively at first, made frustrating wrong turns, and stumbled on unexpected local treasures. We made countless cost-benefit trade-offs along the way about which legal attractions to linger at and which ones to simply frame in a snapshot and move past. Eventually, the lines on the map became less blurry and the street markers more familiar. By the time we reached our destination, we felt comfortable navigating through all three legal systems, at least in the context of Silvia's case.

We hope you feel the same way. The ultimate goal was for readers to be able to close the book covers with a high level of confidence about "the basics" of how one common variety of products liability case would travel through the tort litigation systems of the U.S., Germany, and Argentina. As authors of the first entry in the Contextual Approach Series, we would like to hear what you think worked or didn't work. In the meantime, we propose a closing toast to Silvia Winter. Despite our desire to stay neutral, we couldn't help rooting for her. May she find better days, and products, ahead.

APPENDIX

CASE LAW REPORTING AND CITATION STYLE

One of the most interesting comparative law revelations of this book to students of the common law is likely to be the large impact of judge-made law in civil law countries. Case precedent is theoretically irrelevant in civil law systems, but as detailed in this book, nearly all specific products liability principles in both Germany and Argentina were constructed by judges rather than legislators, although the courts usually were heavily influenced by scholarly writers. Because most tort and products liability issues are not expressly or extensively addressed in codes or statutes, courts necessarily stepped in to fill the gaps in response to the evolutionary pressures of modern life. But, in large part because case law has no official precedential value in the civil law tradition, judicial decisions are not as extensively and systematically reported in civil law systems as in the U.S. Researching German and Argentine case law, even apart from language barriers, can be challenging. Because we discuss case law from all three countries in this book, we offer a synopsis of how cases are reported and cited in the U.S., Germany, and Argentina.

United States. The U.S. is unique among the three nations in having a uniform, easily accessible case reporting system for both federal and state judicial opinions. The National Reporter System, maintained by West Publishing Co., greatly facilitates case research in the U.S. Although the U.S. Supreme Court and some states continue to publish their own case reporters, standard practice is to cite to cases as they appear in the National Reporter System. Federal cases are reported in the Supreme Court Reporter (U.S. Supreme Court), Federal Reporter (U.S. Courts of Appeal), and Federal Supplement (U.S. District Courts). Separate federal topical reporters include the Bankruptcy Reporter, Federal Claims Reporter, Federal Rules Decisions, and Military Justice Reporter.

State decisions are reported in seven different regional reporters as follows: Atlantic Reporter (Connecticut, Delaware, Maine, Maryland, New Hampshire, New Jersey, Pennsylvania, Rhode Island, Vermont), North Eastern Reporter

(Illinois, Indiana, Massachusetts, New York, Ohio), North Western Reporter (Iowa, Michigan, Minnesota, Nebraska, North Dakota, South Dakota, Wisconsin), Pacific Reporter (Alaska, Arizona, California, Colorado, Hawaii, Idaho, Kansas, Montana, Nevada, New Mexico, Oklahoma, Oregon, Utah, Washington, Wyoming), South Eastern Reporter (Georgia, North Carolina, South Carolina, Virginia, West Virginia), Southern Reporter (Alabama, Florida, Louisiana, Mississippi), and South Western Reporter (Arkansas, Kentucky, Missouri, Tennessee, Texas). New York and California get their own reporters in the National Reporter system (New York Supplement and California Reporter). Not all, or even most, U.S. judicial decisions are published in the National Reporter System. Individual courts generally designate which cases are to be published.

U.S. cases follow a uniform system of citation style. Cases are cited by the names of the parties, followed by the volume of the reporter in which the opinion was published, the name of the reporter, the page on which the opinion begins, the page on which the specific material referred to appears (called the "pinpoint cite"), the court that decided the case, and the year the case was decided. Here's an example:

> Greenman v. Yuba Power Products, Inc. [parties], 377 [volume] P.2d [Pacific Reporter, 2d Series] 897 [first page of opinion], 898 [pinpoint page cite] (Cal. 1963) [California Supreme Court and year of decision].

U.S. case law is widely available online through paid subscription services such as Westlaw and LexisNexis and also many free websites. Most federal and state court systems post their opinions and sometimes other court documents online. Legal resource sites such as washlaw.edu, findlaw.com, and others maintain extensive collections of links to the law in all U.S. jurisdictions.

Germany. German case law, particularly higher court decisions, is extensively reported in Germany, but most of it is done online. Only a handful of German cases have been translated to English. The most prominent reporting system is for decisions of Germany's Federal Supreme Court: the BGHZ, which is both an abbreviation of the court's name (*Bundesgerichtshof für Zivilsachen* or Federal Court of Justice for Private Law Matters) and the name of the publishing organ for the court's decisions. Most influential case law in Germany emanates from the Federal Supreme Court, yet not all of the high court's decisions get published in BGHZ. Decisions get selected for publication in the BGHZ if they are deemed to provide guidelines, change previous high court judgments or are otherwise regarded as having high importance.

As in many civil law countries, German court decisions also are reported, often in summary form, in private legal journals, such as law reviews. Many law reviews cover specific areas of law, picking up those trial and high court decisions that fit within their legal spectrums. One of the most prominent journals is the *Neue Juristische Wochenschrift*, commonly known as NJW, which publishes selected judicial opinions and scholarly articles.

Another factor that makes German case research confusing for common law students is the terse citation format. The parties in German cases are not identified by name so as to maintain their anonymity. Citations to opinions published in the BGHZ are short and to the point. They begin with "BGHZ," followed by the volume in which the decision appears, the page on which the opinion begins, and the pinpoint page citation in parentheses, as in this example:

> BGHZ [Federal Supreme Court] 53 [volume], 245 [beginning page] (256) [pinpoint page cite].

Here's an example of a case citation in the *Neue Juristische Wochenschrift*:

> BGH [Federal Supreme Court], NJW [published in *Neue Juristische Wochenschrift*] 2001 [year of publication], 426 [beginning page] (427) [pinpoint page cite].

With no party names as a reference point, famous German cases become known by shorthand descriptors such as the *Fowl Pest* case or *Second Mineral Water Bottle* case.

More and more German case and statutory law can be found online. Some particularly good online sources (all in German) are http://www.dejure.org (large body of code, statutory, and case law), http://www.gesetze-im-internet. de (codes, statutes, ordinances), http://www.juris.de (comprehensive source of federal and state statutes, court decisions, and articles), and http://www.lexis-nexis.de/ (LexisNexis Germany). For English translations of selected code provisions, statutes, and cases, visit http://www.ucl.ac.uk/laws/global_law/ and http://www.utexas.edu/law/academics/centers/transnational/work/.

Argentina. Researching case law in Latin American countries is complicated by problems similar to those discussed for Germany, except perhaps even more accentuated. No single, official reporting source exists for judicial opinions in Argentina. Most Argentine case law is reported through private publications. There are four basic case law reporters, of which *Fallos de la Corte Suprema*, a publication of select Supreme Court rulings, is the only official reporter. The other three main services—*La Ley*, *Jurisprudencia Argentina*, and *El Derecho*—are privately owned legal publications that publish both judicial opinions and academic articles written by noteworthy jurists and scholars. Cases are selected for publication based on their importance or relevance as determined by the discretion of the publishers' staffs.

These three private services do not cover all parts of the country. They publish only cases decided in large judicial districts such as Buenos Aires, Mendoza, Rosario, Córdoba, and La Plata. Finding reports of cases decided in other parts of the country can be difficult even for Argentine lawyers, and is a task usually reserved to lawyers who practice in those provincial and small jurisdictions. As a consequence, Argentine national legal development tends to follow the trend of cases decided in the most populous jurisdictions. Other courts have almost no influence in the development of the country's law and are seldom cited outside of their jurisdiction.

No uniform citation format is in place. Lawyers and scholars usually adhere to the citation format used by the particular court to which they are referring. The format used in this book is patterned roughly after the citation format for Argentine cases prescribed by *The Bluebook: A Uniform System of Citation* (18th ed. 2005). While the format is a bit unwieldy, given the difficulty of locating Argentine case law, it is better to include more information rather than less. Citations include the following information in the following order:

• The name of the deciding court;
• An abbreviation of the court's name in brackets;
• The date of the decision;
• The name of the parties, sometimes including a reference to the type of case, such as "suit for damages" or *daños y perjuicios*;
• The name of the reporter or other publication where the case appears, first spelled out and then abbreviated in brackets;
• The year of publication, the volume in which the decision appears, and page number, all within one set of parentheses and divided by dashes (year-volume-page).

Two dates (the decision date and the year of publication) are included because decisions often are not published until many months after they have been handed down. The following citation of a landmark products liability case decided by the National Civil Court of Appeals in Buenos Aires provides an example that tracks the above list. Because brackets are used in the citation format, to avoid confusion we did not add bracketed explanations as we did above for the U.S. and Germany:

Cámara Nacional de Apelaciones lo Civil, Sala C [CNCiv.], 4/26/56, "Sánchez Cesáreo R. y otro c. Club Italiano," La Ley [L.L.] (1956-83-410).

For most Argentine cases referenced in this book, all of the above citation information is included, but some of the cases we cited are unpublished or lack complete publication data.

Currently, the best online source for researching Argentine law is Lexis-Nexis Argentina (http://www.lexisnexis.com.ar), which offers a growing collection of statutory and case law, albeit in Spanish. The database contains a fairly complete archive of modern cases decided in large jurisdictions such as Buenos Aires. Some other helpful online sources (all in Spanish) include: http://www.info.gov.ar/ (updates on current legal events, selected case law, and links to official documents of various government agencies and departments), http://pjn.gov.ar (official website of the federal judicial branch that includes case law and judgments), and http://scba.gov.ar (official website of the Supreme Court for the province of Buenos Aires offering institutional map, case law, and a legal search engine).

Selected Bibliography

Many of the sources listed below proved helpful in composing this book. The bibliography focuses on the U.S., Germany, and Argentina, and, except for two treatises on Argentine products liability law, is limited to sources available in English. Some online sources are listed in the preceding appendix.

General Comparative Law and Legal History

Vivian Grosswald Curran, Comparative Law: An Introduction (Carolina Academic Press 2002).

Nigel Foster & Satish Sule, German Legal System and Laws (Oxford University Press 2002).

Lawrence M. Friedman, A History of American Law (Touchstone 3d ed. 2005).

Mary Ann Glendon, Michael W. Gordon & Paolo G. Carozza, Comparative Legal Traditions in a Nutshell (West Group 2d ed. 1999).

Frederik G. Kempin, Jr., Historical Introduction to Anglo-American Law in a Nutshell (Thomson West 3d ed. 1990).

John Henry Merryman, The Civil Law Tradition: An Introduction to the Legal Systems of Western Europe and Latin America (Stanford University Press 2d ed. 1985).

John Henry Merryman, David S. Clark & John O. Haley, The Civil Law Tradition: Europe, Latin America, and East Asia, Cases and Materials (LexisNexis 1994).

M.C. Mirow, Latin American Law: A History of Private Law and Institutions in Spanish America (University of Texas Press 2004).

Rudolf B. Schlesinger, Hans W. Baade, Peter E. Herzog & Edward M. Wise, Comparative Law (Foundation Press 6th ed. 1998).

Comparative Tort and Products Liability Law

Richard Best, *A Comparison of Civil Liability for Defective Products in the United Kingdom and Germany*, 3 GERMAN L.J. No. 4 (April 1, 2002).

THE BOUNDARIES OF STRICT LIABILITY IN EUROPEAN TORT LAW (Franz Werro & Vernon Valentine Palmer eds., Carolina Academic Press 2004).

COMPENSATION FOR PERSONAL INJURY IN A COMPARATIVE PERSPECTIVE (Bernhard A. Koch & Helmut Koziol eds., SpringerWien 2003).

EUROPEAN GROUP ON TORT LAW, PRINCIPLES OF EUROPEAN TORT LAW: TEXT AND COMMENTARY (SpringerWien 2005).

WILLIAM C. HOFFMAN & SUSANNE HILL-ARNING, GUIDE TO PRODUCT LIA-BILITY IN EUROPE (Kluwer 1994).

INTERNATIONAL COMPARATIVE GUIDE TO: PRODUCT LIABILITY 2005 (Global Legal Group 2005).

INTERNATIONAL PRODUCT LIABILITY LAW: A WORLDWIDE DESK REFERENCE (Gregory L. Fowler ed., Aspatore Books 2003).

JOCELYN KELLAM, THE CONTRACT-TORT DICHOTOMY AND A THEORETICAL FRAMEWORK FOR PRODUCT LIABILITY LAW: A COMPARISON OF THE ELE-MENTS OF LIABILITY IN AUSTRALIA, FRANCE AND GERMANY (Baden-Baden: Nomos 2000).

THE LIMITS OF EXPANDING LIABILITY: EIGHT FUNDAMENTAL CASES IN A COMPARATIVE PERSPECTIVE (J. Spier ed., Kluwer Law Int'l 1998).

BASIL MARKESINIS, MICHAEL COESTER, GUIDO ALPA & AUGUSTUS ULLSTEIN, COMPENSATION FOR PERSONAL INJURY IN ENGLISH, GERMAN AND ITAL-IAN LAW (Cambridge University Press 2005).

C.J. MILLER AND RICHARD S. GOLDBERG, PRODUCT LIABILITY (Oxford 2d ed. 2004).

Mathias Reimann, *Liability for Defective Products at the Beginning of the Twenty-First Century: Emergence of a Worldwide Standard?*, 51 AM. J. COMP. L. 751 (2003).

Rebekah Rollo, *Products Liability: Why the European Union Doesn't Need the Restatement (Third)*, 69 BROOK. L. REV. 1073 (2004).

Symposium on Products Liability: Comparative Approaches & Transnational Lit-igation, 34 TEX. INT'L L.J. 1 (1999).

Symposium—Products Liability in Latin America, 20 ARIZ. J. INT'L & COMP. LAW 1 (2003).

UNIFICATION OF TORT LAW: CAUSATION (J. Spier ed., Kluwer Law Int'l 2000).

UNIFICATION OF TORT LAW: CONTRIBUTORY NEGLIGENCE (Ulrich Magnus & Miguel Martín-Casals eds., Kluwer Law Int'l 2004).

UNIFICATION OF TORT LAW: DAMAGES (U. Magnus ed., Kluwer Law Int'l 2001).

UNIFICATION OF TORT LAW: FAULT (P. Widmer ed., Kluwer Law Int'l 2005).

UNIFICATION OF TORT LAW: LIABILITY FOR DAMAGE CAUSED BY OTHERS (J. Spier ed., Kluwer Law Int'l 2003).

UNIFICATION OF TORT LAW: MULTIPLE TORTFEASORS (W.V.H. Rogers ed., Kluwer Law Int'l 2004).

UNIFICATION OF TORT LAW: STRICT LIABILITY (B.A. Koch & H. Koziol eds., Kluwer Law Int'l 2002).

UNIFICATION OF TORT LAW: WRONGFULNESS (H. Koziol ed., Kluwer Law Int'l 1998).

WALTER VAN GERVEN, JEREMY LEVER & PIERRE LAROUCHE, CASES, MATERIALS AND TEXT ON NATIONAL, SUPRANATIONAL AND INTERNATIONAL TORT LAW (Hart 2000).

Comparative Civil Procedure

Oscar G. Chase, *American "Exceptionalism" and Comparative Procedure*, 50 AM. J. COMP. L. 277 (2002).

John H. Langbein, *The German Advantage in Civil Procedure*, 52 U. CHI. L. REV. 823 (1985).

PRE-TRIAL AND PRE-HEARING PROCEDURES WORLDWIDE (Charles Platto ed., Int'l Bar Ass'n 1990).

WORLD LAW GROUP MEMBER FIRMS, INTERNATIONAL CIVIL PROCEDURE (Shelby R. Grubbs ed., Kluwer Law Int'l 2003).

U.S. Products Liability Law

DAVID A. FISCHER, MICHAEL GREEN & WILLIAM C. POWERS, JR., CASES AND MATERIALS ON PRODUCTS LIABILITY (Thomson West 4th ed. 2006).

MARK A. GEISTFELD, PRINCIPLES OF PRODUCTS LIABILITY (Foundation Press 2006).

TERRENCE F. KIELY & BRUCE L. OTTLEY, UNDERSTANDING PRODUCTS LIABILITY LAW (LexisNexis 2006).

JAMES A. HENDERSON & AARON D. TWERSKI, PRODUCTS LIABILITY: PROBLEMS AND PROCESS (Aspen 5th ed. 2004).

DAVID G. OWEN & JERRY J. PHILLIPS, PRODUCTS LIABILITY IN A NUTSHELL (Thomson West 7th ed. 2005).

DAVID G. OWEN, PRODUCTS LIABILITY LAW (Thomson West 2005).

David G. Owen, John E. Montgomery & Mary J. Davis, Products Liability and Safety: Cases and Materials (Foundation Press 5th ed. 2007).
Restatement (Third) of Torts: Products Liability (American Law Institute 1998).
Marshall S. Shapo, The Law of Products Liability (CCH, Inc. 4th ed. 2001).

German Tort and Products Liability Law

Basil S. Markesinis, Vol. II., The German Law of Obligations, The Law of Torts: A Comparative Introduction (Oxford/Clarendon 3d ed. 1997).
Basil S. Markesinis & Hannes Unberath, The German Law of Torts: A Comparative Treatise (Hart 4th ed. 2002).
Manfred Wandt, *German Approaches to Product Liability*, 34 Tex. Int'l L.J. 71 (1999).

German Civil Law—General

Anke Freckmann & Thomas Wegerich, The German Legal System (Sweet & Maxwell 1999).
Peter L. Murray & Rolf Stürner, German Civil Justice (Carolina Academic Press 2004).

Argentine Products Liability Law

Jonathan Miller, *Products Liability in Argentina*, 33 Am. J. Comp. L. 611 (1985).
Juan Javier Negri, *Argentina, in* Products Liability: An International Manual of Practice (Warren Freeman ed., Oceana Publications, Inc. 1990).
Liliana Schvartz, Defensa de los Derechos de los Consumidores y Usuarios (García Alonso 2005).
Federico C. Tallone, Daños Causados por Productos Elaborados (Hammurabi 2002).

U.S. Tort System—Commentary

Carl T. Bogus, Why Lawsuits are Good for America: Disciplined Democracy, Big Business & the Common Law (N.Y.U. Press 2001).

JOHN G. FLEMING, THE AMERICAN TORT PROCESS (Clarendon Press 1988).

WILLAM HALTOM & MICHAEL McCANN, DISTORTING THE LAW: POLITICS, MEDIA, AND THE LITIGATION CRISIS (University of Chicago Press 2004).

ROBERT A. KAGAN, ADVERSARIAL LEGALISM: THE AMERICAN WAY OF LAW (Harvard University Press 2003).

English Translations of German and Argentine Codes

CIVIL CODE OF ARGENTINA (including amendments reflected by Argentine online updating services as of January 28, 2001) (Julio Romanach, Jr., trans., Lawrence Publishing Co. 2001).

THE GERMAN CIVIL CODE (as amended through January 1, 1992) (Simon L. Goren, trans., Fred B. Rothman & Co. 1994).

GERMAN COMMERCIAL CODE & CODE OF CIVIL PROCEDURE IN ENGLISH (Charles E. Stewart ed., Oceana Publications 2001).

About the Authors

Andrew J. McClurg is a nationally recognized torts scholar and teacher. He holds the Herbert Herff Chair of Excellence in Law at The University of Memphis Cecil C. Humphreys School of Law. From 2002–06, he was a member of the founding faculty at the Florida International University College of Law. Previously, he was the Nadine H. Baum Distinguished Professor of Law at the University of Arkansas at Little Rock, and also has taught at Wake Forest University, the University of Colorado, and Golden Gate University. McClurg's books and law review articles have been cited by numerous courts and in more than 175 different journals. McClurg is the recipient of five teaching awards, including four *Teacher of the Year* awards. Before joining academia, he served as a law clerk to a federal district court judge and worked four years as a trial lawyer.

Adem Koyuncu is both a lawyer and medical doctor. He is a lawyer in Cologne in one of the German offices of Mayer, Brown, Rowe & Maw LLP, a major U.S. firm, where his practice includes German tort and products liability litigation. Prior to joining the firm, he worked several years in the pharmaceutical industry. He is the author of two books and several articles in the field of products liability law, particularly as it relates to the pharmaceutical and medical device industry. His book, *The Liability Triangle: Pharmaceutical Company-Physician-Patient*, earned him the Science Award 2005 of the German Society for Law and Politics in Health Care. Koyuncu received both his medical and law degrees from the University of Cologne, Germany. He worked as a physician prior to becoming a practicing lawyer. He is an active national lecturer and presenter.

Luis Eduardo Sprovieri is a partner in the Buenos Aires office of Baker & McKenzie, serving as coordinator of the firm's products liability group for Latin America. He is also a specialist in the fast-growing field of mass tort litigation in Argentina. Before joining Baker & McKenzie, he worked for almost two decades for the Argentine judiciary, reaching the position of Civil Court

Clerk in Buenos Aires, the largest jurisdiction in the country. After obtaining an LL.M from Duke University School of Law, he served as consultant to the World Bank's legal department in Washington D.C., where he worked on legal and judicial reform in Latin America and co-authored the World Bank publication, *Argentina: Legal and Judicial Sector Assessment.* He is the author of several articles on tort law and civil procedure, subjects he has taught as an assistant professor at the Catholic University of Argentina. He also practiced as a plaintiffs' personal injury lawyer in Buenos Aires.

INDEX